Violent Peace

D0700930

Violent Peace

*Militarized Interstate Bargaining
in Latin America*

David R. Mares

COLUMBIA   UNIVERSITY   PRESS   NEW   YORK

Columbia University Press
Publishers Since 1893
New York, Chichester, West Sussex
Copyright © 2001 Columbia University Press
All rights reserved

Library of Congress Cataloging-in-Publication Data

Mares, David R.
   Violent peace : militarized interstate bargaining in Latin America / David R.
   Mares.
      p. cm.
   Includes bibliographical references and index.
   ISBN 0–231–11186–X (cloth) — ISBN 0–231–11187–8 (pbk.)
      1. Latin America — Foreign relations. 2. Conflict management — Latin
   America. 3. Latin America — Military policy. 4. Pacific settlement of
   international disputes. I. Title.
   F1415 M298 2001
   327.8 — dc21

                                                               00–064424

Casebound editions of Columbia University Press books
are printed on permanent and durable acid-free paper.
Printed in the United States of America

c 10 9 8 7 6 5 4 3 2 1
p 10 9 8 7 6 5 4 3 2 1

To Jane, Alejandro, and Gabriel

Contents

Preface

Interstate Competition in a Heterogeneous World: The Importance of Understanding Violent Peace

The world is a heterogeneous place. Words do not mean the same across ideological, cultural and political divides. One group's "freedom fighters" are another's "terrorists" and vice versa. Disagreement abounds concerning whether the term "free markets" means that one factor of production, capital, should flow without political encumbrance, while another, labor, is highly restricted, although both produce short-term displacements and long-term benefits. For some "democracy" implies only that the political rights of individuals are safeguarded, while for others it incorporates social justice for all. The same person can call prisoners who produce goods and services for the market "prison labor" in China but see them only as "repaying a debt to society" in the U.S.[1]

Whatever the sources of disagreement, and they are virtually infinite,[2] "peace" requires that we find ways of engaging in interstate competition short of "war to eliminate the bad guy so that we may all live in peace." Yet the current state of the study of international relations does not meet these needs. Instead it is seeking the holy grail, as we churn out study after study purporting to find that a particular type of state, liberal and democratic, is so inherently pacific that everywhere states achieve this form, the "Pacific Union" reigns. By the way, we also know which states are "Liberal" and "Democratic" because they don't fight each other.[3]

This book focuses on why military force is often used when states have disagreements. It takes conflict as a given in international relations, but does not assume that military violence is an inevitable result. It takes the possibility of decreasing the use of military force, not its elimination, as a subject of major importance for students of international relations. Many disputes will be definitively resolved, but others will develop. International society will continue to confront the same fundamental task: how can nations that disagree on important matters nevertheless coexist without threatening or using military force against each other?[4]

Most analysts of international politics as well as policymakers combine elements from Realist and Liberal paradigms: military power matters, but under particular circumstances rival states do cooperate in the security realm.[5] In a nutshell, anything that *credibly* increases the benefits of cooperation while decreasing the costs of cooperation, relative to the benefits and costs of conflict, makes cooperation more likely. No big surprise here. Debates essentially revolve around whether costs and benefits are increasing or decreasing in particular circumstances and whether credibility is achieved or not.

This book proposes a conceptual scheme for analyzing the effective determinants of whether disputes become militarized and how far down the continuum toward war they progress (figure 1).

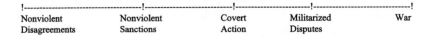

| Nonviolent Disagreements | Nonviolent Sanctions | Covert Action | Militarized Disputes | War |

FIGURE 1 Continuum of Interstate Conflict

The argument put forward in this book is that leaders use foreign policy to provide collective and private goods to their domestic constituencies. The threat or actual use of force is part of an overall strategy designed to modify the status quo. That change may aim to unilaterally resolve a dispute, transform a situation in bilateral negotiations, bring in third-party international actors, or even to alter domestic political fortunes. The key question for a leader is whether the use of military force will benefit her constituencies at a cost that they are willing to pay and whether she can survive their displeasure if the costs are high.

The willingness of constituencies to pay costs varies with the value that they attach to the good in question. Their ability to constrain the leader varies with the institutional structure of accountability. The costs of using military force are influenced by the political-military strategy for the use of force, the strategic balance with the rival nation and the characteristics of the military force used. A leader may choose to use force only when the costs produced by the combination of political-military strategy chosen (S) + the strategic balance (SB) + the characteristics of the force used (CF) are equal to or lower than the costs acceptable to the leader's constituency (CC) minus the slippage in accountability produced by the domestic means of selecting leaders (A). Force will not always be used when these conditions are met, but force will not be used in their absence.

Why Latin America?

The concept of "regional security complex"[6] helps us evaluate this argument about the determinants of the use of force. This is an analytical construct that distinguishes a group of nations from the entire international system based on their particular security relationship. The regional security complex is not simply a geographic designation. States whose individual securities cannot be meaningfully separated from that of another form part of the same complex; e.g., South Korea and the U.S. The security interdependencies may be explicit and purposeful, or they may be the result of "security externalities," in which the costs and benefits of a bilateral security relationship spill over to affect other states.[7] A good example of a security externality is the threat that Brazil felt in the 1920s from U.S. military interventions throughout the Caribbean basin.[8]

This book uses the Latin American experience of the past century to support these claims and to suggest ways to manage competition among heterogeneous states in order to minimize conflict and stimulate cooperation. Latin America is a particularly appropriate place on which to focus. The region is a microcosm of international relations. Numerous states, at different levels of economic development, engage in constant interactions on issues in which their interests are not harmonious. Liberal economic policies have fallen in and out of favor and democracy has spread across the region and receded in three waves over the last century. The U.S. has demonstrated a consistent resolve to intervene in all disputes, militarized or not. A variety of international institutions, global and regional in nature, have sought to promote the peaceful resolution of conflict. Wars have occurred as recently as 1995, militarized disputes number in the hundreds, there are periodic arms races and arms control agreements, and many disputes have been settled via negotiations. The historical record thus provides important variation on the dependent variable of this study, the use of military force.

The historical record does not support simple explanations. Democracies have threatened and even fought each other (Colombia and Venezuela in 1987 and 1995; Ecuador and Peru throughout the last 15 years). Increased economic integration has not stopped states from threatening and fighting each other (Colombia and Venezuela in 1995; El Salvador and Honduras in 1969; Ecuador and Peru in 1995). Deterrence has failed (Argentina and Great Britain in 1982) and succeeded (Argentina and Chile in 1978). Great powers have stopped the fighting (the U.S. in Central America 1906–7), mediated crisis (Great Britain between Chile and Argentina in 1902 and the U.S. in the Ecuador-Peru war of 1995), and stood aside while the battlefield took its course (the U.S. in the Paraguay-Bolivia war of 1932–35, the Ecuador-Peru war in 1941, as well as the Malvinas/Falklands war of 1982 between Great Britain and Argentina). International institutions have served as fronts for the interests of the region's great power (the Pan American Union and the Organization of American States for the U.S.). These institutions have also been irrelevant (in the invasion of Panama and Granada, as well as during the Chaco War), and provided a forum for mediation (the OAS in the One Hundred Hours War between El Salvador and Honduras in 1969).

In short, Latin America over the last century has been a microcosm of international politics. Although little studied as a laboratory for interstate conflict management, its empirical richness facilitates analytical thinking about the use of military force in other regions after the Cold War.

Organization of the Book

The book has three parts. Part 1 introduces the issue of violent peace, providing theoretical (chapter 1) and empirical (chapter 2) material for the analysis that follows in Part 2. Chapter 1 presents the conceptual framework I use to think about the use of military force in foreign policy. A model of militarized bargaining is developed and the design of the research for assessing its plausibility is discussed. Chapter 2's historical description of wars and militarized disputes in Latin America provides evidence for the phenomenon of violent peace. It also demonstrates the suitability of the region for illustrating the plausibility of the model of militarized bargaining.

Part 2 presents a variety of quantitative, as well as qualitative, analyses of the use of military force. The first three chapters provide theoretical and empirical critiques of the three major paradigms for understanding conflict dynamics in the region: hegemonic management by the U.S. (chapter 3); democratic peace (chapter 4); and the military distribution of power (chapter 5).

The next two chapters illustrate how the militarized bargaining model contributes to explaining the use of military force in interstate disputes. Chapter 6 examines the militarization short of war of the Beagle Channel dispute between Argentina and Chile in 1978, with some discussion of the contrasting case of the militarization leading to war over the Malvinas between Argentina and Great Britain in 1982. Both cases have the same initiating country, run by a military dictatorship, yet two different ways of using force in foreign policy. Chapter 7 examines one enduring rivalry over time, the Ecuador-Peru conflict over the Amazon. This longitudinal analysis allows us to hold countries and issue stable over time. The Beagle and Amazon cases allow insight, respectively, into a military dyad and a democratic dyad.

The Conclusion summarizes the advantages of utilizing the militarized bargaining model for understanding Latin America's violent peace. By helping us to understand the decision to use force, the model also indicates what combination of policies might diminish the likelihood that states will resort to military force in their international relations.

Many people and organizations have contributed to this book. Financial support for different phases of the project came from grants by the University of California's Institute on Global Conflict and Cooperation and the San Diego branch of the Academic Senate, Committee on Research. Harry Hirsch generously provided funds from discretionary funds of the chair of the department of political science for editing.

I was fortunate to benefit from stays at a number of research centers while researching and writing. FLACSO-Ecuador was particularly forthcoming during the summers 1995, 1996, and 1997; Adrian Bonilla deserves a special thank you for his hospitality and encouragement. Francine Jacome and Andrés Serbín facilitated my research at INVESP, Caracas, Venezuela in 1995. The Center for International Affairs, Harvard University, provided a stimulating setting for revising the MS.

Early versions of various chapters were presented at workshops and seminar series at the University of California, Davis; the David Rockefeller Center for Latin American Studies, Harvard University; the Security Studies Seminar at MIT; the Naval Postgraduate School, Monterey, California; the Inter-American Dialogue in Washington, D.C.; the Fundación Arias para la Paz y el Progreso Humano in Costa Rica; the War College of the Ecuadorian Air Force; the Mexican Ministry of Foreign Relations in Mexico City; the Instituto de Altos Estudios de la Defensa Nacional, Caracas, Venezuela; the Centre for International Relations, Queen's University, Kingston, Canada; and the Dutch Foreign Ministry in Amsterdam. Participants were generous and encouraging and I thank them for their comments.

A number of my colleagues at UCSD read all or parts of the MS and made extremely helpful suggestions: Victor Magagna, Gary Jacobson, Peter Gourevitch, Gary Cox, and Arthur Lupia. I also received important research assistance from Steven A. Bernstein and Daniel Lake. Conversations with a trio of Chileans (Augusto Varas, Francisco Rojas and Emilio Meneses) over the years of the project were especially stimulating.

Grant Barnes and Leslie Bialler did the final editing and offered wonderful encouragement. I owe a special thanks to Kate Wittenberg of Columbia University Press for her confidence, patience, and encouragement in bringing this project to fruition.

My family—Jane, Alejandro, and Gabriel—deserve infinite gratitude for tolerating my physical and mental absences during the many years I put into this book.

The success of the project owes much to those named above and others too numerous to single out. The shortcomings, however, are mine alone.

David R. Mares
September 2000

Violent Peace

Part 1

The Issue

1   The Origins of Violent Peace: Explaining the Use of Force in Foreign Policy

Latin America represents a theoretical puzzle for the study of international relations. International relations analysts are usually attracted to the region because of its purported "long peace.[1]" They are intrigued that this pacific outcome occurs despite the absence of what have been identified in the literature as possible determinants of a "long peace": nuclear weapons,[2] democracy,[3] economic interdependence,[4] western culture,[5] or an advanced level of economic development.[6]

A detailed examination of the empirical record in chapter 2, however, indicates that there has not been a long peace in the region, whether one defines peace as the absence of "war" (defined by at least 1,000 battlefield-related deaths), or the absence of serious military confrontations. The empirical record raises three puzzles for analysts and policymakers concerned with understanding and possibly decreasing violent conflict. Why are these states using military force against each other? Given the prevalence of the use of force in relations between states in the region, why haven't there been more major wars? And, in the context of the current spread of democracy, why are so many democracies using force against each other?

These questions are best answered through the development of a general explanatory model of the use of force in foreign policy. In this model I conceptualize the decision to use force as an optimization problem in which decisionmakers weigh the costs of militarized conflict against their constituents' willingness to accept those costs. The decisionmaker cannot fully control either of these two factors. In addition, her balancing of these factors occurs within a context in which constituencies affect the decision-maker's ability to retain her position of power.

This argument assumes the rationality of behavior, but is not a rational unitary actor model of foreign policy. At defining moments, when a state's existence or international position is at play, we can assume that virtually all citizens want their leaders to defend the country, with military force if necessary. In those cases, it is analytically useful to collapse domestic politics and think about rational unitary actors conducting international politics. But this approach only means that we expect domestic actors to have homogeneous preferences about survival, not that they do not exist or act. When we focus on issues other than survival and international position, however, domestic actors' policy preferences become heterogeneous and the rational unitary actor approach becomes less useful.[7] Military force may still be used, but we have to break into the black box of domestic politics to understand it.

In brief, my argument is that leaders use foreign policy to provide collective and private goods to their domestic constituencies. The key question for the leader is whether the use of military force will benefit her constituencies at a cost that they are willing to pay and whether she can survive their displeasure if the costs are high. This is not, however, another "democratic peace" argument. As Doyle has pointed out, even those who accept the argument that democratic states (however one defines democracy)[8] are less likely to use force against each other still have to explain why force is used at all in these relationships.[9]

In my argument, the willingness of constituencies to pay costs varies with the value that they attach to the good in question. Their ability to constrain the leader varies with the institutional structure of accountability. The costs of using military force are influenced by the political-military strategy for the use of force, the strategic balance with the rival nation, and the characteristics of the military force used. A leader may choose to use force only when the costs produced by the combination of political-military strategy chosen (S) + the strategic balance (SB) + the characteristics of the force used (CF) are equal to or lower than the costs acceptable to the leader's constituency (CC) minus the slippage in accountability produced by the domestic means of selecting leaders (A). Force will not always be used when these conditions are met, but force will not be used in their absence.

$S + SB + CF \leq CC - A$ may lead to the decision to use force
$S + SB + CF > CC - A$ no force will be used

The answers to the second and third puzzles (why so "few" wars and why democracies use force against each other), build upon this model of the use of force. Wars are few relative to militarized clashes because the use of military force is a bargaining strategy, not an ideal option. Wars do not occur without any advance warning.[10] War is preceded by some degree of informal or formal bargaining in which the international and domestic costs of escalating to war are evaluated by both sides. Major war requires mobilization strategies that affect all citizens and depends upon the opponent's ability to resist. Few issues are likely to produce the domestic incentives for citizens to pay such high costs. Escalation to war should occur only when decisionmakers perceive that the costs of escalating do not outweigh the willingness of constituencies to pay, considering their ability to depose the leadership. Thus even large-scale use of military force by one side does not always produce "war"—for example, the Peruvian attacks on Ecuadorian outposts in 1981, or the U.S. invasions of the Dominican Republic (1965) and Panama (1989), or its mobilizations against Haiti (1994). The militarized bargaining model tells us where to look to understand both the attacks and non-responses.

Three of the model's variables are particularly helpful in understanding violence among democracies. First, citizen preferences concerning negotiation and the use of force vary, just as only a few democracies choose the death penalty over life imprisonment, and only one subjects minors to death.[11] Second, some uses of force entail very few domestic costs, hence democratic constituencies may be confronted with minor costs. Finally, even within democracies there are significant differences in the vulnerability of a leader on any one particular issue. Democratic leaders will, therefore, at times find the use of force to constitute an "appropriate" policy option even against another democracy.

This opening chapter elaborates on the conceptual and theoretical origins of the militarized bargaining model. The core of the approach is that the use of military force is best thought of in a bargaining context. I draw on historical data from Ancient Greece as well as modern international politics to support this view. The concept of "militarized bargaining" is developed and illustrated. Selection of the five key variables is theoretically justified and they are operationalized for use in the text.

Conceptualizing the Decision to Use Force

For roughly three centuries before their conquest by Macedonia, Greek city-states consistently engaged in battles against each other. As Victor Davis Hanson describes it, *polei* would organize their hoplites, meet in a clearing, and attack. Attack meant pushing against each other in organized formations, and when one side pushed through, the battle was over, as there could be no regrouping of the broken ranks. Few died in the process. If a battle were expected another day, a truce allowed the exchange of dead and wounded and the victor erected a trophy. In addition, when invading armies were not engaging other hoplites, they would cut and burn the orchards, vineyards, and grainfields of their adversaries. Given the horticultural characteristics of grape vines, olive trees, wheat, and barley, however, this activity did little long-term damage, as the hoplites, farmers themselves, fought after the harvests, and the vines and trees would grow back after their "pruning." Hanson argues convincingly that these battles made sense in a context in which the Greeks wished to avoid long wars, but had important disagreements with each other.[12]

Greek use of organized military violence in this period was thus ritualized, ubiquitous, and largely inconclusive. City-states generally neither perished nor lost their autonomy. The destruction of a city was a very costly affair, requiring hoplites to spend much time away from homes and fields. If we were to define "war" as a large-scale enterprise (as we moderns do with our definition of a minimum of 1,000 battlefield related deaths), and "peace" as the absence of war (as do those who speak of the "long peace" between the U.S. and Soviet Union), we would have to say that the Greeks in this period experienced a "violent peace." Military force was used frequently in their inter-*polei* relations, but major war among Greeks was avoided for almost 300 years, until the outbreak of the Peloponnesian War.

The termination of this type of warfare was largely the result of changes in strategies and the characteristics of force, which lowered the costs of using force and raised the stakes of conflict. After repeated contact with Persian armies in the fifth century B.C. the Greeks began to engage in varied operations, so that military organization turned away from an overwhelming reliance on hoplites. Athens' social-economic structure and wealth enabled it to field armies over the long period of time required to besiege cities. In addition, Athenian naval supremacy allowed it to maintain the constant vigilance necessary to subjugate its former allies in the Delian League and create an empire. Technological developments subsequently made siege warfare a less costly affair. As a result of making long-term war more feasible there was no inherent limit to the damage war could inflict. The stakes of warfare among the Greeks were raised, provoking the Peloponnesian War and subsequently enabling the Macedonian conquest of Greece.[13]

Is the concept of a "violent peace" relevant to the modern world? Perhaps more so than a focus on the occurrence of war. Not only is warring a rare event in the 19th and 20th centuries,[14] it has become even rarer after WWII in most of the world (see chapter 2). Yet, during the Cold War the U.S. and Soviets engaged in multiple threats of military violence, including nuclear war, as well as funding and supplying proxy wars. We cannot understand the foreign policy dynamics of the Cold War if we conceptualize it primarily as a long period of war avoidance between the U.S. and Soviet Union.[15] And, as the next chapter illustrates, for over a century Latin America has also experienced a "violent peace."

The concept of a "violent peace" forces us to consider the use of officially sanctioned military violence across national boundaries when war is not the intended result. War might occur, but as a result of escalation dynamics unknowable, unforeseen, or miscalculated by those who made the initial decision to use military force. In short, the decision to use military force should be thought of as a bargaining tactic rather than a decision to settle an interstate dispute through war. This book focuses on discovering the conditions under which states bargain with military force, as well as when those bargaining tactics are likely to lead to war.

A Model of Militarized Bargaining

International politics is largely a bargaining situation: two or more actors, with common and competing interests, interact with each other in addressing, directly or tacitly, the terms of their relationship. Because the international system is anarchic and actors are primarily self-interested, any interactions dealing with high-value issues carry the risk that one side will renege on the cooperative aspects of the relationship. These risks may be mitigated through a variety of mechanisms, but they do not disappear even when states enter into formal negotiations and agreements.[16]

Policymakers usually negotiate without any recourse to military force. Under some circumstances, however, state leaders draw upon their military capabilities to influence the terms of their international relationships. The uses of those military capabilities range from mere verbal threats to an application of military force that produces large-scale violence. These uses of a state's military capabilities represent *militarized bargaining*.

Militarized bargaining is used in a variety of situations. These can be fruitfully typologized as "pre-negotiations" (activities undertaken before the actors decide to formally begin a process leading to a cooperative solution to their problem), "distributional bargaining" (in which the outcome is conceptualized as zero-sum), and "problem-solving negotiations" (in which the parties focus on solving common problems).

Pre-negotiations may lead to formal negotiations or be oriented to pro-duce some political benefits independently of whether or not negotiations begin. For our purposes, the relevant point is that the contending parties are not addressing their issue because one side finds the status quo of no agreement to be an outcome superior to that it perceives as likely from negotiations. The purpose of pre-negotiation, therefore, may be to convince the reticent party either that the costs of the status quo are becoming higher or that the benefits of a possible agreement are increasing.[17] It can suggest that war is a possible result and that, even short of war, the overall rela-tionship will suffer and the reticent party will need to divert resources into preparing for armed clashes. Introducing military considerations into the relationship is not what Fisher, Ury, and Patton have in mind when they counsel a party confronting another who refuses to negotiate to create "ob-jective conditions that can be used to establish deadlines."[18] But it may be the only option available to the state seeking change, short of capitulating on the issue.

When negotiations are absent, the government of the revisionist state may also seek to communicate credibly to its domestic constituency, as well as to other governments, that the issue is still alive. These are not "diversionary conflicts," in which a policymaker under pressure at home provokes an international crisis in order to rally domestic support around a new issue. Low-level militarized signaling could be a way for a policy-maker to satisfy some of his nationalist constituency cheaply. Militarized bargaining can thus help a decisionmaker to defuse pressure for resolution when such efforts might have little possibility of success or cost his core constituencies more than they would be willing to pay.

Using military force as a threat has many attractions as a tool in *distri-butional bargaining*. Given the commitment problems inherent in any bar-gaining situation, an action which can be decomposed into steps allows a player to build a reputation for following through on threats.[19] Military force can be disaggregated into public pronouncements, mobilization or display, use of force causing minor damage or few deaths, and use of force resulting in great damage or many deaths.[20] In addition, because the use of military force has the potential to escalate to war, its use even at low levels makes it more difficult for the initiator to back down without some concessions; thus it serves to bind the initiator to his position.[21]

Even if one side seeks to engage in *problem-solving negotiations* it may be advantageous to use military signaling to either expand the other's bar-gaining range or to credibly communicate that one will not expand its own. Figures 1.1 and 1.2 illustrate the bargaining situation in a problem solving negotiation. The two vertical axes represent the payoffs to the two parties. The horizontal line divides the payoffs into positive or negative and conse-quently represents a zero payoff. Any point on the line is an actor's Best Alternative to No Agreement (BATNA). Each party's preference curves begin high on their payoff axis and move outward toward the other party, crossing

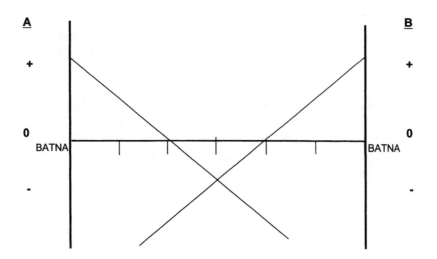

FIGURE 1.1 Bargaining Scenario: No Cooperative Solution Possible

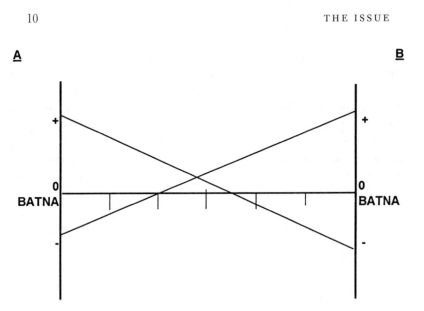

FIGURE 1.2 Bargaining Scenario: Cooperative Solution Possible

the horizontal line along the way. If the two parties' preference curves cross at or above the horizontal line, agreement is possible.

There are two situations in which militarized bargaining might be appropriate in problem-solving negotiations. If the preference curves do not intersect above the horizontal line, militarizing the dispute at low levels might extend the other party's curve outward, as a result either of fearing a worsened bilateral relationship or because a third party might influence it to make a settlement possible. The other case could arise when there is disagreement about where within the cooperative space the agreement will be.[22] The point of militarized bargaining in this situation is not to bully the other party into an agreement, but to influence the other party's costs slightly. Bullying tactics would destroy a problem-solving relationship and push the parties into distributional bargaining.

Theoretical Foundations

Although Schelling's seminal work on strategic interaction in international politics recognized the potential importance of linking issues in dispute,[23] the traditional model of interstate bargaining perceives issues as largely one dimensional.[24] This approach fits reasonably well with the assumption of a rational unitary actor because preferences can be assumed and held constant. But the work of negotiation analysts using a problem-solving bargaining model forces us to open up the black box of decision-making to discover which issues can and cannot be linked, as well as the extent of the bargaining range. In other words, the bargaining scenario in which states find themselves depends upon domestic demands in both countries. If a decisionmaker cannot convince his constituency to accept extra dimensions, he will of necessity identify the issue as one-dimensional. In addition, if a support coalition does not form within the defender's domestic selectorate for opening discussions with a dissatisfied party, no bargaining range will exist. We need, therefore, to incorporate domestic politics to explain foreign policy decisions.[25]

My model builds on the work of numerous scholars. From Alexander George and the "second wave" of deterrence theorists, I take the insight that a focus on the simple overall military balance is not sufficient to explain the use of force in interstate relations.[26] My aim is to make more systematic the argument that certain nonmilitary variables, under specifiable conditions, will determine whether a state can deter a challenge to the status quo.

I have also incorporated insights from analysts who study the foreign policies of small states in alliances, whether those be formal or informal. These studies have shown convincingly that often the "tail wags the dog" and that the problems of "moral hazard" provide important latitude for small states to engage in violent behavior at times.[27] I put these findings in the context of a general model of the decision to use violence internationally. In my general model, small states differ from larger states only in their capabilities, not in their reasoning or desires. Hence, an argument about when weak or strong states choose to utilize military force should be deducible from the general model once we make adjustments for the appropriate distribution of capabilities, military and otherwise.

Another school of analysts which will find their work reflected here is the retrospective voting/expected utility school which links the policy behavior of leaders to their particular requirements for remaining in office. I found Reed's analysis of heterogeneous politicians particularly fruitful for modifying the approach used by the group of analysts which has flourished around Bruce Bueno de Mesquita.[28] I conceptualize decisionmaking in many of the same ways, but differ in both the core interests that drive policymaking and the preference orderings of citizens. They define core interests simply as "physical security," which I find too limiting. What drives my model is the notion (and the empirical reality) that the use of force in international politics does not disappear when the survival of the state is no longer in serious question. We need to ask and answer the question, "Why?" rather than assume it away. Another difference in our approaches is that I do not assume that citizens always prefer to negotiate rather than fight. Because of these two major differences the utility calculations of decisionmakers will thus differ dramatically in my model as compared to theirs.

This model of the decision to use force internationally is based upon six theoretical assumptions that define the general context in which foreign policy is made. These assumptions are

- international anarchy
- rational, forward looking and self-interested behavior by the actors
- the existence of a hierarchy of national goals
- heterogeneous constituencies in domestic politics
- decisionmakers who try to use foreign policy to remain in power
- incomplete information, both domestically and internationally.

I begin with the assumptions of anarchy and rational, forward looking and self-interested behavior by the relevant actors. Anarchy is simply the absence of an overarching authority that can make agreements among states binding and punish those who violate such agreements. Actor rationality is instrumental, meaning that actors choose to behave in ways they expect will help them get what they want. They are also self-interested and forward looking, by which I mean that they put their own needs first and think about whether the agreements made today will hold up tomorrow. Competing states in an anarchic realm and actors in the domestic arena who are forward looking confront a commitment problem in their relationships with those who promise to behave in certain ways. The severity of this commitment problem varies depending upon the costs actors pay for breaking their commitments.[29]

Anarchy sets the context within which the actors compete, but it does not determine all of their goals. I find the assumption that states seek to secure their sovereignty (understood as the ability to decide oneself how to respond to challenges and opportunities at the international level[30]) more useful than the assumption that they seek power.[31] In any strategic interaction situation, the options players have are affected by the relative distribution of resources relevant to the matter at hand; this is true even when cooperative interactions are possible.[32] Consequently, states will care about their relative standing, also known as international position.

Historically, there have been instances in which states, even great powers, did not confront credible threats to either their survival or the maintenance of their position, or when it was not possible to move up in position. This experience is as true for great powers as for smaller powers.[33] At these times military force may still be used in international politics, but in order to advance other interests of states, not to defend their core interests. Krasner argued that at such a moment the U.S. followed its ideological interests in Vietnam.[34] Ideology, however, is an ambiguous concept, and in any case one would really be speaking about the ideology of the social forces dominating the state apparatus, since a state cannot have an ideology. For purposes of social scientific analysis, material rather than ideological interests are more useful. Thus, under international conditions of significantly reduced immediate threat, we are most likely to find goals that are defined by the material interests of the governing coalition in the state.[35]

I assume, therefore, that a *hierarchy of goals* exists for a state under conditions of international anarchy: survival, position and the advancement of national interests defined domestically. Once we introduce domestic politics into the argument, we move beyond the rational unitary actor model. I make two assumptions about domestic politics, one focusing on the domestic constituencies which select the government's leadership (the electorate in a democracy, and in nondemocratic polities the groups without whom a leadership could not survive) and the other concerning the foreign policy-maker(s).

The *selectorate* is assumed to have both *homogenous and heterogeneous characteristics*, depending upon the foreign policy issue. In the foreign policy arena, the selectorate is assumed, first and foremost, to want its leadership to provide for the security and position of the nation. Even in a dictatorship, the selectorate will want to determine the decisions concerning how the country will respond to international challenges and opportunities, as well as to continue to exploit the disenfranchised at home. Security and position are collective goods for the selectorate. All members of the selectorate will benefit from their provision, whether they contribute the taxes, blood or skills required to supply security and position (if they don't benefit because the leadership excludes them, they have already ceased being part of the selectorate).

As the threats to the security and position of the nation decline, the selectorate will demand that its leadership provide them with private goods. Private goods in foreign affairs are those whose benefits are consumed by specific groups. Examples would be the acquisition of nonstrategic territory (that which is not necessary for defense or lacks the natural or human resources which generate national wealth) for cattle ranchers, fishing rights for a particular group of fishermen, or the protection of citizens migrating illegally to other countries. Hence, the selectorate displays heterogeneous characteristics when it comes to the demand for private goods.

The selectorate is also heterogeneous in its preferences concerning how to behave internationally with respect to the use of force. Advocates of a Liberal Peace paradigm assume that citizens will always prefer to negotiate than use military force, though they would prefer to use military force than capitulate to demands made via military threats.[36] The reality of citizens capitulating rather than fighting (British public opinion at Munich) or supporting the use of military force against another democracy rather than negotiating (the British vis-à-vis Fashoda, and Venezuela against Colombia[37]), are too important to be ignored. I leave the selectorate's preference orderings to be determined empirically.

We can now turn to the *decisionmakers*. The relevant decisionmaker is not a bureaucrat or simply an appointed administrator. In foreign policy matters, the head of government (whether president, prime minister, or dictator) must authorize decisions that involve the use of official military force (including standing orders to respond with force if borders are violated). Even in a military dictatorship, policy decisions are made with the expectation that civilian supporters will either benefit from that use of force or not pay costs beyond what they are willing to accept. To ignore these questions would cost the military the support of their civilian allies, thereby threatening the government's ability to remain in power.[38]

The goal of the decisionmaker is to remain in power, either individually or as a group if a leadership period is of fixed duration (e.g., the election to the Presidency of a member of the same party). Policy choices are best understood from this perspective. While domestic policy choices probably matter more for selection,[39] in cases where foreign policy is disputatious it must matter to important actors domestically (or else there would have been a settlement). Bueno de Mesquita and Siverson have demonstrated the negative costs which losing a war can have on a leader's ability to remain in power.[40] But there is no reason why the foreign policy arena cannot also provide positive benefits. In short, I assume that policymakers perceive a positive payoff with the selectorate for delivering goods from whichever sphere, domestic or foreign.

Analysts of international relations are used to thinking about the possibility of domestic political gain in terms of diversionary fights.[41] There is no reason to limit the possibilities of domestic payoffs to those derived from in-group–out-group dynamics. A leader who takes a major step toward resolving a contentious issue can benefit at these times, because he will be able to demonstrate his ability to rise above "partisan" politics and act for the good of the nation. For example, faced with a Congress which would not pass his proposed legislation and hounded by charges of corruption, Guatemalan President Jorge Serrano reversed a century-long policy and recognized the existence of Belize. The military, important supporters of the President, were pleased with this move as it made their internal and external security tasks more manageable by reducing the threat of war with the British guarantors of Belizean sovereignty.[42]

Incomplete information. Decisionmakers have to make decisions without knowing everything about their own costs and benefits, nor about their rival's. Incomplete information gives added value to private information and provides incentives for parties to mislead rivals. In addition, what decisionmakers "know" may be erroneous. Rather than treat this as a cognitive problem of misperception, I follow Bueno de Mesquita and company in viewing this as a problem of incomplete information.[43] Nevertheless, I go beyond their treatment of the topic by incorporating the possibility that one's knowledge of one's own costs may itself be incomplete.[44]

If information were complete, rival states would know each other's bargaining range and whether cooperation was possible. If their bargaining ranges overlapped, they would also know the commitment of each to a specific point in the cooperative space. With incomplete information rivals are not sure where they stand or whether third parties might be enticed to become involved. Decisionmakers may thus pursue militarized bargaining with only an estimated guess as to whether this tactic will either get negotiations started or influence those already under way. In addition, incorrect information about one's ability to influence a rival's policy can also produce an overly optimistic decision to challenge. The information a decisionmaker has about his country's own capabilities to effectively carry out the chosen policy may also be erroneous.

Because of the strategic interaction among rival leaders and the problem of incomplete information internationally and domestically, one cannot simply examine the outcome of the militarized foreign policy and deduce initial policy preferences of the leadership. Rather, analysis must begin by setting out the general context of foreign policy making, examining its particular manifestation for the issue and countries in question, and tracing the politics and updating of information along the decision path.

Explaining Militarized Bargaining

Militarized bargaining is simply the use of military force by one state to influence the behavior of another. The specific context in which militarized bargaining may occur has two characteristics. First, a disagreement exists between two or more nations. Second, at least one of the actors has a military capability. Anytime these two situations occur, there is a potential for a state to use military force to influence the behavior of another.

Policymakers contemplating force are hypothesized to consider the interaction among five factors that bridge the international and domestic spheres. Policymakers evaluate each factor in accordance with the theoretical assumptions of the model. The five factors are:

- the *political-military strategy* within which force would be used
- the *strategic balance* among the parties involved
- the *characteristics of the force* to be used
- the *willingness of constituencies to absorb costs* associated with the use of force
- the *degree of accountability of the policymakers* to their constituencies

Political-Military Strategy. The utility of force as a policy instrument has to be evaluated in the first instance in terms of its contribution to the policymaker's ability to advance her constituencies' interests. Only after ascertaining its potential usefulness does it make sense for policymakers to weigh the costs and benefits of using force.

There are different ways in which to advance those interests, depending upon the state of the relationship between the contending parties. These alternatives can be usefully summarized in five political-military strategies.

- keep the issue alive
- affect bilateral negotiations
- defend the status quo
- attract the support of third parties
- impose a solution

If the leader perceives the costs of any likely resolution of the dispute to be greater than those which his constituency is likely to accept, he will not pursue a solution today. But since the constituency wants a solution favorable to its interests at some point, the leader can score points at home by *keeping the issue alive* internationally. If the country is in possession of the resources in dispute, keeping it alive means simply continuing to control the asset *de facto*. But if the country does not control the asset, keeping the issue alive can be done by any combination of diplomatic protest, economic obstructions, or low-level military signals. The combination selected will depend upon the extent of the leader's credibility problems with the rival or third parties and the acceptability of associated costs to his domestic constituency. Low credibility will bias actions toward more severe acts, whether diplomatic, economic, or military. A constituency with great aversion to costs will bias policymakers toward less severe diplomatic, economic, or military actions, e.g., a verbal threat to send forces to disputed territory, "if necessary."

If the leader believes that negotiations could produce an outcome acceptable to his constituency, there will be an incentive to *negotiate bilaterally*. But the rival may believe any likely outcome of negotiations to be unacceptable to her constituency, and therefore avoid negotiations or negotiate with a very narrow bargaining range, in essence, *defending the status quo*. In these circumstances each state wants to communicate its resolve and its high valuation of the asset in dispute. A low-level use of military force could be an attractive option for signaling. In addition, since each state's position on the issue is a function of the costs domestic constituencies are willing to pay, low-level use of military force by one party may be directed at raising those costs to the other. The rival's domestic constituencies are expected to induce their leaders to broaden the government's bargaining range. If the negotiating process includes, or could potentially include, *third parties*, the use of military force against a rival may be a signal directed toward the third parties in order to get them to pressure one's rival to negotiate or widen its bargaining range.

Finally, leaders could choose to attempt to resolve the issue unilaterally by *imposing a solution* and thereby provide their domestic constituencies with the largest possible good. Low-level military force is unlikely to produce such an outcome, except in the case where one state can credibly communicate that it is willing to follow up such low-level use with large-scale attacks.[45] Consequently, we should see this strategy accompanied by the large-scale active use of military force.

None of these strategies is inherently appropriate for a leader to pursue. Discerning which strategy, if any, a leader is likely to pursue requires examining the specific case. Case details will illuminate where the disagreement stands, the determinants of the costs associated with each strategy, and the constraints on the costs a leader can impose on his constituency. The actual costs for using military force are determined by the strategic balance and the characteristics of the force to be used.

Strategic Balance. The strategic balance is a relative measure. I use it here to refer to the factors which influence the likely costs produced by the strategies each actor can use in particular disputes, rather than in its more narrow military sense, as in "strategic nuclear weapons." As numerous studies of small-state conflict behavior have demonstrated, a focus on the *absolute* capability of a nation, even incorporating nonmilitary factors, is inadequate for analyzing interstate conflict dynamics.[46]

The appropriateness of a measure of the strategic balance depends upon the particular political-military strategy one is utilizing and the political-military strategy one is confronting. The strategic balance is defined by the resources that are relevant to those strategies and thus helps us understand the bargaining situation between the actors. While others have made this point using variations in military strategy, risk assessments, and time frames,[47] I add diplomatic and economic factors to the range of relevant resources. Because of incomplete information, however, the strategic balance is never entirely clear to either party.

Three broad categories of resources are useful in considering the strategic balance: diplomatic, economic, and military. The relevant *diplomatic resources* revolve around the ability to garner external support for, and blunt external criticism of, one's strategy in the dispute. This is affected not just by the skill of the diplomatic corps, but also by the standing which one's position on the disputed issue has in the international political order of the era. Great powers may claim that their interests and values are universal, use force in the defense of those interests, and face little international sanction. Smaller powers, however, must couch the defense of their interests within the context set by the reigning great power political order or be willing to face international sanctions. When smaller states can link their actions to the interests of great powers, new opportunities for advancing their interests arise. It may be possible to gain support for their own use of force, or aid in defending against a rival's use of force, or perhaps even to increase international pressure on the rival to negotiate the previously nonnegotiable. Alternatively, when a small state has interests that are of minor consequence to the great powers, its rival's diplomacy might serve to convince the great powers that any benefits they might garner from becoming involved in the dispute would be outweighed by the associated costs.

Economic resources include both those that can be used in a nonmilitary way to influence behavior by a rival and those for building up national capacity to use military force. In evaluating whether to use military force, policymakers will consider both aspects of economic power. When economic leverage is sufficient to gain one's goals at acceptable costs, force is unlikely to be used.[48] But when that economic leverage is deemed insufficient, how economic resources affect a state's ability to mobilize, use, and resupply military forces becomes paramount.

A state's economic infrastructure (railroads, highways, and airports) can dramatically affect the logistical costs of using force. The ability to raise revenue for defense can be an important consideration because it highlights the domestic opportunity costs involved in using force, thereby making it more likely that opposition to its use will form. For example, the inability of a poor state to tax the wealthy imposes a severe constraint on state expenditures. Military expenditures thus come more openly, while economic and social welfare spending decreases. When the domestic elite are focused on moderating the polarization of society they are unlikely to support a leader who wishes to spend the government's meager resources in militarized bargaining with a neighbor.

Honduras in the 1960s and 1970s provides a good example of this economic constraint on the use of force and helps explain why El Salvador believed it could quickly defeat Honduras with a blitz in 1969. Honduras also illustrates how diplomacy might overcome this constraint: after the 1979 victory by the communist-oriented Sandinistas in neighboring Nicaragua, the U.S. flooded Honduras with both economic and military aid. Economic constraints on Honduras' military capabilities were thus obliterated, until the U.S. perceived that the Sandinistas were defeated and lost interest.[49]

Military resources include the quality and quantity of personnel, type and quantity of armaments, and doctrines for utilizing those resources. Studies of great power foreign policy tend to emphasize the quantitative aspect of such resources because the social and economic disparities that underlie qualitative differences among great powers are not large. But the experiences of Iraq in the Gulf War, Israel in the Middle East, and Chile in South America demonstrate the importance of quality differentials where they exist.

Characteristics of Force. Two characteristics of the military force contemplated also affect the costs of using force: mobilization requirements and force alternatives. The attributes of the *domestic mobilization* process affect the time domestic and international opposition has to organize, as well as the personal disruption experienced by the relevant publics. A society's decision to have a military defense establishment with certain characteristics reflects its perception of vulnerability in the international system as well as the domestic politics of the civil-military relationship,[50] and is not simply an outcome of the desire to use military force in any particular foreign policy dispute. Nevertheless, the defense establishment's characteristics will affect the way in which a leader chooses to use force. Most studies that examine this aspect of the use of force are concerned with its impact on escalating a crisis with an international rival.[51] Yet the cost implications for the domestic constituencies of the decisionmaker should also be of concern. The use of force which relies on a reserve-based military produces the highest domestic economic costs as workers are taken away from their jobs and employers have to scramble to replace them temporarily. The use of a standing military force produces the lowest mobilization costs.

Force alternatives also influence the likely level of political costs to the leader. Political costs will primarily be the result of the level of casualties and the budgetary costs of the operation. Given similar training and equipment, the relative vulnerability of ground forces is highest, with air and naval forces generally much lower. The cheapest use of force from the perspective of casualties would be a naval bombardment from offshore or a drone-piloted airstrike, followed by manned aircraft, and the costliest is the use of the army to penetrate territory. However, decisionmakers must also consider the economic costs generated by using these different means. For some countries, the consumption of jet fuel, rockets, etc. in even a small military action may exhaust the defense budget. The leader would then be forced to confront the political costs of raising more money for the defense establishment.

While knowing the costs of using military force is a necessary component of any decision to use it, policymakers must also assess how their constituencies value these costs and what they are willing to pay for the foreign policy good. In addition, we need to consider the ability of the constituency to hold the policymakers accountable for their action.

Constituency Acceptance of Costs. In this model, constituents are defined narrowly as those whose support is required for a leader to remain in office. In a democracy voters in general are not constituents; rather, it is those voters who voted for the policymaker[52] as well as those voters whose support might be necessary for re-election. In a dictatorship, constituents include military officers and economic elites, but they do not include the large segments of the urban poor who are supportive of strong authority. The identification of constituents cannot be done in any general way, but must be analyzed in the specific cases.

Constituencies are heterogeneous with respect to what they want their foreign policy leaders to provide beyond the collective goods of national survival and international position. Their private demands will be related to their social-political and economic characteristics. Hence, fishermen will want access to rich fisheries, while migrant workers will desire freedom to cross borders and humane treatment once across.

Constituents are also heterogeneous in the costs they are willing to pay to receive those goods. The amount of money, blood, and inconvenience a constituency is willing to pay for a collective or private good is another empirical question to be answered in case analysis. But we can make a few general suggestions about payment schemes constituencies will likely find attractive. Collective goods have to be couched in nationalist rhetoric in order for the vast majority of society to contribute to their provision. The low level of draft dodging and tax evasion during modern wars demonstrates the success of nationalist sentiment for overcoming collective action problems. Constituencies seeking private goods will prefer to have costs distributed entirely away from them or at least broadly with other groups, including nonconstituents. In general, private goods delivered to a constituency at costs below actual costs will be received with greater enthusiasm by the constituency. This distribution of costs is made easier if the constituency and policymaker describe the private good in ways that imbue them with nationalist sentiments (e.g., fisheries as part of the national patrimony).

Degree of Accountability. The sensitivity of the leadership to its constituency's cost evaluations is determined by the institutional structure of leadership accountability, which includes selection intervals and the leadership's ability to perpetuate itself in office via selection of colleagues. The democracy-nondemocracy distinction is not sufficient for this variable.[53] The literature clearly demonstrates that the institutional rules governing who votes and when, as well as how votes are counted, vary across democracies and make a significant difference in who wins and policy outcomes.[54] There is also an inherent problem in any principal's control of her agent; consequently, "slippage" will inevitably occur between what the majority of citizens want and what their legislators, presidents, and government bureaucrats actually do.[55] The experience of the United States demonstrates that even within well institutionalized democracies, leaders may have the means and willingness to use force in a dispute without getting explicit authorization from the legislature or the public.[56] Finally, studies have shown that non-democracies are also less likely to go to engage in violence against other nondemocracies than against democracies.[57] The "nondemocratic peace" therefore bears analysis as well. My model, since it does not privilege democratic institutions per se, sheds light on the decision to use force in all types of political regimes.

The earlier assumption that the leader desires to stay in office makes the determinants of retaining office central in our discussion of constraints on the leader. Three factors are crucial in determining the degree of accountability of policymakers to their constituencies: selection intervals, reselection possibilities, and legacy possibilities.

Selection intervals for the leader affect the swiftness with which the use of military force can be sanctioned at home. The time it takes to call the policymaker to account is important because a leader may be able to deliver other goods after using military force which will dilute the anger felt by a constituency that paid costs at the prior moment.[58] Five gradations distinguish the vulnerability of a decisionmaker on this factor, and vulnerability makes for accountability. The least vulnerable leader is a personalist dictator. He faces an unlimited time period in office; removing him at any particular point in time requires a major upheaval in domestic politics. Next in vulnerability is a leader who faces a fixed time period in office, and can be removed beforehand only through an impeachment process for criminal behavior. Leaders in presidentialist systems are in this situation. Prime Ministers of a majority government have fixed terms, but can be deposed beforehand through a vote of no confidence. Since they lead a majority government, such votes should be rare. Leaders of authoritarian governments that depend upon the support of a small group (e.g., a military junta) may have irregular terms but are subject to swift replacement. They are, consequently, quite vulnerable to their constituency. The most vulnerable leader is the Prime Minister in a coalition government. The coalition is likely to be constituted by parties who have major differences (otherwise they would be in the same party); as a result, votes of no confidence are an ever-present danger for the decisionmaker.

Re-selection possibilities constrain leaders by giving them an opportunity to remain in office if they continue to please their constituencies. Four possibilities are analytically useful for our discussion. A leader who has no possibility for reselection can only be controlled by the possibility of ouster before her term expires. The decisionmaker who can be reselected for a consecutive term will be more controllable in his first term. In the case where a fixed number of terms is specified, he reverts to the situation of no reselection in the final term. The leader who can be reselected only after a specified period has passed (usually one term) is likely to be more adventuresome on policies that she expects to have a medium-term payoff, even if short-term costs might be high during her first term. The leader who is most controllable by his constituencies will be the one who confronts unlimited possibilities for reselection.

Leaders can be constrained in the absence of reselection if they can influence the selection of their successor. These *legacy possibilities* are fundamentally determined by the strength of the political groupings to which the leader belongs. In democracies these groups take the form of political parties which compete for the selectorate's votes. Although parties exist in authoritarian polities, it is the party elite who determines both who the party's candidates are and whether they will win. Strong political groups or parties make it more likely that a leader who delivers to his constituency but cannot be re-selected will be succeeded by a colleague from his group or party.

We now have three elements to consider in this causal factor of accountability. Selection intervals have five variations, reselection possibilities have four, and legacy possibilities are two. That makes 11 variations, with 132 possible combinations. These are far too many to list, but Table 1.1 presents some of the most interesting combinations, in ascending order of accountability, along with some examples.

TABLE 1.1 Illustrations of Variations of Leadership Accountability
(in ascending order)

Type	Examples
1. Personal dictatorship	Iraq under Hussein, Nicaragua under Somoza
2. Fixed term, authoritarian dominant party state with unlimited reelection	Indonesia under Suharto, Communist Cuba
3. Fixed term, no reelection, weak parties, and presidential	Ecuador, 1979–94
4. Fixed term, authoritarian dominant party state with no reelection	Mexico, Islamic Iran
5. Fixed term, limited reelection, strong parties and presidential	U.S., Venezuela, Chile, Argentina
6. Fixed term, parliamentary, majority party government	UK
7. Irregular term, swift replacement	Argentine military junta, 1976–83
8. Fixed term, parliamentary, with coalition government	Israel, 1997

Hypotheses

The argument of this book is that whether a state will engage in milita-rized bargaining depends in part upon its ability to provide benefits to a leader's domestic constituencies at a cost that they are willing to pay. It is an argument about the necessary, though not sufficient conditions for force to be used in international politics.

The model generates the following hypotheses about the likelihood of a state using military force in its foreign policy. A leader may choose to use force only when the costs produced by the combination of the political-military strategy chosen (S), the strategic balance (SB) and the characteristics of the force used (CF) are equal to or lower than the costs acceptable to the leader's constituency (CC) minus the slippage in accountability produced by domestic means of selecting leaders (A).

When $S + SB + CF \leq CC - A$, a leader may decide to use force
When $S + SB + CF > CC - A$, a leader will decide not to use force

Once a dispute has become militarized the decision to further escalate follows the same logic. Policymakers update their information on the status of each variable, but the calculations yield the same predictions: force may only be used in each instance if $S + SB + CF \leq CC - A$.

Evaluating the Argument

My analytic framework for explaining the determinants of militarized bargaining is most appropriately tested by structured and focused comparative case studies that employ a process-tracing methodology.[59] While the case studies will be focused on the dynamics of decisionmaking when considering whether or not to use force, I have also provided brief historical backgrounds to the conflict for readers unfamiliar with the specific cases. Structured comparisons are carried out by addressing the following questions in each case analysis:

- What political-military strategy did the leader have in mind when he chose whether or not to use force?
- What was the strategic balance between the rival states at the time of the decision to use force and how did the leaders perceive the balance?
- What were the domestic costs produced by the characteristics of the decision to use force and were those costs anticipated by the decisionmakers?
- What groups made up the constituency of the leader at the time of the decision and what did they perceive the costs of the use of force to be?
- Did the leader attempt to evaluate his constituencies' views on the use of force and did he feel constrained by them?
- Was the behavior consistent with the hypotheses produced by my model of militarized bargaining?

The Argentina-Chile and Ecuador-Peru enduring rivalries are used to demonstrate the plausibility of the model. Enduring rivalries are particularly appropriate conflict groupings with which to study force initiation dynamics. These rivalries consist of disputes which are repetitive, severe, durable, and continuous (at least five militarized disputes within a 25-year period with no more than 10 years between incidents, unless the issue in dispute remained the same).[60] The problem of selecting on the dependent variable (the occurrence of a MID) is mitigated when one examines an enduring rivalry in which, as occurs in these cases, years may pass between instances of force although the issue continues to be contentious.

Examining leaders' decisions concerning the use of force in an enduring rivalry allows us to more clearly examine how variations in the five variables affect leaders' calculations. Latin America provides a rich empirical history for anyone investigating violent conflict. There are periodic arms races, governments fall in and out of international favor, nationalist fervor ebbs and flows, and polities move away from and toward democracy. Even within democratic structures there have been significant constitutional reforms over time which affect the separation of powers as well as the sensitivity of leaders to the electorate. Because of these shifts, the Latin American experience should be particularly ideal for evaluating arguments about the effect of democracy per se on the use of force internationally.[61]

Quantitative tests of my argument are not yet possible, as the existing data sets do not include at least four of my five variables (the accountability variable can be extrapolated from existing data). Given the paucity of information concerning Latin American militarized interstate disputes one needs to virtually reconstruct each of the hundreds of MIDs to develop the relevant data set. Hopefully, the analysis in this book will stimulate such efforts.

Testing this framework requires examining the relationship between leaders and their key constituencies. If the model is correct, we should not see militarized behavior occurring out of the blue. Instead, we should find leaders attempting to calculate the costs to key supporters of the decision to use force, as well as their ability to devise and implement a strategy to gain their policy goals within a relevant strategic balance. If national survival or international position is at stake, the calculations should be straightforward, both in terms of which resources matter in the strategic balance as well as what costs domestic constituencies will be willing to pay. On issues other than national survival or international position, however, leaders should pay particular attention to the variety of signals by key groups hoping to influence the decision: polls, public demonstrations, editorials, statements by acknowledged spokespeople for particular interests, etc.

The model gains support to the extent that we see leaders strategically calculating both domestic and international costs before undertaking military actions. If leaders consistently take these factors into consideration this framework will be useful. The Conclusion to the book addresses how to incorporate this framework into a more complete argument about the sufficiency factors for militarized bargaining to occur.

2 Latin America's Violent Peace

Analysts of international conflict tend to ignore Latin America, believing that little military conflict exists and that whatever wars in which these nations may engage are minor.[1] Even those who specialize in the politics of the region, including Latin Americans themselves, tend to perceive interstate conflict as sporadic and generally, a non-issue.[2] This chapter examines the historical record to demonstrate that the use of violence across national boundaries has been a consistent trait of Latin America's international politics. In fact, violence in the region escalates to war in much the same proportion as in the rest of the world, with the exception of the Middle East.

The historical record of military conflict makes the Latin American experience appropriate for evaluating competing explanations for why decisionmakers choose to use force. This chapter serves as a historical overview of the empirical experience analyzed in parts 2 and 3. In the first section, I define the security complex to which Latin America belongs and identify its security *problematique*. A second section quantitatively examines the history of Latin American wars and MIDs, both intra- and inter-regionally. A concluding section examines past and current Latin American efforts to eliminate the use of violence in the region's international politics.

The Latin American Security Complex and Its Problematique

The primary security concerns that tightly link a group of countries in Latin America's security complex arise from both self-perceptions and political competition. These factors link the U.S., Latin America, Belize, Guyana, and Suriname into a security complex,[3] but have historically kept Canada out. Even Canada's decision to join the Organization of American States has not yet effectively incorporated it into the security complex.

Self-perceptions linked the former Spanish and Portuguese colonies with the former British colony that defined itself in opposition to the mother country (the U.S.), but not with the one which never severed those political links (Canada). After independence the idea of a "Western Hemisphere," culturally and politically distinct from Europe, permeated the diplomatic rhetoric, if not actual foreign policy, of these states. The U.S. itself articulated this view, officially in the Monroe Doctrine and popularly when it sided with a Venezuelan dictator against the British in the 1890s.[4] Latin American diplomats even discussed the desirability of developing "American" (i.e., western hemispheric) international law. At various times different Latin American countries tried, unsuccessfully, to make the Monroe Doctrine (promulgated unilaterally by U.S. President James Monroe in 1823) a security policy of the Americas as a whole.[5]

But self-perceptions are usually a deceptive guide to behavior and outcomes when they clash with material interests and power. The U.S. has always opposed multilateralizing the Monroe Doctrine, while in the early nineteenth century Simón Bolívar in Colombia, as well as Argentine leaders, quickly discovered that the U.S. would not jeopardize its relations with Europe to defend other American nations.[6] In the mid-nineteenth century Mexico found to its dismay that South American states were unwilling to play a role in limiting U.S. expansion at the expense of its American neighbors. Further examples of perceptions themselves not defining security complexes abound in the twentieth century. Among the most notable instances were Brazil's frustrated claims to membership in the great power concert in the Council of the League of Nations, Argentine perceptions that it belonged to a British-centered security complex during World War II, and revolutionary Cuba's belief that it could leave the regional security complex.[7]

Central American balance of power dynamics, the Nicaragua-Colombia territorial dispute, and the 1995 war between Ecuador and Peru provide more contemporary examples of the indirect links among distinct bilateral conflicts. In 1993 Colombia accused Nicaragua of seeking missile boats from North Korea in order to contest Colombian sovereignty over the San Andres Islands. Nicaragua denied the charges, noted that it was downsizing its military establishment in accord with Central American confidence-building measures, and cited the sale of helicopters to Ecuador as an example. These purchases, in turn, increased the operational capacity of the Ecuadorian armed forces and contributed to its provocative behavior in the disputed territory. Peru responded with a full-scale attack on Ecuadorian positions.[8]

The security externalities that combine with self-identification to make "Latin America" a security complex[9] develops from three different arenas: international, regional, and domestic. At the international level, the U.S. is a great power that, irrespective of Latin American wishes, has historically identified all of Latin America as belonging to its unique sphere of influence. U.S. power and geography meant there would be no great power concert or balancing in Latin America. The U.S. has never recognized the right of any other great power to a sphere of influence, yet has insisted on its right to unilaterally pursue and defend its interests anywhere in the Western Hemisphere.[10] U.S. foreign policy has been consistent on its right to regional paramountcy from the Monroe Doctrine in 1823 through the Hay-Pauncefote Treaty (1901), the Roosevelt Corollary to the Monroe Doctrine (1904), the Inter-American Treaty of Reciprocal Assistance (1947), and the invasion of Panama in 1989. The security implication for Latin America has been that U.S. defense interests produce fundamental security externalities for each and every Latin American nation.[11]

A second security externality is a remnant of Spanish colonialism and nation-building after Independence. Latin American interstate conflicts historically have most often revolved around how to resolve the overlapping ecclesiastical, administrative, and military colonial boundaries affecting the territories of national states. One reason why Latin American international politics appears so geared to legal argumentation is because most states have numerous colonial documents supporting expansive claims over territory.

The prevalence of disputed territorial borders in the region means that the method of resolution of a particular conflict, whether diplomatic or military, takes on more general significance. This may explain why some countries, frustrated by their own diplomatic failures to solve territorial disputes, supported Argentina's military seizure of the disputed Malvinas Islands in 1982. For example, Peru, which provided military and diplomatic aid to Argentina, was itself engaged in a long-standing dispute with Ecuador in which the latter rejected Peru's territorial gains by force of arms in 1941.

A domestically rooted externality develops out of the highly stratified social structure in Latin America and the developing nature of its economies. When the social structure in one country is threatened by revolutionary upheaval, elites in the rest of Latin America begin to worry. These Latin American perceptions of threats to regional stability are re-reinforced by the U.S. in two ways. The U.S. attempts to organize regional opposition, and thus engages in rhetorical excesses, if not the actual fabrication of "evidence" of revolutionary internationalism.[12] In addition, the willingness of the U.S. to act militarily in these situations raises the specter of internationalizing domestic conflict (as occurred in Central America during the 1980s).

Transborder spillovers of revolutionary upheaval are not merely perceptual overreactions by Latin American and U.S. elites. Historically, many of those seeking to change the social structure within their country have both appealed for support from and offered assistance to their Latin American brothers and sisters facing the same problems. Sandino's fight against the U.S. intervention in Nicaragua during the 1920s, Cuba's Revolution, Chile's Popular Unity administration, and the Nicaraguan Sandinistas in the 1970–80s all had significant extranational participation.[13] Neofascist agents from Brazil's Estado Novo traveled South America in the 1930s to build a regional front against "Communists," while Perón's Argentine labor movement and Peru's progressive APRA party tried to reproduce themselves elsewhere on the continent. Che Guevara tried to reproduce the Cuban Revolution in the heart of South America. Even Caribbean democrats cooperated loosely in the notorious Caribbean Legion to overthrow dictators.[14]

Note, however, that Latin America's security complex does not include an issue that characterizes developing countries in other regions: the nation itself is not an issue.[15] Political regimes claiming to represent the nation often have legitimacy problems, but in the twentieth century these have not led to separatist movements. Indigenous people, as well as the descendants of Africans brought to the Atlantic coast in Central America, have demanded their rights as citizens, and in cases where communities are split physically by national boundaries, dual citizenship. Not even the recent political movements for varying degrees of autonomy by some of these communities call for full independence.[16]

If Latin America can be thought of as a security complex, what is its security *problematique*? From a Latin American perspective, extracontinental threats largely ceased to be major issues once the U.S. became powerful enough to defend the hemisphere. (Mexico did worry about a Japanese attack during World War II, but neither Brazil nor Argentina was seriously concerned about German aggression; indeed, when the U.S. provided Brazil with equipment and supplies to defend its "bulge" on the Atlantic, the Brazilians chose to focus resources on their southwestern border with Argentina.[17]) Although Germany tried alternately to woo and threaten Mexico, Chile, Argentina, and Brazil, these American states understood that the costs of playing balance of power politics were enormous, the chances of the U.S. accommodating such an alliance small, and the threat from Germany if they did not ally, minor.[18]

Given the forced isolation of the region from great power politics, its security *problematique* arises from the region's own internal characteristics. In a security complex characterized by disputed borders, unequal levels of economic development and broad disparities in the distribution of power, the main security threats for Latin American states revolve around sudden attempts at military resolutions of long-standing border issues, massive movements of migrants, and the spread of revolution. Included in this regional security agenda are the manner and timing of U.S. intervention in the hemisphere. U.S. unilateralism and its inconsistent application (meaning that a country cannot count on U.S. aid if attacked)[19] produce security benefits and costs for Latin American states that are largely beyond their capacity to control. The unpredictability of U.S. behavior thus becomes a security risk.

The History of Militarized Disputes in the Region

Table 2.1 lists the 23 wars in which Latin American nations participated after their wars of Independence, both in the Western Hemisphere as well as in Europe (World War I and World War II) and Asia (World War II and Korea). The standard international relations definition of war, which requires at least 1,000 battlefield related deaths, is quite arbitrary, but accepted in the field. My analysis conforms to standard usage in the interest of developing a study which can be used by researchers outside of the region. In consequence, many of the events that observers of, and participants in, the

TABLE 2.1 Latin American Wars Since Independence

Year	Name	Participants
1825–28	Uruguayan War	Argentina v. Brazil
1836–39	Peruvian Confederation	Chile (Argentina) v. Bolivia, Peru
1841	Peruvian-Bolivian	Peru v. Bolivia
1846–48	Mexican-American War	United States v. Mexico
1851–52	La Plata War	Brazil v. Argentina
1861–67	Franco-Mexican War	France (United Kingdom, Italy) v. Mexico
1864–70	War of the Triple Alliance	Paraguay v. Argentina, Brazil, Uruguay
1863	Ecuadorian-Colombian War	Ecuador v. Colombia
1865–66	Spanish-Chilean War	Spain v. Chile, Ecuador, Peru, Bolivia
1876	First Central American War[a]	Guatemala v. El Salvador
1879–84	War of the Pacific	Chile v. Peru, Bolivia
1885	First Central American War[a]	Mexico, El Salvador v. Guatemala
1906	Second Central American War	Guatemala, Honduras, El Salvador v. Nicaragua
1907	Third Central American War	Honduras, El Salvador v. Nicaragua
1932–35	Chaco War	Bolivia v. Paraguay
1932	Leticia War[b]	Peru v. Colombia
1939–41	Zarumilla War[c]	Peru v. Ecuador
1969	Soccer War	El Salvador v. Honduras
1982	Malvinas/Falklands War	Argentina v. Great Britain
1995	Cenepa War	Peru v. Ecuador

Latin American Combat Participation in Other Wars[d]

1918	WWI	Brazil

TABLE 2.1 *(continued)*

Year	Name	Participants

Latin American Combat Participation in Other Wars[d] *(continued)*

Year	Name	Participants
1944	WWII	Brazil, Mexico
1950	Korea	Colombia

[a] MID labels both the 1876 and 1885 conflicts as "First Central American War"

[b] 868 battlefield deaths, below the 1,000 COW cutoff. See discussion in text.

[c] The revised MID set limits deaths to over 500.

[d] In WWI the Germans sank Brazilian shipping and a Brazilian naval squadron participated in Allied patrolling of the northwest African coast. During WWII Brazil fought in Italy, sustaining 400 dead and capturing 13,000 German and Italian troops; Mexico flew 785 ground attack missions in the Pacific. Colombia sent 4,000 troops to Korea, suffering 120 dead, proportionately equivalent to 1,612 U.S. dead. English, *Armed Forces of Latin America* pp. 101, 109, 318, 171, respectively

Source: MID data base, revised version to 1992"; Osny Duarte Pereira, *La seudo-rivalidad argentino-brasileno* (Buenos Aires: Corregidor, 1975) notes 8,000 Brazilian deaths in the Uruguayan War. On the War of the Peruvian Confederation, St. John, *The Foreign Policy of Peru*, pp. 34–40; Peru-Ecuador 1996 field research.

region call "war" are excluded from this analysis;[20] they are, however, included in the analysis of militarized disputes.

Two exceptions merit comment. The Leticia War in 1932 produced 868 battlefield-related deaths. The 800 Peruvian losses in a population estimated at 5.65 million in 1930 were the equivalent of more than 17,000 losses in a U.S. population estimated at 123 million in 1930 and would be more than 38,000 for a population of 270 million in 1996![21] The 1941 Zarumilla War (a.k.a., The Maranon War) between Ecuador and Peru was downgraded in the revised MID set, with combined battlefield-related deaths of more than 500. Yet in this conflict Ecuador lost 40 percent of the territory it claimed and Peruvian troops penetrated deep into undisputed Ecuadorian territory, which they held until Ecuador signed a peace treaty.[22] It strains credibility not to accept these military clashes as "wars." I include them in the list of Latin American wars, but not in the discussion of wars across regions, since I do not know if other regions had similar "near misses." I have not, however, included the 1937 attack by Dominican forces on Haitian migrants that killed up to 12,000. Because the Haitian government responded diplomatically, not militarily, the Dominican action produced a "massacre," but not a "war."[23] For similar reasons I do not include the 1999 attack by the North Atlantic Treaty Organization (NATO) on Yugoslavia as a "war."

Of the 23 wars, 17 have been among Latin American nations. Nine of those Latin American wars occurred in the nineteenth century and eight in the twentieth century. The wars of the first 60–80 years of independence had tremendous consequences: states were created, confederations of states ceased to exist, and the position of states in the regional hierarchy was dramatically altered. Uruguay was created by British mediation as a result of the Argentine-Brazilian war of 1825. The creation of Panama in 1903 was partly the result of civil war in Colombia, but the dispatch of U.S. forces to the region to prevent the central government from defeating the secessionist movement was a fundamental determinant. Gran Colombia split into three states, one of which (Ecuador) struggled constantly to keep itself together. The breakup of the United Provinces of Central America led to the establishment of five independent states, and 70 years of war to attempt to re-create it under either Guatemalan or Nicaraguan leadership.

War also had implications for the regional distribution of power: a Central America united under the auspices of one state would make that state a more important player in regional politics. Perhaps the greatest impact of war on the regional hierarchy of states comes from the War of the Peru-Bolivia Confederation (1836–39) and the War of the Triple Alliance (1864–70). Those wars thwarted two powers which appeared poised to create the most powerful states in the region; that Bolivia and Paraguay are today the poorest states by far in South America is testimony to the importance of the stakes of war at the time.

The stakes of international conflict in Latin America declined around the turn of the century (after roughly 1885 in South America and 1907 in Central America). National existence and international hierarchy solidified as national identities took hold, states developed centralized and effective governments, hinterlands were colonized, and military capabilities increased. A threshold was crossed in Latin America's regional relations and we can usefully consider it the end of the "National Period."[24]

It may be tempting to deprecate the significance of Latin America's twentieth-century wars, noting that they fall just over the threshold, with the exception of the Chaco War (Bolivia and Paraguay sustained approximately 100,000 deaths). In studying the use of violence, however, we should not rigidly adhere to definitions out of context. In the 1969 war Honduras (the poorest country in the region at the time) suffered 2,000–5,000 deaths as a result of the Salvadoran invasion, equivalent to the U.S. today losing approximately 200,000–500,000 people. The U.S. lost "only" 53,000 service people in Vietnam, but few call it an insignificant war. In addition to the loss of human life, the 1969 war effectively interrupted for twenty years the Central American economic integration project that had been progressing rapidly and stimulating strong growth in the region.[25] In the Zarumilla War, Ecuador lost 40 percent of the territory it claimed to Peru. Over the next 42 years there were 20 militarized disputes between the two parties, resulting in another war in 1995.

War may occur in Latin America, but is its frequency significantly less than in other regions? Tables 2.2 and 2.3 use two different conceptions of

TABLE 2.2 War Occurrence by Region
(Among Sovereign States in the International System)

Total Wars 1816–1997 (standard comparison)

Europe	Asia	Africa	Middle East	Latin America
30	22	5	10	21*(23)

20th Century Wars to 1997 (standard comparison)

Europe	Asia	Africa	Middle East	Latin America
15	19	4	9	6*(8)

*Because of our comparative interest here, the Leticia and Zarumilla Wars have not been added since I do not know if other regions have near misses in the battlefield related deaths count.

Source: MID data base, hostility level 5, revised version to 1992, plus author's addition of the following post 1992 wars: Europe two (Croatia-Yugoslavia; Bosnia, with Croat and Serb participation), Latin America one (Ecuador-Peru).

TABLE 2.3 Post World War II Wars, 1945–1997
(security community comparisons)

Area	number
Middle East	9
Europe	4
Southeast Asia	4
Indian Subcontinent	4
Latin America	3
Africa	2
Northeast Asia	1
North America	0

Source: Militarized Interstate Dispute data set, revised edition. For the period after MID II, I have added two European wars (Croatia-Yugoslavia, and Bosnia) and one Latin American war, Ecuador-Peru.

region for thinking comparatively about Latin America's experience with war. Table 2.2 uses the four standard regions in the literature to situate Latin America comparatively. In terms of total international wars since 1816 (the start date for quantitative studies of war) Latin America is not exceptionally peaceful. Europe (30) is by far the most warlike, followed by Asia (22) and Latin America (20, not counting the Leticia and Zarumilla Wars), each of which has significantly more experience with war than the Middle East (10) or Africa (five). Latin America's ranking is not entirely different when we just examine the twentieth century, when virtually all of the African, Asian, and Middle Eastern wars occurred. (The distribution of wars in these regions is a function of the way in which war is coded in the literature. Only conflicts between recognized members of the international state system count as "interstate" wars, the other conflicts are either "colonial" wars or "extra-systemic" wars.) The frequency of Latin American wars (six) in that century keeps the region in the middle of the group: well below Europe (15) and Asia (19), slightly below the Middle East (nine), but above Africa (four).

Table 2.3 focuses on post World War II wars. It organizes the regional categories into groups that actually share immediate security concerns and interact over security issues (e.g., India and Korea, both in Asia, have few security-related interactions). The new distinctions include a North America category consisting of Canada, the U.S. and Mexico. (The fact that Mexico is in two regions, North and Latin America, does not affect the tallies since the country has been involved in no post World War II wars.) Viewed in this light, the Latin American experience appears even less unusual. In the post World War II period Latin America has experienced more wars (three) than northeast Asia (one) and Africa (two), and just one fewer than Europe, Southeast Asia and the Indian subcontinent (each with four). Only in comparison with the Middle East's nine wars can we think of Latin America (and the rest of the world!) as being relatively peaceful.

If we turn our attention to interstate disputes in which official military violence is threatened or used without producing war, Latin America appears even more violent. In the twentieth century alone, Latin American states threatened, used military force against each other, or were the subject of threats or actual use of force by non-Latin American countries more than two hundred times. The occurrence of militarized interstate disputes (MIDs) actually increased in the twentieth century.[26]

Latin America's MID behavior also fails to distinguish the region in comparative perspective. The occurrence of MIDs in the international system has increased over time, even taking into account the increase in number of states in the system.[27] Examining the MID behavior of individual nations, we find that of the 21 most dispute prone non–great-power states between 1816–1976, seven are Latin American.[28] Among the 44 enduring rivalries over the period 1816–1992, Latin American states were involved in 10, including the two longest rivalries in the study (Ecuador-Peru more than 100 years, and Chile-Argentina with 112 years).[29] And finally, analysis of dispute behavior between 1816–1976 indicates that the patterns of MID behavior can be generalized across geographic boundaries.[30]

Table 2.4 analyzes the MID data in terms of five categories: total MIDs; average number of years between militarized disputes; the escalation of MIDs to war; total participants; and whether force is used by the initiator of the conflict. Data limitations precluded analyzing the behavior of the target countries in a MID. Also, the data are analyzed only from the end of the National Period through 1992 because my research on MIDs after 1992 did not produce reliable evidence about the initiating action.[31]

From table 2.4 we can see that MIDs occur on average more than once every year (every 0.87 years in South America, every 0.79 years in Central

TABLE 2.4 Latin American Militarized Interstate Disputes
(After the National Period)

Total MIDs

	Total MIDs[a]	Years per Dispute	War/MID
South America 1884–1993	127	110/127 0.87	3/127 0.024
Central America 1907–1993[b]	110	87/110 0.79	3/110 0.027

Participation Characteristics

	Total Participants	Force[c] by Initiators	Force[c] by Targets
South America 1884–1993	290	91/147 0.62	—[d]
Central America 1907–1993[b]	170	51/73 0.70	—[d]

[a.] Excluding W.W.I, W.W.II and Korea. see explanation in text.

[b.] Includes Central America, Panama, Mexico, Cuba, Haiti and the Dominican Republic

[c.] Force is defined as having a hostility level of 4 or greater in the MID data set (using rather than merely threatening or displaying force).

[d.] Data has too many missing force values to be meaningful.

Source: MID data set

America). Disputes tend to begin with the overt use of force, rather than merely a threat: 62 percent in South America and 70 percent in Central America. Unfortunately, we do not have sufficient data to evaluate the response of the target of such threats. Although disputes do escalate and become militarized, it is extremely rare that they develop into war (1,000 battlefield deaths): only around 2.4 percent for South America and 2.8 percent in Central America. This behavior is well in line with the general finding that disputes involving only non-great powers "have a very high likelihood of involving the use of force, but the probability of these disputes escalating to war has been quite small."[32]

Contemporary Latin American Disputes

Many analysts, commentators, and policymakers consider serious intra-Latin American disputes, as well as their possible militarization, as belonging to another era, specifically that characterized as pre-redemocratization and Cold War, if not pre-economic liberalization and free trade. Chapters 3 and 4 present quantitative and qualitative analyses over time to dispute the notion that conflict in the region is time bound in any significant way. In this section I simply demonstrate that violent interstate conflict continues in the contemporary period.

The contemporary era can be defined in two ways for an examination of MID behavior in Latin America; alternative dating criteria reflect views about why Latin American states used violence before the contemporary era. For some observers a watershed in Latin American politics began after 1979 with redemocratization (Ecuador started the latest "wave" in 1979), while others are more inclined to utilize 1989, when the fall of the Berlin Wall signaled the end of the Cold War.

Disagreements with other states are inherent in the very nature of sovereignty. The question is not whether disagreements among Latin American states ceased once they re-democratized or the Cold War ended; rather it is whether they stopped using, or significantly decreased the use of military force in their international bargaining over these disputes.

My definition of democracy uses the Polity III rankings up to 1993,[33] with countries scoring 6 or better on the 0–10 democracy scale. For analysts who believe 6 to be too low, we need to remember that Chile in the 1960s scored a 6; few students of Latin America would claim Chile was nondemocratic at the time.[34] By the 1990s most Latin American democracies garner scores in the 8–10 range. I have disagreements with Polity III rankings for El Salvador, Guatemala, and Honduras. The first two countries were engaged in serious civil wars in the 1980s, during which human, civil, and political rights were drastically curtailed for large portions of the population. I date their democratic transitions at a later time when their peace agreements were implemented, that is, 1992 and

TABLE 2.5 Contemporary Democracies in Latin America

Haiti 1990–91, 1994–	Dominican Republic 1978–	Cuba–NO
Costa Rica 1948–	Guatemala 1993 (**1997**)	Honduras 1990 (**1986**)
El Salvador 1984–(**1992–**)	Nicaragua 1990–	Panama 1990–
Colombia 1957–	Venezuela 1958–	Guyana 1992–
Ecuador 1979–	Peru 1980–91 (1994–)	Brazil 1985–
Bolivia 1982–	Paraguay 1989–	Chile 1990–
Argentina 1983–	Uruguay 1985–	Mexico–2000

Source: Polity III TO 1993, democracy score of 6 or better; Mares classifications after 1993. Mares revisions in parentheses and discussed in text.

1997, rather than 1984 and 1993, respectively. Honduras began its transition to democracy in 1982 and by the second presidential election in 1986 (rather than its third in 1990) had adopted the institutional and procedural mechanisms to give elections real meaning, as well as promote civil and human rights sufficiently to merit a 6. After 1993 the characterizations are mine and generally follow Polity III, except that I return Peru to democracy in 1994 for reasons explained in chapter 7.

The data in table 2.6 provide information on the intra-Latin American MIDs occurring from 1980–1997. The MID II database terminates in 1992 and the latter years are compiled from my own search carried out with limited funds and therefore likely to understate the true occurrence of MIDs. The highest level of hostility reached in the MID is provided either directly from the MID data base or based on my calculation according to MID criteria. The last column of the table indicates whether or not the countries in the dispute were democratic.

Examination of table 2.6 reveals that there has been no shortage of MIDs among Latin American states after 1979. The period 1990–94 appears to represent a significant decrease in MID activity, but by 1995 Latin America seems to return to its historical pattern of multiple MIDs per year.

The empirical record of the relationship between democracy and the use of military force in foreign policy is particularly interesting in table

TABLE 2.6 Intra-Latin American MIDs 1980–98

Year	Dyad	Hostility Level [a]	Democracy
1980	Colombia/Nicaragua	3	yes/no
	Chile/Argentina	4	no/no
1981	Ecuador/Peru	4	yes/yes
	Nicaragua/Honduras	3	no/yes
	Venezuela/Guyana	3	yes/no
	Chile/Argentina	4	no/no
	Argentina/Chile	4	no/no
1982	Argentina/Great Britain	5	no/yes
	Venezuela/Colombia	4	yes/yes
	Venezuela/Guyana	4	yes/no
	Guatemala/Mexico	2	no/no
1983	Nicaragua/Costa Rica	4	no/yes
	Argentina/Brazil	4	no/no
	Argentina/Chile	3	no/no
	Ecuador/Peru	4	yes/yes
1984	Guatemala/Mexico	4	no/no
	Peru/Ecuador	4	yes/yes
	Argentina/Chile	4	no/no
1985	Honduras/El Salvador	3	yes/no
	Nicaragua/Costa Rica	4	no/yes
	Ecuador/Peru	4	yes/yes
	Ecuador/Peru	4	yes/yes
1986	Dominican Rep/Haiti	3	yes/no
	Nicaragua/Honduras	4	no/yes
	Nicaragua/Costa Rica	4	no/yes
	Venezuela/Colombia	2	yes/yes
1987	Dominican Rep/Haiti	3	yes/no
	Nicaragua/Costa Rica	4	no/yes
	Colombia/Venezuela	4	yes/yes
1988	Honduras/Nicaragua	3	yes/no
	Panama/Costa Rica	4	no/yes
	Colombia/Venezuela	4	yes/yes
	Ecuador/Peru	4	yes/yes
1989	Honduras/Nicaragua	4	yes/no
	El Salvador/Honduras	4	no/yes
	Peru/Ecuador	3	yes/yes
1990	None		

TABLE 2.6 (*continued*)

Year	Dyad	Hostility Level [a]	Democracy
1991	Honduras/Nicaragua	4	yes/yes
	Peru/Ecuador	3	yes/yes
1992	None		
1993	None		
1994	Ecuador-Peru	2	yes/yes
1995	Ecuador/Peru	5	yes/yes
	Ecuador/Peru	4	yes/yes
	Colombia/Venezuela	4	yes/yes
	Nicaragua/Honduras	4	yes/yes
	Nicaragua/Colombia	2	yes/yes
1996	Nicaragua/Honduras	4	yes/yes
	Nicaragua/El Salvador	4	yes/yes
	Honduras/El Salvador	4	yes/yes
1997	Honduras/Nicaragua	4	yes/yes
	Nicaragua/Costa Rica	3	yes/yes
	El Salvador/Honduras	3	yes/yes
	Venezuela/Colombia	4	yes/yes
	Belize/Guatemala	4	yes/yes
1998	Ecuador/Peru	3	yes/yes
	Costa Rica/Nicaragua	3	yes/yes
	Nicaragua/Honduras	3	yes/yes

[a] Hostility Levels: 1 no use; 2 threat; 3 display; 4 use < 1,000 battlefield related deaths; 5 war

Sources: MID II to 1992; 1992; *Keesing's International Archives*; *ChipNews/Santiago Times*; *NotiSur & EcoCentral*; *Hoy* (Quito, Ecuador); and *La Nacion* (San Jose, Costa Rica); democracy classification from Table 2.5

2.6. From 1980–97 there were at least 52 MIDs. Of these MIDs 15 occurred among interstate dyads combining democratic and nondemocratic regimes, 27 MIDs were between democratic pairs, and only 10 MIDs occurred among nondemocratic dyads. Incredibly, after 1990 all of the 16 MIDs occurred between democratic dyads, although table 2.5 indicates that there were still many nondemocratic countries in the region. El Salvador and Guatemala experienced post Cold War MIDs only after democratizing in 1993 and 1997, respectively. Peru, which shifted back and forth between democracy and authoritarianism in this period, became engaged in militarized disputes only during its democratic years. Even with this incomplete data table 2.6 clearly disputes the arguments that democratic states are absolutely peaceful.

Table 2.6, although incomplete, also provides strong evidence for rejecting the claim that the Cold War means the end of militarized behavior. Since the end of the Cold War there have been 16 MIDs, including one war, between Latin American countries.

What specific issues are associated with the use of interstate violence in Latin America? Table 2.7 lists the 11 major, 4 minor, and 4 latent disputes covering a wide variety of issues which confront the region today. A dispute is classified as major if one side is actively discussing revision of the status quo or a MID has occurred in the current activation of the dispute. A minor but active dispute is one in which disagreements over implementing an agreement occur, but in which no party has utilized military force. A latent dispute is one in which disagreements exist, but neither side raises them for discussion or other action.

Border demarcations dominate the list of current grievances, but competition for fishing and petroleum resources is also significant. Migratory flows add fuel to the tensions generated by border and resource disputes, most significantly between Colombia-Venezuela, El Salvador-Honduras and Costa Rica-Nicaragua. It is a particularly difficult issue between the latter two countries. The crisis of the Nicaraguan economy has produced about a half million illegal migrants (1/7th of the Nicaraguan population) to Costa Rica; the money they send back represents an important source of income for many Nicaraguan families. Costa Rica expelled many undocumented workers, then relented to pressure and declared an amnesty for those entering before November 18, 1999. Despite Nicaraguan concerns, the Costa Rican government has repeatedly reiterated that it will not extend the amnesty.[35]

Even when a dispute has been "officially resolved" at the negotiation or arbitration stage, problems persist in the implementation stage. Many examples exist in the current "peaceful" environment. Although the Hondurans and Salvadorans have accepted the World Court decision delimiting the border between them, there have been military mobilizations and confrontations by vigilante groups on the border. Tempers

TABLE 2.7 Interstate Disputes in Contemporary Latin America

Countries	Issue
Major Disputes	
Guatemala-Belize	Border Demarcation
Honduras-El Salvador	Implementation of Interamerican Court of Justice decision on border demarcation; migration
Honduras-El Salvador-Nicaragua	Maritime demarcation in Gulf of Fonseca; depletion of fisheries
Honduras-Nicaragua	Maritime demarcation in Atlantic; migration
Nicaragua-Costa Rica	Border demarcation; migration; transit rights in San Juan river
Nicaragua-Colombia	Territorial dispute over San Andres & Providencia Islands
Colombia-Venezuela	34 points on border in dispute; migration; guerrillas; contraband, including but not limited to drugs
Venezuela-Trinidad & Tobago	Maritime boundaries; natural resources
Haiti-Dominican Republic	Migration, border demarcation
Ecuador-Peru	Border demarcation (resolved 1998)
Bolivia-Chile	Territorial dispute: outlet to the Pacific
Minor but Active Disputes	
Chile-Peru	Final implementation of 1929 treaty covering Peruvian access to Chilean port at Arica
Panama-Colombia	Guerrilla incursions into Panama
Colombia-Costa Rica	Territorial sea in the Pacific
Latent Disputes	
Venezuela-Guyana	Territorial dispute: Venezuela claims 40% of Guyana

TABLE 2.7 *(continued)*

Countries	Issue
Antarctica (12 countries)	Treaty puts national claims on hold
Argentina-Great Britain	Malvinas/Falklands, Georgias & Sandwich Sur
United States-Cuba	US naval base in Guantanamo

Source: Francisco Rojas Aravena, "America Latina: Alternativeas y Mecanismos de Prevencion en Situaciones vinculadas a la Soberania Territorial," in *Paz y Seguridad en las Americas* October 14, 1997, p. 4; U.S. Department of Defense, *United States Security Strategy for the Americas* Washington, DC September 1995 pp. 12–14 and my own research.

are flaring over whether repatriation of citizens on the "wrong" side of the border should be forcibly carried out, as well as what the compensation should be for the property of those choosing to move.

Ecuador and Peru spent four years negotiating a resolution of their dispute after the 1995 war. Military forces were separated in the immediate area of fighting by a peacekeeping force and a number of secondary issues were soon resolved. But diplomatic negotiations stalled over Ecuadorian insistence on sovereign access to the Amazon. Only after troop mobilizations in August 1998 produced another war crisis were the two countries able to make the concessions necessary for resolution.[36]

The Bolivia-Chile dispute reactivated in 1996 after 20 years of dormancy. During 1976–78 Bolivia was engaged in what appeared to be fruitful negotiations to resolve the issue created by Chilean seizure of Bolivia's Pacific coast province in the 1879 War of the Pacific. By the provisions of a 1929 treaty resolving the Peru-Chile dispute resulting from the same war, however, Peru had to second any Chilean grants of sovereign access to the Pacific for Bolivia which traversed previously Peruvian territory. The Peruvians vehemently protested the 1976–78 negotiations, and a war scare ensued, convincing the Chileans to cease discussions. Bolivia severed full diplomatic relations with Chile in 1978. In 1996 Bolivians began actively discussing the issue and the new government of President Hugo Banzer brought up the issue at the United Nations in the fall of 1997. Although the dispute has not militarized to date, Bolivia has attempted to garner international support by accusing

Chile of maintaining half a million mines on their border. (Chile also maintains mines on its border with Peru and Argentina.)[37]

Latin American Efforts to De-Legitimize the Use of Force

Two centuries of the Latin American experience demonstrate the ubiquity of the use of force in interstate relations. Latin Americans have often been troubled by this frequent use of force. Some of the region's great liberators and statesmen believed that political integration could pacify the region. Political integration would build on cultural and political regime affinities (Spanish American and Liberal Republican), integrate markets, and turn interstate military competition into the politics of federalism.[38] Bolívar himself created Gran Colombia, consisting of present-day Venezuela, Ecuador, and Colombia. Peru and Bolivia became a confederated state, and the Central American communities formed the United Provinces of Central America at independence.

The integrationist approach to common security was defeated throughout Latin America by the force of arms. To avoid civil war, Gran Colombia disbanded in 1830. Chile and Argentina feared the potential of the Peru-Bolivia Confederation. War ensued and although Argentina was defeated, Chile prevailed in 1836–39.[39] The United Provinces of Central American succumbed to civil wars in 1838–42. The independent countries fought over the question of union until 1907, after which the issue was abandoned to the diplomats.[40]

The Latin American experience stands in marked contrast to the U.S. approach. The U.S. perception of security (as well as destiny) lay in incorporating all westward territory to the Pacific Ocean. Rather than reject the use of military force as a path to security, the U.S. embraced it as a legitimate and useful tool to develop continental security if negotiated integration failed. The price, nevertheless, was high for all states involved. Indigenous peoples were herded into reservations, Mexico was despoiled of almost half of its territory, and the U.S. Civil War was the second bloodiest war of the nineteenth century (second to the Napoleonic Wars).

Political integration was not the only means by which Latin American statesmen sought to banish violence from the region. Latin Americans joined with the U.S. in perceiving the Americas as a special place, far from the power politics of Europe. This uniqueness was expected to produce a special style of international politics. For the U.S., uniqueness meant that it would remake the hemisphere in its own image and be the hemisphere's leader. Latin Americans, however, were generally more interested in delegitimating the use of force (military and otherwise) by powerful states in their disputes with weaker states. "American Law" was expected to protect the sovereignty of all states, rather than give great powers rights to police small power behavior. Hope in an "American system" remained, even when it became clear that this perspective did not prevent the U.S. or even Latin American states from violating the sovereignty of American states, or that not all Latin American states rejected the great power legal international order.[41]

In a rebuke to European practice, Latin American diplomats and jurists formulated the first attempts to legally limit the ability of nations to use force to collect debts owed their national citizens by foreign governments (Calvo and Drago Doctrines). Latin American efforts to limit the use of force extended to the U.S. as well. In the early 1900s the U.S. claimed to be promoting civilization, democracy, and stability by refusing to recognize governments which had come to power in nondemocratic ways. Recognition was critical since the Marines and the Navy were dispatched throughout the world when no "legitimate" government was in place to protect the lives and property of U.S. citizens. In addition, lack of international "legitimacy" of a government helped a domestic opposition to arm itself and call on outside support. The U.S. used this policy on recognition to reward pro-U.S. actors and punish those who sought European connections to balance the U.S.'s growing domination. Many Latin American countries consequently sought to make recognition of governments in power automatic, rather than subject to U.S. scrutiny of their "legitimacy."[42]

Latin Americans also tried to marginalize the use of force among themselves by treaty. Between 1826 and 1889 at least 50 conventions among Latin American states forswore the use of force to resolve disputes.[43] Yet this was the period of the bloodiest wars in the Latin American security complex. Between 1929 and 1936 seven major treaties and protocols forswore the use of force, but none was ratified by every state. Even ratification was often accompanied with reservations; the U.S. itself engaged in this practice. And once again, this was a period of intense interstate violence in the region (the Chaco War, the Leticia War, the Dominican massacre of Haitian migrants, and the build-up to the Zarumilla War in 1941 all occurred at this time).

Mediation and arbitration by both regional and extra-regional actors have also been tried. From 1885–1925 arbitral settlements of interstate conflicts in Latin America flourished.[44] Their use declined over time, but El Salvador and Honduras and Chile and Argentina arbitrated their border disputes in the 1980s and 1990s. The resolutions by the arbiters have not been easy to implement, and were rejected by Ecuador in 1910 and Argentina in 1978. The Central American countries dragged their feet on the 1992 World Court ruling, but in 1998 agreed to work out the terms of implementation.[45] Chile and Argentina settled thirteen of fourteen border disagreements after 1984, including many which had already escalated to militarized conflict, including a near border war in 1978. Domestic protests of the 1994 arbitral decision favoring Argentina in the Laguna del Desierto controversy initially made Chile reluctant to submit the final disagreement to arbitration, but the government ultimately did so.[46]

In the 1980s South Americans borrowed the Zone of Peace concept from Australia and New Zealand in an effort to keep the Cold War from undermining regional security. The declaration of a South American zone of peace was directed at the superpowers, not the states within the region. The Contadora Initiative for peace in Central America, supported by most South American governments, fit well within this approach to security. The Contadora proposals focused on limiting the two superpowers' military influence in the region and gaining acceptance of Nicaragua's sovereign right to have a one-party state and the size of armed forces it perceived necessary for defense. Since the Zone of Peace approach did not seek to change the manner in which states in the Western Hemisphere themselves managed their disputes it lost relevance with the end of the Cold War.[47]

The Central American presidents, under the leadership of Costa Rican President Oscar Arias, embarked on a different path to end the civil wars and regional tensions of the 1980s. The Esquipulas agreements focused on democratic resolution of civil strife and targeted military establishments as one of the obstacles. They therefore called for a significant reduction in the size of defense establishments, with Arias himself arguing for their abolition. Although the Central American civil wars ended, and initial progress was made in questioning the need for defense establishments, only Panama (and Haiti in the Caribbean) abolished its military.[48] (There is a certain irony in the fact that the governments that abolished their militaries were in power only because the U.S. militarily invaded Panama in 1989 and had used the Navy and Air Force against Haiti in the early 1990s).

Arms control has also been popular in the region. At the turn of the century the British brokered the *Pactos de Mayo* naval arms agreement between Argentina and Chile. More recently, the treaty of Tlatelolco focused on nuclear nonproliferation in the region.[49] Negotiated force levels in Central America helped diffuse the level of tension in the early 1990s. A ban on bombers was discussed in the 1970s, but Peru's opposition apparently killed it, although Ecuador disposed of its small bomber force (three planes). The Andean Group presidents renounced weapons of mass destruction in December 1991 (Declaration of Cartagena). At the extreme, disarmament itself has been advocated. After achieving parity with Chile for the first time in one hundred years, Peru called for regional disarmament in 1975, but no one seems to have taken the proposal seriously.[50] The OAS is currently attempting to both institutionalize and stimulate the arms control process.[51]

Only in the U.S.-Mexican relationship since the 1930s can we find evidence of a security relationship in which the use of military force is not a factor. Mexico lost half its territory to the U.S. in 1848, suffered a war scare in the 1880s, and experienced two military interventions during the Mexican Revolution (1914 and 1916). But after 1928 both sides began to accommodate each other: Mexico toned down some aspects of its Revolution and the U.S. accepted others, including a socialist-like rhetoric and nationalization of the petroleum industry. Mexicans had come to appreciate that militarizing their relations with the great power could not benefit Mexico and the U.S. came to accept the importance of Mexican domestic stability. While they subsequently had a border demarcation disagreement (in the Chamizal), neither sought to militarize it.

Even in this case, however, the perception that military force is unable to produce security in this complex relationship is increasingly under challenge. Faced with an inward flow of drugs and people the U.S. has been steadily militarizing its southern border in a largely futile attempt to control these new "threats." The U.S. public and their leaders may not believe war is thinkable with Mexico, but they are coming to believe that using military force against Mexico is a legitimate way to address particularly pressing problems.[52]

Conclusion

Contrary to common understanding of the public and scholars alike, the Latin American experience includes its full share of militarized conflict. Review of quantitative data spanning the nineteenth and twentieth centuries from across the region demonstrates that Latin America is not uniquely shielded from this malaise of nation states. While not as war or violence prone as some regions (notably Europe) it does use force more than others do (mainly North America, Africa, and Northeast Asia). The region is thus not an anomaly for security studies and can provide a data set for evaluating competing arguments about the determinants of the use of military force.

Sporadic efforts to delegitimize the use of force in interstate disputes demonstrate that states in the region understand the benefits of such a principle. A reading of the historical record, nonetheless, demonstrates that American nations have been reluctant to place full confidence in it. The issue of interstate conflict in Latin America was, and continues to be, important. There are many issues which produce tensions in international affairs among Latin American countries as well as with the U.S. That conflict rarely escalates to full-scale war and cooperation often wins out, at least in the short term. The threat to use military force, nevertheless, is ubiquitous, while the actual use of that force occurs too often to see it as aberrant behavior.

Why are militarized posturing and conflict ubiquitous in Latin America? In exploring this question we examine whether factors unique to the region, namely, the dominance of U.S. interests and behavior, illuminate these conflicts; or whether theories of international relations with cross-regional applications provide insights into Latin American behavior as well. If the latter, are models which contrast the foreign policy behavior of democracies and authoritarian regimes useful to further our understanding; is Latin American conflict simply the inexorable result of power confronting power; or are Latin American leaders responding rationally to incentives at the international and domestic levels? Part 2 systematically explores these approaches, ultimately demonstrating the advantages of a militarized bargaining approach for understanding interstate conflict in Latin America.

Part 2

Analyzing Latin America's
Violent Peace

3   The Myth of Hegemonic Management

In searching for an understanding of conflict dynamics in Latin America, we first examine the only region-specific theory—namely, the view that the U.S. has managed interstate relations, particularly conflict, in Latin America.[1] The outcome is purportedly regional interstate peace and internal civil violence directed against those social groups which would oppose either the U.S.' paramount position in the hemisphere or the economic system the U.S. champions. Hegemonic management of conflict is a myth that dies hard. It is based on wishful thinking (e.g., Monroe Doctrine); a selective reading of history (e.g., a focus on interventions to overthrow governments with which it disagreed); and a theoretical argument (as the only great power in the region no one can long contest its views on fundamental issues).

This chapter examines the hegemonic management thesis from four different perspectives. Each demonstrates the weakness of distinct versions of the argument and together they provide a resounding rejection for both the benevolent and malevolent hegemonic management theses. The first section lays out the different ways in which analysts across the political spectrum have conceptualized hegemonic management. The next section undertakes a historical analysis of the periods in which hegemonic management seemed to be on the verge of working, but subsequently collapsed (1920s, followed by the 1930s and 1945–61, followed by 1962—present). In the first period Latin American states tried to use the U.S. to settle their own security challenges on favorable terms. When that failed (since the U.S. could not give both sides what each wanted), the Latin American states returned to nationally centered conflict management strategies. A third section presents a quantitative analysis of the impact of regional and systemic polarity on the MIDs that occurred during the past century. The final section examines the hegemonic mismanagement thesis, specifically the claim that the Cold War led to greater conflict in the region.

This chapter finds that both those who favor and those who oppose hegemonic management dramatically overstate U.S. influence on conflict dynamics in this security complex. The dynamics of interstate conflict and cooperation are too complex to be captured by a perspective that a state powerful enough to be paramount can determine the behavior of other states in the region.

U.S. Hegemony in the Americas: Conceptual Clarifications and Implications

Hegemony is a contentious notion in the study of international relations, particularly in the security realm. A hegemon is not just paramount, but is defined by its ability to provide a collective good, in our case, peaceful interstate relations. Thus the outcome of its power, not its absolute or relative strength, indicates whether the U.S. has been hegemonic in Latin America. The relevant metric for discussing hegemony is related to what is necessary to provide the particular collective good in question.

A hegemon in the security arena is a state with the resources to effectively limit the escalation of disputes into the use of military force and, when force is used, to constrain it before such use proves influential in resolving a disputed issue. A regional hegemon is a state that can perform this function for all states in the region. The hegemon's ability to impose constraints on the use of force by regional states provides the collective good. A hegemon not only enforces the proscription against the use of force, but also can exclude recalcitrant states from consuming the collective good: the hegemon imposes punishment in the form of overt or covert intervention, with or without participation by the other states benefiting from the security provided by the hegemon.

It is important to note the distinction between collective security and hegemonic management. A collective security system provides security for each and every member of the community against each and every other member of the community.[2] But in a situation of regional hegemony, no one can protect the regional states against the hegemon. In other words, the regional hegemon provides security for the states in the region against each other, but not against itself.

One may legitimately ask, "What kind of security is this?" The answer depends on the security problematique of the states in question. Great powers certainly would not find any security in this situation; that is why hegemony in the security realm at the global level has been absent in any but a unipolar system. But lesser states may have both fewer options and greater needs. In the context of Latin America's threefold security problematique (governments threatened by domestic overthrow, coercion by neighbors and intervention by the U.S.), hegemonic management might provide security vis-à-vis the first two issues.

In addition, hegemonic management may resolve the third security issue as well. If regional states have no hope of countering the regional hegemon, they might as well learn to live within the constraints of how the regional hegemon defines good behavior. The security dilemma is eliminated as the subordinated Latin American states trade sovereignty (the ability of a government to decide how it will respond to opportunities and challenges), for peace and prosperity. At least this is the argument of those who see hegemonic management as providing benefits.

An analysis of the collective good produced by the regional hegemon facilitates identification of the conditions that characterize hegemony in a regional security complex. Regional hegemony is directed toward two sets of actors. For non-great powers within the security complex regional hegemony means abiding by the rules of behavior set up for the region by the hegemonic state. Rival great powers pose an important challenge to a would-be hegemon in a security complex because they have the ability to contest modes of conflict management. A hegemon's policy is thus to keep other great powers outside of the security complex, recognizing that if they establish their own interests here, they can and will contest the rules of behavior reigning in the security complex.

Some analysts see regional hegemony as producing more, rather than less, conflict. Both extraregional and regional interests are expected to drive the hegemon to impose its worldview on subordinate states. The regional hegemon will most likely be competing for power and influence with states outside the region. Given its capabilities, it will demand that subordinate states ally with it against rivals even though these weaker states may have no interest in taking sides. In addition, the hegemon will seek privileges for its national and private interests within the region. Since subordinate states have their own national and private interests, tensions will develop and the hegemon will often attempt to settle these via the use of force.

How, then, is hegemony constituted? Hegemony is fundamentally about power and control. Analysts have identified three manifestations of power, each operating at a different level.[3] Direct control is the most obvious and characterized by traditional power politics; it is achieved via the use of targeted sanctions and carrots. Subordinate states follow the hegemon's rules because the explicit costs of contesting them outweigh the expected benefits. A more indirect control occurs by structuring the general context that shapes the rules of the game and incentives faced by states. In this manner states find that to achieve their wealth and security goals they must behave according to the standards embodied in the institutional order created by the hegemon. The hegemon does not act directly, but its preferences structure the rules of the game.[4] The most subtle form of control is the influence over the ideas and ideologies which determine the legitimacy of action *in the actor's own mind.*

This third face of hegemony embodies a Gramscian notion of false consciousness. We can note the dominance of the "U.S. way of life" (a middle-class material culture emphasizing consumption and individualism) in much of Latin America, but it is extremely difficult to analyze it from a traditional social science perspective. We also know that in the realm of ideas and ideology the U.S., as the first American colony of a European power to attain independence, had a tremendous impact upon an important segment of the Latin American elite. Latin American conservatives were frightened and appalled by the materialist and Protestant culture of the U.S., but by the mid-nineteenth century they were losing out in most of the civil wars to their liberal rivals.[5]

Liberals throughout the region could look to the U.S. for inspiration and guidance on structuring not only the relationship between state and society, but also the relations among the newly independent states. The idea of an American brotherhood, distinct from European power politics and whose commonalities would provide for hemispheric peace and prosperity, gained ideological sway. Despite abuses of this notion by the U.S. and Latin American states themselves, it never completely disappeared.[6] Latin American Liberals, however, unlike their U.S. counterparts, were attracted to authoritarian solutions to deal with internal dissent.[7]

American distinctiveness was also colored for Latin Americans with an appreciation for European culture and ideas. Europe was the mother region for Latin American elites, who by and large perceived indigenous cultures as uncivilized. The call for European migration, not only to fill in the land, but also to increase the representation of the white race, kept these links alive. Thus in 1889 when the U.S. attempted to insulate the western hemisphere from Europe in an American *zollverein*, Latin America rejected the plan on the grounds that it did not want to isolate itself from its European heritage.[8]

Each face of hegemony operates differently, but the control inherent in each is used to create and maintain a certain international order. In the case at hand, that order is purported to govern regional conflict management. In this chapter I examine the resources which allegedly contribute to the U.S. ability to directly manage conflict via military intervention, covert intervention, and economic sanctions. I then turn to the empirical record of conflict in the hemisphere to evaluate its consistency with patterns expected under either the first or second faces of hegemony.

Establishing Paramountcy, 1823–1945

The unilateral doctrine proclaimed by U.S. President James Monroe in 1823, as well as Thomas Jefferson's prior stipulation of hemispheric security policy in 1808, articulated the ideal security context for a great power: hegemony. The Monroe Doctrine declared that, in the geographic area of its greatest vulnerability (the western hemisphere), the U.S. demanded that all extracontinental powers keep out their military forces and political systems. In return, the U.S. promised that it would not intervene in the zones of strategic importance to those powers. This recently independent country was announcing its isolation from European power politics as well as regional domination.[9]

The process of establishing U.S. paramountcy in the hemisphere varied among the three subregions of Latin America, the Caribbean, and Central and South America. Variation depended upon the capabilities and interests of the European powers in remaining as well as the capabilities and interests of local states. Great Britain realized in the 1890s that the U.S. was willing to risk war to enforce its claims to hegemony in the region,[10] and, in the face of growing problems in South Africa, Turkey and the Continent, was willing to let the U.S. protect British interests in the region.[11] Germany posed a different problem. While, as early as 1901, the Foreign Office was willing to follow the British lead in acquiescing to U.S. predominance, as long as it safeguarded German commercial and financial interests, the Kaiser and his naval planners for several years perceived a war with the U.S. as most likely. By 1905, however, the realization that Germany would have to fight a two-front war in Europe effectively ended German interest in a naval competition in the Caribbean.[12] Thus the U.S. established military dominance in the Caribbean Basin by 1905.

Political, commercial and financial paramountcy took longer. On the Caribbean islands of Cuba and Hispaniola (Haiti and the Dominican Republic) the establishment of direct U.S. control was swift and more thorough than elsewhere. The United States began its official and direct intervention in the Caribbean in 1898 with the Spanish American War. While the war was ostensibly fought to give the Cubans the independence for which they had struggled for decades, the U.S. seized Puerto Rico for itself and limited Cuban independence after expelling the Spanish. The Platt Amendment to the Cuban Constitutional Convention of 1901, which the U.S. insisted upon before it would end its occupation of the island, gave the U.S. the right to intervene in Cuba virtually any time it desired.[13]

The next step in advancing U.S. hegemony came as a result of great power "rights" to unilaterally discipline small powers that infringed upon the rights of citizens of great powers. A security problem was created for the U.S. and Caribbean states by European creditor nations using force anytime they feared that Latin American states were unable or unwilling to pay. The U.S. public and policymakers viewed the specter of British, German, French and Italian warships bombarding Latin American ports and seizing their customs houses as an affront to the security concept embodied in the Monroe Doctrine. President Roosevelt's solution entailed U.S. military intervention to collect debts and pay European creditors. The 1904 intervention in the Dominican Republic became the first operation under the Roosevelt Corollary to the Monroe Doctrine. Within a few years the U.S. became frustrated at collecting debts for the Europeans and began replacing European with U.S. loans, formally guaranteed by Customs House Treaties. Now the Marines would protect U.S. financial interests when they seized control of customs houses or governments.[14] These treaties and loan agreements provided the "legal" justification for U.S. intervention throughout the Caribbean Basin through the 1920s.

Central America represented a twofold security problem for the U.S. In addition to the question of financial default came the repeated Central American wars instigated by Guatemala and Nicaragua. Independence had precipitated the creation of a unified Central America, but it broke into five republics shortly thereafter. For the next seven decades the two largest Central American nations, Guatemala and Nicaragua, attempted to re-create the Central American Federation by force of arms. El Salvador, Honduras, and Costa Rica were constantly invaded by one of the two aspiring local powers, provoking the other to come to the rescue of the besieged state.

The key external actors in Central America were Great Britain, Mexico, and the U.S. We have already noted the process by which Britain came to accept U.S. hegemony. Mexico, however, was quite active in the region, accepting U.S. military dominance but disputing its political control until incapacitated by revolution in 1910.

Mexican projection into Central America gained new life after Porfirio Díaz brought order and stability to the country in the 1880s. A number of factors contributed to heighten tensions with Guatemala. A disputed border between the two, a remnant of the days when Central America formed part of the Mexican Empire, created great antagonisms between the two countries. Guatemalan Liberals sent aid to a revolt in Chiapas, Mexico and Mexico dispatched troops to the border with Guatemala for a war that the military believed inevitable. Guatemala sought U.S. protection from possible Mexican aggression. A Guatemala-U.S. alliance on its southern borders worried Mexico because the U.S. had despoiled Mexico of half of its national territory in the north a few decades earlier. Finally, Guatemala aggressively sought to re-create a Central American Union under its control.[15] If successful, either Guatemala, or the U.S. through Guatemala, would leave Mexico with a powerful neighbor on both of its territorial borders.

Although Foreign Minister Matías Romero thought a war with Guatemala could lead to territorial expansion, President Porfirio Díaz worried that the U.S. could use such a precedent against Mexico at some future date. Aware that he could not act unilaterally, Díaz searched for allies. He noted to the French and British Ambassadors that European and Mexican interests coincided in denying the U.S. control of a canal through Nicaragua. Díaz appealed for "moral" support in hopes that military aid to Central America would not be necessary. Mexico also attempted to influence the selection of governments throughout the region.[16] But these efforts to defeat U.S. allies in Central America and establish Mexican influence failed.

Three factors contributed to the failure. European great powers did not see Mexico as a sufficiently credible ally with which to contest the U.S. in the region. In addition, Guatemalan nationalists were able to withstand Mexican diplomatic pressure as well as a show of military force on the border, because the U.S. continued to view Guatemala as the key to a unified Central America in which it could have great influence. When Guatemala appealed to the U.S. for support in the face of Mexican pressure, the U.S. sent the Mexicans a veiled warning by reassuring Guatemala that, although Mexico had legitimate interests in the area, the U.S. was confident that it would not resort to force.[17] Finally, Mexico felt severely constrained in what it could offer Costa Rica, Nicaragua, and El Salvador.[18] Costa Rica appealed for a secret alliance with Mexico to thwart Guatemala's continued efforts at union. But Mexico rejected such direct action because the U.S. might perceive the alliance as an indication of Mexico's intent to dominate Central America.[19]

The failure of indirect domination and renewed U.S. interest in the region led Mexico to change its approach to Central America. Although U.S. Secretary of State William Blaine's desire to set up an arbitration mechanism for disputes throughout the hemisphere failed,[20] he was able to impose it in Central America. In 1890 the U.S. decided to arbitrate the conflict between Guatemala and El Salvador. Mexico insisted that it be included as an arbitrator and the U.S. accepted.[21] From the events of 1906–1907, on which more documentation about the collaboration between the two exists, it appears that Mexico's interests lay in limiting U.S. intervention by requiring that it be seconded. The U.S. interest in Mexican collaboration lay in using its presence to help convince the Central American nations that U.S. intervention could be fair despite its preferences for Guatemalan leadership in the region.[22]

Mexico attempted to ally with Nicaragua in limiting U.S. hegemony in the region. Like his Mexican counterpart, the liberal dictator José Santos Zelaya had used his political control and European financial ties to bring peace and prosperity to his country. From that domestic base Zelaya was able to compete for influence in Central America commensurate with the country's geopolitical character. For the area, this was a large country: and it was located in the middle of the region, with an ideal site for a transisthmusian canal. By the early 1900s Nicaragua's problem was not so much Guatemala, as the U.S. intent to secure sole access to a canal and implement the Roosevelt Corollary in Central America.

Zelaya, a nationalist who wanted Central America for the Central Americans, with himself as leader, objected to both these goals. In 1894–95 he had appealed for U.S. support against British efforts to keep him from exercising sovereignty over Mosquito lands in the country's Atlantic region.[23] But the U.S. did not thereby control Zelaya. In 1901 canal negotiations between the U.S. and Zelaya broke down when he refused to accept any U.S. sovereignty over the zone.[24] He also initially refused to accept the right of the U.S. to arbitrate in Central America in 1906, and refused to trade his European loans for U.S. loans guaranteed by a Customs House treaty.[25]

In 1906 war between Guatemala and El Salvador was renewed and, after an unsuccessful mediation attempt by the U.S., Mexico proposed joint leadership of a regional peace conference. Zelaya initially rejected the idea because of U.S. participation. Instead he invaded Honduras, installing his own allies in office. But the preparations of Guatemala and El Salvador to attack and Díaz's appeals convinced Zelaya to attend the conference.[26]

The 1907 Conference set up the neutrality of Honduras and called for a regional peace pact in Central America. At this latter meeting Zelaya attempted to persuade Díaz to support a Central American Union, but failed. Instead, a general peace and friendship treaty was signed and the Central American Court of Justice (with one Justice from each country) was established.[27]

Because the conference failed to resolve the underlying issue of who would dominate Central America, intrigues continued. Guatemala and El Salvador fomented rebellion in Honduras to decrease Nicaraguan influence. Nicaragua continued to provide a haven for political opponents of other Central American governments to plot revolt. And El Salvador and Guatemala themselves were on the verge of war. The U.S. attempted to mediate without Mexican participation, but Mexico insisted on its rights in the region and the U.S. hesitated to break openly with Mexico. In 1909 Mexico sent gunboats to the region in a joint effort with the U.S. to keep peace.[28]

By 1909, however, the U.S. decided that the political and financial situation in Central America required implementation of the Roosevelt Corollary. This meant that Zelaya had to go. The U.S. pressured Mexico to participate in a new regional treaty which would exclude Nicaragua and give both the U.S. and Mexico the right to intervene unilaterally.[29] Mexico perceived a new intensity in U.S. policy and initially sought to limit the scope and degree of potential intervention by convincing the U.S. that Díaz could persuade Zelaya to abandon his aggressive Central American policies.[30]

Although Zelaya accepted Díaz's suggestion that he expel active political refugees from Nicaragua, the U.S. continued to see Zelaya as an obstacle to its plans for the region. In this context, Nicaraguan conservatives saw an opportunity to regain power. With the help of Guatemala and of the U.S. consul in Bluefields,[31] the conservatives revolted. Zelaya's troops quickly routed most of the rebels, but Zelaya ordered the execution of two U.S. mercenaries. Seizing this pretext, the U.S. severed relations and President Taft informed congress that U.S. direct military intervention was probable.[32]

Mexico was quite alarmed at this turn of events. Díaz himself tele- grammed the U.S. State Department offering to get Zelaya out of Nicaragua and asking the U.S. to keep its Marines out of Nicaragua. Díaz also sought to replace Zelaya with another Liberal, as a counterweight to Conservative control of Guatemala. Díaz sent a special envoy to Washington to discuss asylum for Zelaya in Mexico if the U.S. did not object. Zelaya recognized that he might be winning the military battle only to lose the political one, so he ordered hostilities to cease and attempted to initiate conversations with the U.S.[33]

But the U.S. now saw a way to eliminate its regional competition with the nationalist Liberals and their Mexican allies. It rejected negotiations and protected the remnants of the Conservative forces with U.S. warships and Marines. With help from the U.S. and Guatemala, the Conservatives emerged victorious in the civil war in 1910. The State Department presented the new government with the conditions for U.S. recognition. Among those conditions was acceptance of a U.S. loan guaranteed by a Customs House treaty giving the U.S. the right to intervene in Nicaragua, i.e., acceptance of the Roosevelt Corollary.[34]

And what of Mexico? Faced with outright U.S. aggression against Nica- ragua in 1909, Mexico broke with the U.S. on joint security efforts. It was reported to have sent arms and money to back the Liberals' fight against the U.S.-favored Conservatives.[35] But in August 1910 the Nicaraguan Liberals lost the civil war and in November Mexico itself fell victim to revolution. While the U.S. became bogged down in the quagmire of Nicaraguan Con- servative politics, Mexico's attention was forced inward.

The collapse of the Nicaraguan and Mexican governments permitted the U.S. to firmly establish military, political and economic dominance in Cen- tral America and the Caribbean by 1910. U.S. Marines arrived in Nicaragua in 1912 and would remain until 1933, leaving briefly in 1925–1927. The U.S. Navy took control of Haiti in 1915 (and would hold it until 1934), and the Dominican Republic the following year (until 1924). The Platt Amendment guaranteed direct intervention in Cuban politics until rescinded in 1934.

The achievement of U.S. paramountcy in South America took longer and was never as complete as in Central America and the Caribbean. Military domination was the easiest to gain. The U.S. stood aside in the War of the Pacific, despite its displeasure with Chilean aggression, partly because its navy was inferior to the Chilean navy. The U.S. naval program quickly changed this situation. By 1891 it could coerce the Chilean government into rendering honors to the U.S. flag under pain of a naval bombardment.[36] Vis-à-vis European great powers, the U.S. could also exercise decisive influence in Venezuela by the 1890s. But the British military presence in South America was still formidable (they even established a new coaling station in Peru during World War I[37]), Germany was very active militarily and diplomatically, and even the French and Italians were active in training the armies of lower South America.[38] German defeat in World War I and British withdrawal of their fleet in 1921[39] effectively gave the U.S. military domination of the region.

Following World War I, the U.S. gained economic leadership of South America. The war had two fundamental impacts in this area. European trade and financial relations with the region collapsed as the war demanded a diversion of resources, including ships for transport.[40] In addition, new U.S. strategic thinking developed as the result of wartime experience. The U.S. came to see domination of communications infrastructure (cables), petroleum and bank loans in South America as security matters.[41]

Table 3.1 provides a glimpse of the evolution of South American economic relations after World War I. Britain's stagnation stands in stark contrast to the dramatic gains made by the U.S. The difference is even greater when we consider that one country dominated British-South American economic relations (i.e., Argentina received one-half of all British investment in the region), while the U.S.-South American economic relationship was dispersed throughout the region.[42] Nevertheless, it is clear that the U.S. had a competitor in this arena; hence we should note U.S. leadership rather than paramountcy in economic relations at this time.

During the 1930s the U.S. confronted an economic rival in southeastern South America (Argentina, Brazil, Paraguay, Uruguay) it had assumed vanquished: Germany. While German trade with this region lagged far behind British and U.S. at the start of Hitler's rise to power, by 1938 it had dramat-

TABLE 3.1 U.S. and British Economic Relations with South America

Year	Exports	Imports	Total Trade	Total Investments
1913				
Great Britain	$300 million	$305 million	$605 million	$4 billion
United States	$178 million	$208 million	$385 million	$173 million
1927				
Great Britain	not given	not given	$750 million	$4.4 billion
United States	$465 million	—	$1 billion	$2.29 billion

Source: calculated from Krenn, *U.S. Policy toward Economic Nationalism*, pp. 2, 8.

ically closed the gap. Bilateral trade agreements which tied these South American countries to the German mark promised to catapult Germany into the number one position in the near future.[43]

Political relations were even less dominated by the U.S. Brazil believed it had constructed a "special relationship" with the U.S. at the turn of the century and consistently followed the U.S. lead in hemispheric affairs. It hoped to use that relationship to be "first among equals" in Latin America, but was repeatedly frustrated when neither Europeans, Spanish Americans, nor the U.S. recognized it as such.[44] Other South American countries were much more circumspect in their recognition of U.S. political leadership in the hemisphere after World War I.[45]

World War once again brought dramatic changes to the hemisphere. After 1945 U.S. military domination reached new heights, as it became the chief source for training and arms. In addition, Latin American governments could no longer toy with balancing the U.S. with other great powers, as Argentina did with Britain and Germany, because the only rival great power (the communist Soviet Union) was itself opposed to most of these Latin American governments.[46] Economic relations continued to be diversified enough so that we must refer to U.S. leadership rather than domination in this sphere. Political relations, however, took a new turn with the creation of the Organization of American States and development of the Inter-

American Treaty of Reciprocal Assistance (Rio Treaty). If the U.S. were ever paramount in South America, it would be in this period.

We thus come to the questions at the core of the hegemonic management thesis. Did the U.S. have the resources to act as a hegemon in the security realm? Did the U.S. provide the collective good of peaceful resolution of conflict to the region? In other words, did the U.S. manage security relations in Latin America well enough so that we can attribute either a lack of conflict or the occurrence of conflict to its handling?

The analysis so far suggests that in the Caribbean and Central America the U.S. had attained paramountcy in the military, economic, and political arenas by 1904. In South America its position does not appear as dominant in all of the arenas until after World War II. Military paramountcy came with the withdrawal of the British fleet in 1921, while economic leadership was established quickly after World War I and political paramountcy was not achieved until 1945. In short, the resources upon which the U.S. could draw to provide hegemonic management of conflict were significantly different in the two subregions. We can now turn to the empirical record to see if we can find support for the claim of hegemonic management in either the entire security complex or by subregion (Caribbean and Central America compared with South America).

A Hegemon by its Tail: Deflating Hegemonic "Successes"

Advocates of the benefits of hegemonic management in Latin America can point to a number of cases in which a U.S. coercive or mediative role correlates with a dispute not escalating or being rapidly contained upon escalation. Bryce Wood makes the strongest qualitative argument for the U.S. hegemonic management thesis. In Wood's analysis the dependent variable is not militarized disputes, but rather large-scale violent conflict.[47] Wood asks why there had been no large-scale wars in the half century since the end of the War of the Pacific and suddenly there were three in the 1930s. He points to the influence of great powers in general, as the cause.

According to Wood, until World War I, European and U.S. mediators and arbiters diffused intra–Latin-American conflict. European great powers ostensibly lost the respect of Latin America because of the slaughter in which they engaged during World War I, so the burden of leading Latin Americans toward peaceful resolution of conflict fell to the U.S. For a time the U.S. was willing to provide diplomatic leadership, economic incentives and military interventions to maintain peace, but the costs proved too great and the U.S. retreated behind the Good Neighbor Policy after 1933. Because Latin Americans had not been able to create hemispheric institutions to carry out the role played by the U.S., wars broke out.[48]

Note that this explanation also accounts for the lack of large-scale conflict in Latin America between 1884 and the establishment of U.S. hegemony after World War I. It remains a great power management explanation, just not a hegemonic one. For purposes of evaluating Wood's thesis, therefore, only the latter two periods (1919–1931 and 1932–1954) become relevant. For Wood the 1920s were essentially a hegemonic period because European great powers played no role. In the 1932–54 period of the Good Neighbor Policy, according to Wood, the U.S. ceased military intervention and diplomatic interference in Latin American affairs and, hence, the use of force to resolve disputes gained ascendancy.[49]

To discern whether there is any causal relationship behind these correlations we need to look at the historical record in more depth. The interrelated territorial disputes of Colombia-Peru, Peru/Bolivia-Chile, Ecuador-Peru and Bolivia-Paraguay can help us evaluate the contribution of hegemonic management to conflict resolution. The question is whether hegemonic imposition/incentive or the Latin American states' own evaluation of incentives derived from domestic or nonhegemonic international factors caused the resolution/mitigation of conflict in the 1920s. Examination of the renewed outbreaks in the 1930s allows us to explore whether a decline in U.S. leadership or a reevaluation of the gains and losses by Latin American actors is responsible.

After World War I Bolivia, Colombia, Ecuador, and Peru believed that the U.S. was hegemonic in the area and that they could profit by its hegemony. They looked to the U.S. to solve territorial conflicts in which they were the weaker party because they believed that the U.S. could obtain a "just" settlement, i.e., one that would give the weaker party greater benefits than likely in bilateral negotiations. Domestic factors also proved fundamental in Peru and reverberated throughout the continent. The dictator Augusto Leguía (1919–1930) believed that the existence of territorial disputes would keep foreign capital away, thereby limiting the opportunities for development and corruption. He worried, however, that a nationalist backlash might topple him if he sought to make concessions to Colombia and

Chile to resolve the border disputes. If he could convince his compatriots that he was a nationalist who, in order to save the nation, had reluctantly given in to demands from the all powerful U.S. he might have his cake and eat it too. Hence, Leguía looked for the U.S. to behave rhetorically as a hegemon, although the initiative would come from him.[50]

Chile and Argentina worried that the U.S. might establish hegemony over the region. For Chile, the danger lay in the possibility that the U.S. might impose a solution to the Peru-Bolivia-Chile dispute which would give Bolivia an outlet to the sea and return both Tacna and Arica to Peru, i.e., deprive Chile of the fruits of victory in the War of the Pacific. Argentina, in contrast, perceived a twofold danger: the U.S. could finally block Argentine aspirations to Latin American leadership and might even help make Brazil its stand-in for South America.[51]

The period began with a war scare, as Peru was becoming increasingly frustrated by Chile's refusal to hold the plebiscite that would determine whether Tacna and Arica would return to Peru or become Chilean. While the Treaty of Ancon had provided for a plebiscite to decide the future of these two cities, Chile had opposed holding one because, as former Peruvian cities, they would likely vote to return to Peruvian jurisdiction. Chile attempted to colonize the cities and expel as many Peruvians as possible, but could not be certain that it had achieved enough electoral strength to win a plebiscite. At the same time, Peru worried that Chile had sufficient control in the territory to manipulate an election in its favor. On the grounds that the League of Nations opposed territorial annexation by force, Bolivia and Peru asked the League Assembly in 1919 and 1920 to revise the Treaty to return not only Tacna and Arica, but also Tarapacá to Peru and provide Bolivia with an outlet to the sea. This action proved extremely popular in Peru's 1919 presidential election campaign that brought Leguía to power. In addition, the two countries asked U.S. President Woodrow Wilson to apply his Fourteen Points program to Latin American disputes.[52]

While the League dragged its feet considering the two requests Chile and Peru mobilized their armed forces. The U.S. opposed the use of the League to resolve Latin American disputes and Leguía withdrew the petition.[53] Rumors abounded that the U.S. would intervene to resolve the dispute. Chile worried and Peru happily expected that U.S. interest would provide Peru with a diplomatic victory. Chile tried to head off U.S. intervention by reopening bilateral negotiations, but Peru successfully held out for U.S. mediation. Peru, nevertheless, failed to gain what it sought in the mediation-turned-arbitration: the U.S. refused to help President Leguía overcome domestic opposition to his cooperative stance by officially asking Peru to participate in the process. The U.S. subsequently ruled in favor of a plebiscite (which Peru feared the Chileans would rig), rather than simply turning the disputed territories over to Peru. U.S.-Peruvian relations were spared a crisis when in 1926 U.S. election supervisors concluded that the Peruvians were correct, a fair plebiscite could not be held in Chilean controlled territory.[54]

The U.S. contribution to the resolution (temporary as it turned out) of the Tacna-Arica dispute turned out to be minor. The U.S.-preferred solution, elections, could not be implemented because of the threat that the Chileans would kill and intimidate prospective Peruvian voters. Next the U.S. Secretary of State suggested that the disputed territories be turned over to Bolivia, with that country making indemnity payments to Chile and Peru. While this proposal pleased Bolivia, Peru and Chile rejected it. In 1929 Peru and Chile agreed in bilateral negotiations to split the difference (Peru got Tacna, Chile Arica). A Protocol to the treaty indicated that if one of the parties were to transfer any part of this territory to a third party, the other treaty partner would need to accede. This stipulation pit Peruvian nationalists against Bolivian aspirations because the most likely outlet lay in the Arica region. Bolivia protested diplomatically and with street demonstrations, to no avail. Bolivia thus lost, and Chile gained, an important ally in this territorial dispute.[55]

U.S. paramountcy probably did have an impact at two points, although their contribution to the outcome is not clear. Chile's military dictator, General Carlos Ibañez (1927–29) attempted to enlist first Britain, then Japan, in a trade of Easter Island for armaments and diplomatic support for Chile's position on Tacna-Arica; but neither extrahemispheric great power was interested.[56] This time Leguía was able to get the U.S. to accept responsibility for the final terms of the agreement, thereby providing him with a justification for ceding "national" territory.[57] But he was overthrown within a year, and the new government denounced his subservience to the U.S., as exemplified in the ceding of national territory.

The Peruvian-Colombian border agreement of 1922 also originated in domestic concerns and left neighboring Ecuador feeling that the agreement had been made at its expense. In 1916 Ecuador recognized Colombian rights over disputed territory in the Amazon, expecting to gain an ally against Peru. But Leguía subsequently offered Colombia a better deal: sovereignty in the disputed area north of the Amazon River in exchange for Peru gaining the previously ceded Ecuadorian territory south of the Putumayo River. Colombia would now have settled borders with Ecuador and Peru (so it believed), leaving it with disputes only with Nicaragua and Venezuela. Brazil was also interested in the treaty, as it potentially affected the settlement of its Amazonian frontier with Peru.[58]

The U.S. does not seem to have played a role in Peru and Colombia's coming to the decision to negotiate the Salomon-Lozano treaty, but subsequently supported it. As the treaty confronted problems along the way to ratification, the U.S. played a fundamental role in insuring its confirmation. First, Brazil was brought in after Secretary of State Hughes let the Brazilians know that "he would be pleased" if they could support the treaty. Leguía subsequently began to get cold feet about the nationalist backlash if he submitted the treaty to Congress for ratification. Although he was a dictator, his hold on power could not long survive nationalists joining with other opponents of his regime. The U.S. successfully exerted enormous pressure on Leguía to have the Congress ratify it,[59] which it did in 1928.

The claim for U.S. success in conflict management in the two cases is misplaced. Bolivia had expected the U.S. to use its hegemonic power to regain an outlet to the sea, and instead was confronted with its old ally, Peru, now in a position in which it could define its interests in opposition to Chile's ceding territory to Bolivia. A similar situation occurred with Ecuador, which severed relations with Colombia once the terms of the Salomón-Lozano Treaty became known, and lamented "In times of crisis the weakest is sacrificed, since this is the easiest way out."[60] Finally, Peru's dictator was not able to convince the army and nationalist civilians that the U.S. had forced these agreements upon him. Opposition to him would thus include the charge that he had sold out the national patrimony.[61]

Because these alleged "successes" of U.S. hegemonic management failed to address fundamental problems, disputes were renewed in the late 1920s and early 1930s. They begin with the renewed confrontation between Bolivia and Paraguay over the Chaco and access to the Paraguay River and, along with it, an outlet to the Atlantic Ocean for Bolivia. Bolivia and Paraguay had disputed this largely uninhabited territory since 1878. In the 1920s both sides began colonizing and fortifying the area and stockpiling arms. The U.S. successfully opposed mediation by the League of Nations, claiming American nations should settle the dispute.[62] Argentina unsuccessfully mediated a border skirmish in 1927 and a major confrontation occurred in

1928. After the Chile-Peru agreement of 1929 the Bolivian Vice President told the U.S. chargé d'affaires that this was the "final blow" to Bolivian prestige and that it would not be allowed to happen again.[63]

The ensuing Chaco War (1932–35, with a final peace settlement in 1938), was the bloodiest of the twentieth-century Latin American wars. It was prolonged by competition between Argentina and the U.S. for leadership of mediation efforts, with both leading parallel groups until the U.S. realized that Argentina would undermine any settlement it did not lead. Rather than seek a quick end to the conflict, Argentina sought to mediate an agreement that would confirm its leadership in Latin America.[64]

Another blow up came after Leguía was overthrown. In 1932 nationalists and opponents of the new government seized the town of Leticia in the territory previously ceded to Colombia. Col. Sánchez Cerro's government initially opposed the action, but when it proved popular, especially among the Army and the Civilist Party which supported him, he seconded it. Colombia appealed to the U.S. for diplomatic support, but found that it had to rely on its own military force to push the Peruvians out and on the League to provide a forum in which a resolution could be negotiated.[65]

Colombia's military successes contributed to an arms build up in the region and gave Peruvian militarists and nationalists another defeat to nurse. As a result, when Ecuador began to make incursions along its disputed frontier with Peru in the late 1930s, Peruvians saw the opportunity to not only resolve a territorial issue, but also put to rest a history of defeat. In 1941 they swept across Ecuador in a blitzkrieg and, after much diplomatic maneuvering, the U.S. accepted the results on the battlefield.[66]

In sum, Wood is correct in pointing out that the 1930s became a bloody decade unlike any other since the end of the nationalist wars of the nineteenth century. But nuanced U.S. leadership (intervention and interference produce peace, nonintervention and noninterference produce war) was not the key difference; indeed, the U.S. was a distinctly secondary actor in the 1920s as well as in the 1930s. National interests, both domestic and territorial, produced the context in which the U.S. could broker some agreements and serve as a shield for others. But because the disputes were linked in ways unappreciated by the U.S., although clearly seen by the Latin Americans, the "solutions" of the 1920s upset the status quo without resolving the fundamental problems or leaving any of the actors with an increased sense of security. Thus they led directly to the military confrontations of the 1930s.

The alleged U.S. "success" of the 1920s proved hollow, in light of the impact of the diplomatic maneuvering of the time on the conflicts in the 1929–41 period. In addition, the indicators of success are the result of mistaking correlation for causation (the U.S. had intervened in the 1920s, it did not in the 1930s). Wood's argument did not apply to Central America and the Caribbean, so I left it aside in this qualitative analysis. In turning to some quantitative evidence we go beyond Wood's analysis and thus can incorporate Central America and the Caribbean.

Hegemonic Management in the Security Complex: Some Quantitative Evidence

This quantitative approach to the argument will facilitate our evaluation of the hegemonic management thesis by enabling us to incorporate MID experiences across almost the entire time period of our study, 1884–1993.[67] We can also arrange the data in a slightly different way, which should strengthen the hegemonic management thesis by controlling for some factors that may be affecting the impact of hegemonic management. These modifications separate the period of hegemonic management into two, according to systemic polarity, and split the region in two, South and Central America (the latter including Mexico and the Caribbean). We therefore create a best case scenario for the hegemonic management thesis and thereby demonstrate the robustness of any critique of the hegemonic thesis.

Up to now we have had a rather simple view of regional hegemonic management because we have focused only on the power distribution within the region. But while the regional hegemon may effectively isolate the region from the international system, it itself remains but one of the great powers in the global arena. As a consequence, the regional hegemon is playing in two games, the regional and global. While not significantly constrained by regional states (this is after all the core idea in a hegemonic management thesis), the regional hegemon is interacting with other powerful states at the international level. Consequently, the dynamics of its role in the global system may affect its ability and preferences for policing the region.

For Realists, the polarity of the international system will affect a great power's behavior. Whether the world is multipolar or bipolar will affect the costs and benefits of policing or otherwise managing the region.[68] The chief effect of systemic polarity on regional hegemonic management should be to restrain unilateral action during multipolarity relative to that exercised during a period of bipolarity. The costs of diverting resources (e.g., in Mexico just as the U.S. was becoming involved in World War I) and the potential for provoking an intense search for great power balancers (e.g., Mexico with Germany in 1938, Argentina with Great Britain during World War II) should be higher in a multipolar than bipolar world. Consequently, the occurrence, and escalation, of military disputes should be highest in a pre-regional hegemony period and lowest when systemic bipolarity reigns. Regional hegemony under conditions of systemic multipolarity should produce an indeterminate but intermediate level of MIDs and their escalations.

Not all hegemonic management advocates, however, believe that systemic polarity affects the regional hegemon's ability to regulate interstate relations within the region. These analysts focus on the power disparity between the regional hegemon and other regional states. Regional hegemony means there is no other great power that can be balanced against the regional hegemon, no matter the polarity of the international system. Thus the regional hegemon confronts regional states on the basis of the distribution of power *within* the region. For these analysts the difference in regional MID behavior is between when there is or is not a hegemon.[69]

We now have two sets of hypotheses for the regional hegemonic management thesis, differentiated by whether or not systemic polarity matters. Each set has three components covering number of MIDs, use of force, and escalation to war (table 3.2). Hegemonic management advocates disagree whether the impact of hegemony should be stronger in Central America and the Caribbean than in South America.[70] We can, however, organize the data to reflect such a split and see if any variations emerge across subregions.

Evaluation. Table 3.3 presents the MID data for the two periods distinguished simply by whether the U.S. was hegemonic in the region. We have used the MID I data base because we are interested in whether disputants utilize military force in their disputes, and MID II does not record hostility level by disputant. The original MID set only goes up to 1976, so our analysis will have to end at that time. Since Central America has been in a hegemonic region throughout the period represented by our database, we cannot test the hegemony hypothesis for it and are limited to South America.

The hypothesis that hegemony per se leads to a decrease in MIDs is rejected, as the average number of MIDs in a year increased from 0.89 to

TABLE 3.2 Regional Hegemonic Management Hypotheses

Undifferentiated Regional Hegemony

Hypothesis 1A: The occurrence of militarized interstate disputes should decrease in the period during which the U.S. is hegemonic in the region.

Hypothesis 1B: The use of force[a] in militarized interstate disputes should decrease in the period during which the U.S. is hegemonic in the region.

Hypothesis 1C: Escalation of disputes to war should decrease in the period during which the U.S. is hegemonic in the region.

Regional Hegemony in an International Context

Hypothesis 2A: There should be fewer militarized conflicts when the U.S. is hegemonic in the region. There should also be fewer militarized interstate disputes when the U.S. is hegemonic and the international system is bipolar, than when the system is multipolar.

Hypothesis 2B: The use of force[a] in militarized interstate disputes should decrease in the period during which the U.S. is hegemonic in the region. The use of force in militarized interstate disputes should also be less when the U.S. is hegemonic and the international system is bipolar, than when the system is multipolar.

Hypothesis 2C: Escalation of disputes to war should decrease in the period during which the U.S. is hegemonic in the region. Militarized conflicts are also more likely to be settled short of war when the U.S. is hegemonic and the international system is bipolar, than when the system is multipolar.

[a] defined as a MID hostility level of 4 or 5 (using rather than merely showing force)

1.03. The use of force by both initiators and targets did decline slightly, by 5.6 and 3.6 percentage points, respectively, thereby providing weak support for Hypothesis 1B. Regional hegemony seems to have an impact in this area of militarized interstate disputes, although not as dramatic as many analysts and U.S. policy makers assert since more than three-fourths of all MIDs begin with the active use of force. Hypothesis 1C, concerning escalation to war, is contradicted, as there were no wars in the pre-hegemonic period analyzed and wars did occur in the hegemonic era. (If the data set extended

TABLE 3.3 Militarized Interstate Disputes and the Hegemonic Management Thesis
(Simple Hegemony Version)

Period	Total MIDs	Disputes per years (% of total)	Force* by initiator (% of total)	Force* by target	War (% of total)
South America					
No Hegemony 1884–1918	31	31/35 0.89	26/31 83.9%	13/31 41.9%	0 0.0%
Hegemony 1919–1976	60[a]	60/58 1.03	47/60 78.3%	23/60 38.3%	2[b]/60

*Force is defined as having a hostility level of 4 or greater in the MID data set (using rather than merely threatening or showing force).

[a.] MID I counts the same Argentine-British dispute in 1947 twice. For the purposes of this discussion, I also only count a MID once, no matter how many participants are involved.

[b.] The MID data set does not classify the 1941 dispute between Ecuador and Peru as a "war" (hostility level of 5), but it does record a hostility level of 6 (more than 999 battlefield deaths). Peru invaded Ecuador with planes, paratroopers and tanks, seized control of 40% of what Ecuador claimed as national territory and held other Ecuadorian territory hostage until Ecuador officially signed a peace treaty. Given the deaths and behavior of Peru, I take the hostility level to be incorrectly coded and classify it as a "war."

Source: MID I data set.

to 1982 the Malvinas/Falklands War would also have been included.) Simple hegemony, consequently, seems to have, at best, only a partial and small impact on interstate conflict behavior in South America.

Perhaps disaggregating hegemony by the international constraints on the hegemon may provide more support for the hegemonic management thesis. Table 3.4 presents the data for both Central and South America. South America provides three periods (no hegemony, hegemony within a multipolar world, and hegemony in a bipolar world) while Central America provides only the two hegemonic periods.

Table 3.4 indicates that the distribution of power internationally and regionally has no systematic impact on the occurrence of militarized interstate

TABLE 3.4 Militarized Interstate Disputes and the Hegemonic Management Thesis (Polarity Version)

Period	Total MIDs	Disputes per years (% of total)	Force* by initiator (% of total)	Force* by target (% of total)	War (% of total)
South America					
No Hegemony 1884–1918	31	31/35 0.89	26/31 83.9%	13/31 41.9%	0 0.0%
Hegemony (Multipolarity) 1919–44	16	16/26 0.62	12/16 75.0%	11/16 68.8%	2/16 12.5%
Hegemony (Bipolarity) 1945–76	44	44/32 1.38	33/44 75.0%	11/44 25.0%	0/44 0.0%
Central America					
Hegemony (multipolarity) 1908–41	36	36/34 1 1.05	8/36 50.0%	7/36 19.4%	1/31 3.2%
Hegemony (bipolarity) 1945–76	38	38/32 1.19	27/38 71.1%	16/38 42.1%	1/38 2.6%

*Force is defined as having a hostility level of 4 or greater in the MID data set (rather than showing force).

Source: MID I data set with modifications for South America explained in Table 3.3. For Central America I include the 1937 Haitian-Dominican dispute as a war since up to 12,000 people died. Although in Chapter Two I classified it as a "massacre" such a large scale use of force should not occur under conditions of hegemony. Consequently, I include it here. The 1969 Hundred Hours War between El Salvador and Honduras is also counted twice in MID I, while I count it only once.

disputes in the western hemisphere. There are variations across time periods and South and Central America differ in their conflict behavior.

For South America, hegemony in the hemisphere combined with a bipolar international structure dramatically increases the yearly rate of MIDs compared with that under a multipolar international structure or no regional hegemony (1.38 compared with 0.62 and 0.89, respectively). In Central America, regional unipolarity in a bipolar world correlates with more MIDs (1.19 yearly average under bipolarity and 1.05 during multipolarity). Thus we reject Hypothesis 2A because a less constrained hegemon correlates with more rather than fewer MIDs in both subregions of the Latin American security complex.

Hypothesis 2B postulates that states will use force in their disputes more often when the hegemon is occupied with a multipolar world. South and Central American behavior diverges on this point, but in ways which still do not support the hegemonic management thesis. In South America variations in systemic polarity do not affect the use of force by initiators (75% under both bipolarity and multipolarity). Also in contrast to the Hypothesis, in Central America initiators use force significantly more often when the hegemon is less constrained (half the time under multipolarity, but 71% of the time under systemic bipolarity). Targets in South America behave partially in line with the hypothesis (responding with force 68.8% of the time under multipolarity, and only 28.2% under bipolarity), but still significantly more violence is used during regional hegemony in a multipolar world than in the absence of hegemony. In Central America the behavior of targets during hegemony is the reverse of that in South America. Central American targets are more likely to resort to force (42.1% of the time under bipolarity and in only 19.1% of their MIDs in a multipolar world). Hypothesis 2B is thus also rejected.

The postulated impact of systemic polarity on conflict escalation to war also lacks empirical support (Hypothesis 3B). There are so few wars that it would be hard to make a strong argument about their correlation with anything. But the data clearly show that in both South and Central America war happens when the U.S. is hegemonic and the world is either bipolar or multipolar. Hypothesis 3B is also not supported in South America because regional multipolarity corresponds with 0 wars!

In sum, the argument for a positive theory of hegemonic management of conflict in Latin America's security complex fails to provide any insight into the pattern or dynamics of interstate conflict.

Hegemonic Mismanagement of Conflict

There is also a hegemonic mismanagement thesis. Managers seek to make their "team" produce their product as the manager understands it. But managers may undermine the group's ability to perform by dissipating its energies in side issues that may be more important to the manager than to the group. In the business world, this manager gets replaced for failing to deliver the goods. But in an owner-operated firm, no one may be able to replace the manager if she is incompetent and the company would fail. Under conditions of anarchy and hegemony in a regional security complex, the hegemon has "job security" and thus may run the "company" into the ground.

For some analysts, U.S. management of conflict in the Americas is a case of mismanagement. Rather than produce security for all Latin American nations vis-à-vis each other, the manager (U.S.) promoted distrust and conflict as it forced Latin American states to contribute to the enforcement of its vision of security in the complex. Rather than police the security complex on its own, the U.S. utilized Latin American elites and nations to do its own enforcement.

There are two versions of this thesis, one focusing on nationalism and the other on anti-communism. The basic point is the same: the U.S. saw it (nationalism or communism) as a threat to its own interests in the security complex and moved to sanction and eliminate it.[71] Had the U.S. acted on its own, it would have been implementing a unilateral security agenda which would have punished the "offenders" but kept the other nations secure from the conflict. (Note the discussion in the introduction to this chapter.) But by forcing Latin American countries to become involved in the conflicts between the hegemon and a recalcitrant state, the U.S. subjected those allies to conflicts that were not in their own interests.

The hegemonic mismanagement thesis expects conflict in the Latin American security complex to increase under hegemony. We will test both the nationalist and anti-Communist versions. The evidence for the nationalist version is the same as for the simple hegemony version of the pro-hegemonic management thesis, except that now we expect MIDs to increase rather than decrease. Once again, we cannot test this hypothesis for Central America and the Caribbean since there were only a few years between the end of the nationalist wars and the establishment of U.S. paramountcy. Reviewing table 3.3 we find that in South America the frequency of MIDs did increase, but the level of violence by both initiator and target decreased slightly. There were two wars in the hegemonic period, but examination of the Chaco and the Peru-Ecuador war of 1941 did not indicate that leaders were fighting because of U.S. interests. Consequently, hegemonic mismanagement is a spurious correlation with these two wars.

The anti-Communist mismanagement thesis presents some new possibilities for analyzing the data. According to the anti-Communist version, we expect militarized conflict to increase in the period in which the U.S. was hegemonic after the Russian Revolution in 1918.[72] We can make some modifications in the analysis done so far in order to get a better handle on the mismanagement thesis. MID II extends up to 1993, and the Cold War ends in 1989. There are too few cases between the end of the Cold War and the end of the MID II for inclusion of post–Cold War behavior in the analysis. Since MID II allows us to include the most turbulent period of the Cold War in Latin America, it, rather than MID I is more appropriate for investigating the impact of U.S. anti-Communism on interstate conflict management. As noted earlier, using the MID II data set precludes distinguishing between the use of force by the initiator and target, but we can still ascertain whether a conflict became militarized up to the use of force (4 or 5 in the MID data set). In addition, we can ask how many states participated in the MIDs, an important consideration for an argument which claims that the hegemon pushes other states into disputes which are otherwise irrelevant to them.

Table 3.5 analyzes the data in terms of four categories: total Latin American participants in MIDs; the average number of disputants per year; whether force is used in the conflict; and the number of Latin American participants in regional wars. South America presents us with four cases, the pre-Communist years of 1884–1918 and the anti-Communist period of 1919–1988, also separated by whether we utilize military or a complete paramountcy (military, economic, and political) to claim hegemony. The Central American cases are more straightforward in that all three circumstances occur together. Pre-Communist hegemony should thus correspond to 1908–1918 with Anti-Communist hegemony covering 1919–1988.

Evaluation. Table 3.5 provides some empirical support for the hegemonic mismanagement thesis. In South America, whether one uses the strictly military or multi-factorial definition of paramountcy, more Latin

TABLE 3.5 Latin American Participants in Militarized Interstate Disputes
(The Hegemonic Mismanagement Thesis)

Period	Total MID Participants	Disputants per year	Force* used (% total MIDs)	Participants in Regional Wars
South America				
A. Military Version				
No Hegemony 1884–1918	91	91/35 2.60	38/64 59%	0/91 0%
Anti-Communist Hegemony 1919–1988	226	226/70 3.23	117/186 63%	5/226 2.2%
B. Full Version				
No Hegemony 1884–1942	160	160/58 2.76	67/118 57%	2/160 1.3%
Anti-Communist Hegemony 1943–1988	157	157/48 3.27	88/132 67%	3/157 1.9%
Central America				
Pre-Communist Hegemony 1908–1918	35	35/11 3.18	12/32 37.5%	0/35 0.0%
Anti-Communist Hegemony 1919–1988	142	142/81 1.75	74/99 75%	3/142 2.1%

*Force: Hostility level of 4 or 5 (using rather than showing force); 25 have unknown hostility levels

Source: MID II, excluding W.W. I, W. W. II, and the Korean War

American countries participate in MIDs during the periods of U.S. anti-Communism. (From 2.60 to 3.23 disputants per year, and 2.76 to 3.27, respectively.) In addition, South American conflicts are somewhat more likely to utilize force during this period: 4 percent more violent MIDs when examining the military version of U.S. paramountcy and 10 percent more

MIDs becoming violent when we incorporate political and economic paramountcy.

The table also indicates that Latin American countries are more likely to participate in regional wars during the periods of alleged U.S. hegemonic mismanagement. But these numbers are not very convincing. There are so few participants in wars that the difference between the military and full versions of anti-Communist hegemony is one participant (from two to three total participants). In addition, neither the Chaco nor the Ecuador-Peru war of 1941 can be attributed to anti-Communism. Consequently, only one Latin American participant in a war during the 1919–88 period could conceivably be related to U.S. anti-Communism: the virulent anti-Communist military regime in Argentina during the Malvinas/Falklands War in 1982.[73] But as chapter 6 demonstrates, the anti-communist nature of the regime had little to do with the decision to occupy the Malvinas Islands or resist British attempts to retake them.

In Central America and the Caribbean, the average number of disputants per year declines dramatically with U.S. anti-Communist hegemony, from 3.18 to 2.06. This contradicts the hegemonic mismanagement thesis. But the use of violence in those disputes increases significantly (doubling from 37.5 to 75% of the cases), and the number of participants in regional wars also increases (from 0 to 3), thereby supporting the mismanagement thesis. Nevertheless, the Central America figures are problematic for evaluating the hypothesis because of the vast disparity in time periods analyzed: 11 years for pre-Communist hegemony by the U.S. and 81 years for the anti-Communist period.

Conclusion

This chapter has examined whether the use of force in Latin America results from the unique influence of the United States. The arguments for U.S. determinism follow the logic that either conflict erupts when the U.S. fails to patrol the region, or that U.S. policy actually stimulates conflict. The latter hypothesis, that the U.S. "mismanages" conflict, takes two forms: that the U.S. stimulates conflict either because of U.S. opposition to nationalism, or to communism.

The historical record disputes all these hypotheses. Force is used when the U.S. wants it, and also when the U.S. opposes its use. The strongest evidence exists for the anti-communism argument. Indeed, the period of the Cold War sees increased military conflict in the region. However, though U.S. anti-communism matters, it fails to explain the use of force, since force is used before and after the Cold War, and during the Cold War on issues entirely unrelated to communism. Though the U.S. is uniquely powerful, it is not a hegemon that provides the collective good of peace among nations of the region which have their own interests.

If we want to understand interstate conflict dynamics in the Latin American security complex we need to move beyond the myth of hegemonic management. We turn in chapter 4 to the first of the more general international relations theories. Latin America provides an ideal setting for examination of the democratic peace argument because the region presents rich variation of regime type over time.

4 Democracy, Restrained Leadership and the Use of Military Force

      Many academic analysts and policy advocates focus on domestic institutions as key to understanding the use of force in foreign policy. In this conceptualization, democratic polities "rarely wage war on one another;" consequently, promoting democracy increases the level of international security among democratic states. (Democracy is valued for other reasons as well, but here we are focusing on its alleged implications for conflict management.) Secure in this belief, numerous inter-American analysts and policymakers propose sanctions on those polities that, while still peaceful and cooperative internationally, restructure domestic institutions in such a way as to undermine democratic institutions. The OAS recently adopted a resolution that a threat to democracy in any Western hemisphere nation automatically constituted a threat to the security of all American nations. The Miami Summit of American Nations seconded it and the hemispheric meetings of Ministers of Defense followed suit.[1]

The empirical finding that democracies tend not to engage in large-scale war (defined by 1,000 battlefield deaths) with other democracies[2] is under increasing attack as being an artifice of classificatory schemes: which states are classified as democracies or liberal republics and what time period is considered.[3] The theoretical reasoning to explain the alleged democratic peace has always been contentious.[4] In the case of smaller scale wars and militarized disputes we have even less of a consensus on how democratic states have used military force.[5]

This chapter examines whether democratic institutional constraints best explain the pattern of regional conflict and cooperation in Latin America. Qualitative and quantitative methods are used to evaluate the institutional constraint argument. The qualitative analysis of the first section examines the theoretical logic and decisionmaking processes hypothesized to make institutionally constrained political leaders less likely to engage in the use of force internationally. Quantitative analysis in the next section evaluates the correspondence between democracy and regional conflict behavior. Analyses of general participation rates, levels of hostility, participation rates by individual countries over time, and conflict dyads indicate that the level of democracy is not a systematic or powerful determinant of conflict behavior in Latin America. Democratic institutional constraints appear to sometimes matter for a state's decision to utilize military force in a dispute, but in different ways across subregions and countries. The analysis in this chapter strongly suggests that such factors are at best secondary, and may not even point unambiguously in the direction of nonviolent management of conflict.

Institutional Constraints: Logical Imprecision, Operational Confusion

Institutions themselves do not determine action; rather they provide a context in which social interaction occurs. Both the historical-sociological and rational choice approach to institutions claim that institutions affect the incentives facing actors and structure the relations of power between groups, thereby affecting their behavior.[6] Building on this insight, the democratic peace model claims that something in the nature of democratic domestic institutions makes it difficult for the leaders of a state to use force internationally, in particular against other democracies.

The relevant constraints are of two types, one focusing on elections, the other on multiple veto gates. The electoral focus privileges democratic states as inherently peaceful,[7] while the veto gates argument might be equally effective for constraining nondemocratic governments. The electoral focus makes us consider the interests of the voters and their political leaders, while the analysis of veto gates highlights the institutional role of potential vetoes.

Electoral Constraints

The need for decisionmakers to stand for periodic elections constitutes the most general institutional constraint in a democracy. Elections make it useful to assume that a politician's interest can be condensed to winning elections. The claim is not that politicians have no other interests, but that in order to accomplish whatever her goals are in politics, a politician needs to first be elected. The politician thus needs to offer the voters what they want if she is to be elected or re-elected.[8] If we wish to know how a democratic state will behave, therefore, we need to look to its electorate.

In a nondemocratic polity, leaders do not need to stand for regular and free elections. Because expressing disagreement via rebellion is more costly to participants than filling out a secret ballot, citizens' preferences will constrain a leader less in a nondemocratic than a democratic polity.[9] Nondemocratic leaders still face some constraints imposed by their supporters, but the selectorate will be composed of a narrower cross section of society. Given its small base, the selectorate in a nondemocracy may be able to pursue its goals utilizing military force while shifting the costs (in both money and blood), to the rest of society. In a democratic polity, on the other hand, those who must pay in taxes and lives will be able to effectively communicate their opposition to military adventures.

Although institutional analysts want to avoid incorporating norms, they sneak in via assumptions concerning voter preferences. Individuals are assumed to be driven by the implicit norm that material interests guide their behavior, rather than glory, revenge, or moral purity (e.g., religious, cultural, and national fundamentalism).[10] Since war does not materially benefit the individual soldiers who must do the fighting, individuals will not elect leaders who will take them into costly wars. Because the electoral constraint empowers the pacific people, leaders will have a difficult time fabricating threats to justify the use of force. Politicians recognize this constraint, hence democracies prefer to resolve disputes peacefully.

Any analyst of the third world will immediately be stunned by such a proclamation of pacifist intent. Democratic Britain, France, and the United States share a bloody history in Africa, Asia, and Latin America. Democratic peace advocates have a ready answer: the international system is not comprised solely of democratic states. When a democratic state becomes involved in a dispute with another democratic state, the leaders are similarly

constrained. Consequently, both sides can credibly communicate that neither wishes war and diplomats thus have time to work out the differences.
When a democratic state confronts a nondemocratic state or other political
grouping, however, both sides understand that one is constrained while the
other is not. Hence the democratic state fears being bullied and the nondemocratic state's leaders may believe that they can face down the leaders
of the democratic state.[11] The democrats could thus strike preemptively if
the stakes are high enough, and the people back home would understand
this as a purely defensive action.

In sum, the democratic peace argument does not claim that democracies
are pacifists.[12] If threatened, they will utilize military force to defend themselves, perhaps even preemptively. When democracies make war, therefore,
it is always the fault of the nondemocracy, at the very least for being nondemocratic.[13] If all states were democratic, there would be no war, even
under conditions of anarchy.

The electoral constraint argument merits closer attention before one accepts it as an appropriate depiction of democratic foreign policy. The democratic peace argument becomes logically imprecise once we incorporate a
more realistic and complex model of electoral politics. The difficulties are
threefold and relate to (i) voter preferences; (ii) the structure of the voting
process; and (iii) the process of electoral accountability itself (term limits,
party structure, and transparency of the process).

Voter Preferences

Voter preferences can be usefully discussed in terms of three factors: political
philosophy; distribution of preferences and issue dimensionality; and the
costs of using military force. Only under very restrictive conditions will the
three combine to produce an unequivocal argument for a society's preferences to favor peaceful resolution of conflict.

Political Philosophy
I noted above that democratic peace advocates assume strictly materialist
interests drive citizens. What drives voters in elections, however, is fundamentally determined by political philosophy concerning the appropriate relationship between citizen and state.[14] If a materialist voter preference is
sufficient for peace, the question then becomes whether democratic citizens
everywhere hold the same political philosophy. If citizens are driven by other

concerns, the logic of the institutional constraint argument could drive politicians in democratic societies into diverse positions concerning militarized conflict. Because Latin America has been buffeted by three major political philosophies (liberal, corporatist, and militarist), its experience can illuminate their potential impact on how voters see the legitimacy of using military force.

A liberal political philosophy is individualist and materialist. Society exists for the benefit of its members. The state is subordinated to society. Sovereignty rests in the people, not in the state. In fact for liberals, the state does not exist. There is a government that guides a state apparatus, and that government expresses the will of the dominant political forces. In a liberal government occurrence of free elections means that these forces effectively represent the people. The government exists to defend the individual and not the reverse; individuals seek a peaceful environment in which to accumulate wealth. The people express their will directly via elections and they do it in an individual manner, hence the government finds it difficult to deceive the public. The military is part of the governmental apparatus and as such, subordinated to the will of the people via the civilian government. Citing Locke, Owen notes that all liberals "share a fundamental interest in self-preservation and material well-being. . . . liberalism's ends are life and property, and its means are liberty and toleration."[15]

A corporatist political philosophy conceptualizes the nation as the context in which a society exists. From this perspective, modern society cannot exist in the absence of a national context. In this political philosophy, "the people" is an agglomeration of groups and not of individuals. Individuals define themselves and act in accordance with the group to which they belong. Sovereignty becomes inherent in the "state" itself, rather than in individuals. For corporatists, the nation becomes anthropomorphic as the mother or father of the citizens; consequently, each corporatist group has a responsibility to defend her. The military establishment is understood to be the people in arms and therefore has a special responsibility to defend the state. In political systems defined by corporatist philosophies, the military's internal role is facilitated by constitutional clauses that permit fairly easy declarations of states of emergency.[16] Since the needs of the state come before those of the individual, a corporatist democrat will evaluate the costs of using force differently than will a liberal democrat. Specifically, the former would be willing to pay more individual costs to protect the state than would the latter.

In a militarist political philosophy, the military establishment is believed to be the vanguard social organization in a national process of modernization. According to this conception, since the national defense depends on military capacity, the military are attentive to technological and industrial innovations and seek to keep themselves up to date. Their mission as defender of the state in an anarchic world gives them a vision with which to appreciate the modern reforms that the nation should adopt. The organizational and professional qualities of the military make it contrast with the political and economic forces of the country which continue to focus on defending their own interests and thus cannot bring the country out of underdevelopment. Militarism tends to have an organic vision of the state: it either grows or it dies. The role of individuals is to form part of society and defend it. Individualism represents a threat to the nation because it subordinates the national good to personal good. Within this panorama, both civilians frustrated with socioeconomic progress and military officers anxious to protect the nation perceive that at certain historical moments the military has the moral obligation to assume leadership.[17] Democracies in which a militarist political philosophy reigns might be more likely to accept the use of force to resolve disputes because the military's voice is accorded such a preeminent role when it comes to defending the nation.[18]

A number of problems arise in using political philosophies to reflect citizen preferences on the use of military force in international affairs. First, liberal analysts disagree among themselves as to when a society is dominated by a liberal political philosophy. Doyle marks Great Britain as liberal after the Reform Act of 1832 and the U.S. as liberal from its inception. Owen claims, however, that British citizens did not view the U.S. as liberal until the Emancipation Proclamation abolished slavery in the rebellious states (not in those fighting with the Union) in 1863. U.S. citizens, in turn, believed that monarchy, even a constitutional one, was incompatible with Liberalism; they did not alter this view until after 1884 when the British expanded the franchise once again. Yet North and Weingast identify England as developing "the fundamental institutions of representative government" after the Glorious Revolution of 1688![19] In the absence of systematic criteria determining when a state will perceive another as "liberal" such distinctions in times of crises take on an ad hoc flavor.[20]

A second major problem with this type of analysis lies in the ability of societies to draw from a variety of political philosophies in creating their own political culture. Latin American societies developed with a hybrid political philosophy that expresses the tension inherent in belonging to western culture (and therefore liberal), of having Hispanic roots (and therefore corporatist), and of arriving late to the industrial revolution (and therefore having militarist aspects). This combination means that Latin Americans have always searched for democracy and peaceful resolution of conflict, but feared internal disorder and external defeat. This hybrid political culture does not recognize conflict resolution as having an inherent value, but rather as a mechanism for social-economic development, political stability, and the defense of the motherland.

The foreign policy implication of such a hybrid political philosophy is ambiguous. Latin American democrats historically could support military coups against governments they perceived as unable to govern effectively or to keep competitors from using the democratic process to institute important social and economic changes. One could hypothesize from such behavior that Latin American democrats would decide when to use force based on what was at stake, rather than on principle. Some examples include popular support for democratic Colombia's military buildup after a war scare over territory and resources with democratic Venezuela in 1987 and popular support on both sides during the war between the two democracies, Peru and Ecuador, in 1995.[21]

Some analysts deny that the normative and philosophical understanding of politics can remain independent of the institutional structures of democracy.[22] But the historical experience of Ancient Athens belies such claims: although democratic for more than half a century, democratic Athens attacked democratic Syracuse with a large and costly force.[23] Doyle and Huntington are more credible when they postulate that political philosophies can exist independently of political institutions and hence it is only certain types of democracies ("liberal republics" and "western civilization"[24]) which will have mutually peaceful relations, but only when they both perceive themselves as such.[25]

Distribution of Voter Preferences

The distribution of voter preferences and the dimensionality of issues also affect the ability of voters to constrain their leaders. Polling of voters and public opinion is still in its infancy in Latin America, and foreign policy issues do not generally interest these pollsters, so much of the analysis in this subsection will be theoretical. The comparative and American politics literature recognizes that voter preference distribution and issue dimensionality are important even if we are speaking of societies dominated by liberal political philosophies.[26] The median voter in a liberal society may prefer a peaceful resolution of conflict with other states, but this may not dominate a winning candidate's policy preference. Depending on the relationship between an issue concerning the use of force and other issues, voters may still elect or reelect a decisionmaker who supports the use of violence against the electorate's preferences.[27]

Intransitive preferences at the group level make the aggregation of individual preferences into a coherent social choice problematic.[28] Table 4.1 illustrates the problem. I draw upon three major issues that have concerned voters across Latin America: inflation, guerrilla activity, and a border dispute. In this example, the distribution of preferences across the three issues produces a different preference ordering among the three groups of voters or opinion poll respondents.

Given this distribution of preferences, a cycling problem develops. Fighting inflation is preferred to fighting guerrillas by two of the voters (A and C), and fighting guerrillas beats defending borders (A and B), so we might think that society's preferences would be to focus on inflation-guerrillas-borders. But note that if B and C form a coalition, we now have defending borders preferred to fighting inflation. The majority preference thus depends not on the preferences of individual voters or poll respondents, but on the institutional mechanisms for aggregating votes or opinions.[29]

The cycling problem is aggravated when the issues considered vary along two or more dimensions. The question of whether to use military force can actually tap into three dimensions: whether to use force (yes or no), whether to be involved internationally (isolationist/internationalist), and whether to act in concert with others (unilateral or multilateralist). This range of opin-

TABLE 4.1 Social Choice and Intransitive Preferences

A	B	C
Fight Inflation	Fight Guerrillas	Defend Borders
Fight Guerrillas	Defend Borders	Fight Inflation
Defend Borders	Fight Inflation	Fight Guerrillas

The Cycling Problem: A + C > B and A + B > C but B + C > A

ions produces six distinct attitudes toward foreign affairs: *Unilateralists*, *Multilateralists*, and *Isolationists*, each with versions favoring the use of force (hard-liners) or rejecting it (soft-liners).[30]

In Latin America, *unilateralists* see a competitive international arena in which the nation must participate by relying on its own resources. Argentina provides numerous examples of this perspective in the supporters of Argentine neutrality during World War II, or of its covert intervention in Bolivia throughout the twentieth century, and especially in the mass enthusiasm which erupted in response to the military government's seizure of the Malvinas Islands in 1982. In Peru, we have the popular support for its quick, yet bloody, military ouster of Ecuadorian troops in 1981. *Multilateralists* believe in the utility of acting in concert with others. They can be international institutionalists (e.g., supporters of participation in the OAS, the Rio Group, or participation in international peacekeeping[31]). But multilateralists may also be geopolitical advocates who see the region as engaged in a global geopolitical struggle (e.g., those that supported membership in the Andean Pact, an economic integration scheme built on the idea of import substitution industrialization).[32] *Isolationists* believe the country is better off with minimal ties to the international arena. Examples include supporters of government policy in Guatemala in the late 1970s, 1980s, and Chile from 1972–1989, as well as many Chileans who marched in the streets, demanding General Pinochet's return to Chile after his arrest in 1998–99.

The complexity of public opinion is further increased when we examine specific issues.[33] An opinion poll might theoretically ask if force should be used in resolving disputes. All hard line respondents would answer yes, while soft-liners would answer no. But the resolution of an international dispute can be pursued in a variety of ways. Possibilities include simple cessation, [G in table 4.2] (e.g., Mexico's renunciation of claims to Belize); diplomatic negotiation [N] (there are many examples, both bilaterally and multilaterally); using military force unilaterally to impose a solution [UM] (e.g., U.S. invasion of Panama, Argentine seizure of the Malvinas/Falklands Islands), or using military force multilaterally to guarantee a status quo ante [MM] (as in peacekeeping on the Ecuador-Peru border).

These four policies (G, N, UM, and MM), arrayed across six attitudinal positions produce 24 policy options. Table 4.2 arrays these options across a hypothetical distribution of preferences concerning how a country should respond in an important international dispute. To make the discussion more tractable, I make two assumptions: (1) the public does not perceive its own

TABLE 4.2 Preference Orderings Concerning the Use of Force
(Hypothetical)

Unilateralists		Multilateralists		Isolationists	
Hardliner	Soft	Internationalist	Accommodationist	Forceful	Restrained
20%	10%	20%	30%	8%	12%
UM	N	MM	N	G	G
MM	G	N	G	UM	N
N	UM	UM	MM	MM	UM
G	MM	G	UM	N	MM

Key:
G: give up one's claims in the dispute
N: bilateral negotiations
UM: unilateral military use of force
MM: multilateral military use of force

country as the aggressor in the conflict; and (2) the dispute is not over whether a country has a right to exist. These assumptions fit the Latin American experience in the twentieth century fairly well (see Chapter 2).

Unilateral hard-liners prefer unilateral military action. As internationalists with a regionally competitive geopolitical orientation, they value the need to "win" (e.g., retain territory, control migration, etc.) because it adds to one's resource base and reputation while detracting from that of a competitor. They prefer to win on their own, but would be willing to accept the status quo ante if a multilateral peacekeeping force can guarantee it. Because hard-liners would prefer not to make concessions, negotiations rank low. They would least prefer to give up on the matter in dispute. Their preferences would thus likely be: UM > MM > N > G. Soft unilateralists do not want to use military force, and would prefer to negotiate or give up in the dispute rather than use military force. If force is to be used, being unilateralists, they prefer to act alone. This groups' preferences are likely to be: N > G > UM > MM

Hard-line multilateralists prefer to use international solutions for resolving conflict. In the event that the international community did not use its force in favor of this Latin American country against another, these multilateralists would accept a return to the status quo ante rather than use unilateral force. In addition, they prefer to negotiate rather than impose a solution, if one is necessary. Since they are hard-liners, they prefer to fight than lose anything. For this group: MM > N > UM > G. Soft-line multilateralists prefer negotiation to conceding, but would rather give up than use military force to enforce the status quo ante or impose a solution. N > G > MM > UM.

Isolationists desire to limit the country's international entanglements. Given that resolving a dispute via negotiations or the use of force implies becoming active internationally, both hard-line and soft-line isolationists prefer to walk away from disputes. Preference orderings differ once we move beyond conceding. Hard-liners would next use military force unilaterally, followed by multilateral safeguarding of the status quo ante, and lastly, negotiations (G > UM > MM > N). Soft-liners rank negotiations ahead of the use of any military force, and unilateral over multilateral use (G > N > UM > MM).

Given preference intransitivity across the six groups, we can easily wind up in a policy cycle. Table 4.2 indicates that a majority in this hypothetical example has negotiations as their first choice (40%), but when we incorporate the full range of options, more people prefer multilateral military action to negotiations (48% to 40%). Once again, the ability to put together a stable winning coalition depends on factors outside the groups' preferences on the issue.

Consequently, if voter preferences are intransitive, issues are multi-dimensional, and alienation exists among voters (voter turnout in the new Latin American democracies declined almost everywhere in the 1990s[34]), the candidate who takes median positions on all issues will lose. A candidate can take extreme positions on multiple issues, pulling together a coalition of minority voters to provide the margin of victory. "When this happens, a minority, which supports a candidate for the position he takes on a couple of key issues, regardless of his position on others, is essentially trading away its votes on the other issues to those minorities feeling strongly about these other issues."[35] We thus cannot extrapolate from simple citizen preferences to electoral constraints on government policy.

Costs of Using Military Force

The *costs of the use of military force* are another factor that logically affects voter preferences, since at root the democratic peace argument turns on the disparity between the costs of war to individuals and the benefits accruing to small groups. Three factors stand out. *Domestic mobilization costs* affect the time opposition has to organize, as well as the personal disruption experienced by the relevant publics. A reserve-based military would generate high mobilization costs, while a standing army produces lower costs. *Force alternatives* influence the likelihood that using force will result in casualties on one's own side. The use of ground forces will likely produce the highest casualties, with air and naval forces resulting in fewer casualties. Thus the U.S. government did not land troops in Haiti when confronted with armed mobs on the docks, but had decided to attack with aircraft a few months later when the Haitian government capitulated.[36] One might also hypothesize that some of the popular support in El Salvador, Honduras, and Nicaragua for defending sovereignty in the Gulf of Fonseca depends on the conflict being limited to an occasional confrontation between naval vessels.[37] In addition, *the dyadic balance of power* affects the likelihood of a military dispute spiraling toward war. If the balance greatly favors the voter's side, the likelihood of suffering high casualties diminishes. Thus hard-line Peruvians in 1998 were unwilling to make concessions to Ecuador, even if it meant war.[38]

In conclusion, the two assumptions that voter preferences are against the use of force, and are unambiguously communicated to the decisionmaker, are not appropriate for examining democracies' proclivities toward the use of force internationally.

Structure of the Voting Process

Another problem with the democratic peace argument is that it ignores the nuances in the comparative politics literature concerning the importance of variations in the structure of institutional constraints. Rules governing voters and candidates, as well as party strength, will affect the aggregation of voter preferences and the sensitivity of politicians to their constituency. While rules provide a way to diminish the cycling problem examined in the previous subsection, in the process they become another determinant of society's choices.

Electoral Rules
The voting literature points out that electoral rules which influence when one votes, how many issues are involved in an election, and how those issues are presented to the voters can influence who votes as well as how con-

strained politicians might be on a particular issue.[39] For example, voter turn-out is significantly affected by the costs to an individual of registering to vote, the timing of election day (workday or weekend) and the distribution of the winnings (winner-take-all or some version of proportional distribution).[40] There is no *a priori* reason to expect election results to be the same regardless of whether 30, 60, or 90 percent of eligible voters participate.[41] The structure of the ballot itself can also affect the vote. In Peru's 1996 presidential elections, incumbent Fujimori was strategically placed on the ballot; the use of pictures instead of names, while useful to illiterates, also favored the incumbent.[42]

Distribution of Winnings

Critics of Presidentialist political systems have pointed out that *the distribution of winnings* can affect voter preferences. In societies with minor cleavages, winner-take-all elections decrease the number of parties and push voters toward the center. Where cleavages are great, however, the winner-take-all nature of most Presidential elections may propel voters and their candidates toward extremist positions. These rules diminish the incentive to cooperate because both sides know that the winner does not have to cooperate with the loser in forming a government.[43] In Latin America there are major cleavages around border and migration issues between those who want to resolve the issue and those for whom any concessions constitute treason.

Process of Electoral Accountability

Term limits

Term limits also affect the electoral constraint on politicians. If we assume that politicians seek election and we allow for limitations on terms served by the chief executive, *ceteris paribus*, the degree of electoral constraint will vary as term limitations vary. Presidents who cannot run for re-election cannot be directly sanctioned via the ballot box. In the Americas, variation on reelection restrictions has been great. These range from no reelection (currently, Costa Rica, El Salvador, Guatemala, Mexico, and Honduras) through no-consecutive reelection (e.g., Venezuela since 1958 allows two interrupted terms; Argentina before 1994, Bolivia, Panama, Peru before 1993, while Colombia, Argentina, Brazil, Peru, and Ecuador in the 1990s now allow one), two-term limit (the U.S. since the 1940s, contemporary Peru and Argentina), all the way to unlimited re-election (e.g., the U.S. before the 1940s,

Ecuador until 1979, currently the Dominican Republic, Nicaragua, and Paraguay).[44] The logic of the electoral constraint argument should make, *ceteris paribus*, Presidents facing unlimited reelection possibilities the most constrained of the group.

Party Strength

Party strength should also affect electoral constraints on the Executive. In political systems with strong parties, an executive who cannot be reelected will feel constrained by the desire for her party's candidate to succeed her. And if the President is significantly constrained by the legislature (see the discussion of veto gates below), and party discipline is strong, even a president facing no reelection possibilities may feel constrained by voter preferences.

The strength of party systems varies across Latin America in terms of their institutionalization (stability in interparty competition, parties with stable roots in society, their legitimacy, and stability of their organizational structure and rules). Mainwaring and Scully identify four categories of party strength: institutionalized competitive party systems (Venezuela, Costa Rica, Chile, Uruguay, Colombia and, less so, Argentina); inchoate party systems (Peru, Bolivia, Brazil, and Ecuador); hegemonic party systems (Mexico and Paraguay); and no party system (Guatemala, El Salvador, Honduras, Nicaragua, Panama, Cuba, and Bolivia).[45] Party constraints would be relevant only in the first two categories.

Transparency of the Decisionmaking Process

Transparency will also affect the constraints under which leaders labor. Because politicians are assumed to desire election they will not behave in ways opposed to the interests of the public, *if they expect the public to find out*. While one would like to think that democratic leaders have a more transparent decisionmaking process when the use of force is contemplated than their nondemocratic counterparts, empirical evidence and the existence of covert mechanisms of foreign policy make it impossible to say with any degree of certainty. U.S. presidents have carried out secret diplomacy in such an aggressive manner as to provoke others to act overtly and thus be able to claim defensive action when resorting to force themselves. Repeated *exposés*, in both the domestic and international policy arenas, suggest that either presidents are stupid to think they won't be caught, or that there are sufficient successes to allow presidents to think that they have a good chance of succeeding in their secret policies.[46] The latter seems a more reasonable answer, although by its very nature (success means that we don't know), we cannot test the proposition.

In summary, if the electoral constraint hypothesis were correct, the *content* and *extent* of such constraints should vary across democratic polities. Table 4.3 illustrates the range of electoral constraints across Latin American democracies. In conjunction with the discussion in this section, the table suggests that a blanket assertion that democracy places similar constraints on the use of force in Latin America, simply as a result of being a democracy, is probably too theoretically parsimonious to be useful.

Veto Gates

The argument concerning veto gates claims that the greater the number of institutions and interests required to sign off on the use of force,

TABLE 4.3 Hypothesized Electoral Constraints On the Use of Military Force In Latin American Democracies

Type of Constraint	Variation Across Constraints
Voter Preferences	
Political Philosophy	liberal-corporatist-militarist
Distribution	transitive-intransitive
Issue Dimensionality	single-multiple
Personal Cost of Using Military Force	low-medium-high
Periodicity	regularly scheduled 4 and 6 years
Barriers to Voting	low-medium-high
Distribution of Winnings	winner take all-proportionate
Re-election Possibilities	none-no immediate-one consecutive-unlimited
Party Strength	none-hegemonic-inchoate-institutionalized
Transparency of Decisionmaking	filtered-clear

the less likely a country is to resort to force. Since the use of force is assumed to be costly by these analysts (yet empirically it is often cheap), it is harder to convince multiple groups than it is to convince just one that violence is unnecessary. These vetoes can be formally mandated, institutionalized, or informal and are generally found in the legislature, cabinet, and the military. While nothing in the general idea of a veto is peculiar to a democracy, democratic peace advocates believe that the veto gates are significantly more numerous and influential in a democracy.[47]

Presidentialist systems (all Latin American countries are variants on presidentialism, as is the U.S.) provide the Chief Executive with constitutionally mandated and legislatively delegated powers to administer the business of government. The number and extent of these powers vary across policy arenas and political systems.[48] The study of legislative-executive relations in Latin America focuses on domestic politics, while analysis of these relations in the U.S. context includes foreign policy issues. I extrapolate from the comparative politics literature, and draw suggestions from the U.S. experience, to discuss ways of thinking about the vetoes which confront a Latin American president considering the use of force.

Three basic questions guide the analysis in this subsection. First, does the decision to use force in a dispute require the acquiescence of anyone outside the cabinet? Second, what kind of control over the cabinet does the Executive have? Third, can anyone sanction the Executive for using force? The degree of difficulty of imposing sanctions will also matter for this last question. These can range from the relatively easy (if a majority of the Lower House can stop an action by refusing to fund it) to the difficult (when a constitutional amendment is required). The answers to these three questions will provide us with a good sense of whether veto gates matter in Latin American MIDs, as well as how.

In a presidentialist system the legislative veto over executive use of force depends upon the timing and resources required.[49] When war requires a long-term commitment of troops and large financial outlays, legislative support is generally required to increase the size of the armed forces and pass budgets. Yet even here variation exists across systems, with Chile's current constitution allowing the president, with the consent of the cabinet, to require expenditures in order to avoid "causing serious detriment to the country."[50] In addition, executives may be able to administratively shift funds, as when U.S. President Richard Nixon bombed

Cambodia "on credit" because Congress had restricted funds in order to pressure the administration to end the Vietnam War.[51]

Shorter term or more limited military engagements are harder to effectively control. For example, the U.S. War Powers Resolution of 1973, which was designed to limit the president's ability to use military force (and which has never been accepted as legitimate by a president of either party), allows the president to send troops for 90 days without congressional approval. It also provides for an additional 60 days to withdraw them if Congress demands. Hence by its own terms, the War Powers Act allows the president to engage in a five-month war without Congressional approval. In the days prior to the 1991 Gulf War President Bush felt comfortable drawing on the precedent that the U.S. had engaged in over 200 military engagements without a Congressional declaration of war to argue that he did not need Congressional authorization to begin bombing Iraq.[52]

Secret accounts may also be tapped for low-cost military engagements. In the "Irangate" scandal, the Reagan administration continued funding the Contra war in Nicaragua by selling arms to Iran, despite Congressional prohibitions on both actions. The secret account containing more than $17 million, handled by Venezuelan President Carlos Andres Pérez, and the Ecuadorian President's unilateral control over a special account (*gastos reservados*), might also support a policy the president believed necessary and which Congress was unwilling to fund. Constitutional provisos also guarantee the Chilean and Ecuadorian military guaranteed shares of the revenue generated by the country's major export (copper and petroleum, respectively), for military purchases could also facilitate sustained support of a military mission over Congressional objections. Some Latin American militaries control profitable enterprises, giving them a source of funds independent of congressional control as well.[53]

Mobilizing force to deal with disputed borders (which is the type of conflict in which Latin American countries are most likely to engage), is easier than sending troops to fight in foreign territory because Latin American constitutions contain provisos facilitating the militarization of a region during "exceptional" times.[54] The degree of checks and balances across countries also varies in this matter.

The 1961 Venezuelan constitution gives the president the authority to declare a state of emergency, even preventively, subject to approval of his cabinet (council of ministers) and review by the Congress. The 1991 Colombian Constitution provides the president, upon the approval of all of his ministers, with the ability to declare a "State of Internal Commotion" and issue legislative decrees that suspend laws incompatible with the State of Commotion. He can do so for up to 90 days, renewable for two equal periods, with Senate approval required for the last extension. Because the Congress can censure the ministers, there is an added degree of legislative constraint on this executive action. The 1979 Peruvian constitution, which returned the country to democracy, allowed the president to unilaterally declare a state of siege to confront war, civil war, or its imminent danger but gave Congress the right to override it; the 1993 Constitution limits Congress to being informed.[55]

A legislature may have other means to influence the use of force besides refusing to fund or authorize it. Some presidentialist systems allow for congressional censure of cabinet members as a way to constrain Executive actions. At one extreme of these Executive-Legislative relationships are Ecuador, Chile from 1891–1925, and Peru to 1992. In these cases, congressional censure does not require evidence of criminal wrongdoing on the part of the cabinet minister. When ministers are directly accountable to the legislature and dependent upon it for survival, the Congress has a powerful negative tool to shape presidential policy.[56]

On the other hand, some Latin American democracies give the Executive an important resource to limit the congress' interest in playing out this scenario: the power to dissolve the legislature and call for new elections. Contemporary Chile and Paraguay have the most formal authority since the president can dissolve Congress without provocation. In Uruguay and Peru the president can only dissolve Congress after the legislature has taken steps to censure the Executive (before 1993 the Peruvian president had to wait until Congress censured three of his Ministers, the 1993 Constitution lowered this requirement to two). Although Congress can avoid dissolution by refusing censure motions,[57] such restraint in itself diminishes the legislature's ability to serve as a veto gate on presidential action. With no reelection permitted and the legal power to dissolve Congress the Chilean "superpresident" would seem to be highly unconstrained. This was obviously General Pinochet's intent when his dictatorship wrote the 1980 Constitution. But with redemocratization, the strength of the party system and the continuing influence of the military, presidential power has significantly diminished in contemporary Chile.[58]

The claim that democratic presidents are significantly constrained by institutional vetoes confronts another problem. Whether formal or informal vetoes effectively constrain executives may depend on the context in which the issue of the use of force arises. Chief executives who are more willing to use force in their foreign relations often utilize their legitimate faculties to maneuver the country into a position in which it is threatened and then appeal to the nation for support in "responding" with force. Many members of the U.S. Congress, including ex-President John Quincy Adams, accused President Polk of instigating the war with Mexico in 1846 in order to confront Congress with the choice of supporting or abandoning already committed troops. The House of Representatives passed a resolution, later struck down by the Senate, noting that the President of the United States had unconstitutionally begun the war.[59] Ecuadorians were similarly not informed that their government provoked Peru by establishing military posts in disputed territory in 1994, and thereby perceived Peruvian actions as aggressive.[60]

Democratic polities are also not immune to the use of force as a diversionary tactic. Morgan and Bickers found that as the president's partisan approval rating declines, the likelihood that the U.S. uses military force increases.[61] While those targets may have been overwhelmingly nondemocratic, and hence may support the notion that democracies do not use force against each other,[62] the argument for the power of democratic vetoes is significantly undermined. If the president needed to convince institutional veto holders in order to authorize military action, the correlation between his declining political fortunes and the use of military force would not likely be significant, especially since different parties have usually controlled Congress and the Presidency in the 1946–1976 period examined in the Morgan and Bickers study.

The very notion of covert action in a democracy raises questions about legislative oversight and, through it, institutional vetoes. Covert action oftentimes does not utilize military force and there are very important limits to what one can say about it, given its secretive nature. Still, the subject crops up in discussions of democratic peace.

Russett offers the best defense of the democratic thesis in the face of covert aggression against other elected governments in Latin America (Guatemala 1954, Brazil 1964, Chile 1973 and Nicaragua in the 1980s). He notes that the U.S. fears were "often excessive" and attributes this partly to the Cold War and the "American ideology of the day" which believed that once overthrown by totalitarianism a democracy could not reemerge. Russett recognizes that these criteria make the democratic peace thesis subject to very peculiar international and perceptual circumstances and searches for some "objective" criteria to explain such behavior.

Russett focuses on the stability of the domestic political processes of the nations in question to explain covert action between democracies. Although the formal institutional process indicates who is democratic at the moment, if those institutions confront great domestic disorder the likelihood that they will be jettisoned is sufficient that others will not treat it as a democracy. For example, he argues that the domestic political disorder in Chilean politics during 1971–73 as a result of the "peaceful road to socialism" of the Popular Unity government made the U.S. distrust its democratic character. Hence U.S. action, which he regrets, is explainable within his model.[63]

Russett's defense suffers from serious problems. In 1964 and 1969–70 Chile clearly met his democracy criteria: it was an established and stable democracy.[64] Yet the U.S. covertly intervened in Chilean politics by channeling money into the 1964 presidential elections to help prevent the Socialist (not Communist) Party candidate Salvador Allende from overcoming his narrow defeat in the 1958 elections. This was done covertly not just to avoid the ire of U.S. citizens who might disapprove, but also to avoid a negative reaction from Chilean democrats who would object to another government actively working for one of the candidates in a Chilean election. In addition, before any of the hypermobilization that characterized Chilean politics from 1971–73, the U.S. government covertly attempted to bribe the Chilean Congress not to ratify Allende's election. When that failed, U.S. agents began discussions with military officers in hopes of provoking a military coup that would then turn power over to a Christian Democratic government. The effort failed in 1970 because the Chilean military did not believe that a coup was necessary. The U.S. economic embargo and CIA funding for the miners' strike also helped create economic chaos.[65] In short, Russett ignores the impact of U.S. covert action on the domestic turmoil that he uses to justify U.S. covert action!

In summary, the logic behind the proposition that democratic states resolve their disputes more peacefully among themselves than any other pairing of types of government is indeterminate and ambiguous. Only under very strong assumptions can we hypothesize that democracies will peacefully resolve their mutual conflicts. Those assumptions are (1) that voters cross-culturally value material wealth above all else; (2) that their preferences are transitive; (3) that the issue of the use of force is unidimensional; (4) that veto gates on this issue swing predominantly against the executive; and (5) that democracies can objectively identify each other. If all these assumptions do not hold, whether or not conflict is resolved without the use of force must depend upon factors other than the democratic nature of a polity. The next section demonstrates empirically that even taking one of the most widely utilized definitions of "democraticness" the argument does not hold up well.

Empirical Analysis of Democratic Peace Variants[66]

In this section I test the argument that democracy should lead to a less militarized foreign policy. Democracy scales are provided from *Polity II* and *III*, while MID behavior is taken from the revised MID II data set (1816–1992). I explore the behavior of states in the two subregions of Latin America: South and Central America. I then examine the proposition that democracy matters by distinguishing MIDs in three ways: by general participation in the subregions; by behavior of individual nations; and via dyadic relations among democracies.

The 11-point democracy scale (0–10) used in *Polity II* is built on a weighting of four components which can be found in all political regimes and which help us understand the difference in the general level of constraint confronting political leaders.[67] The components are competitiveness of political participation; competitiveness of executive recruitment; openness of executive recruitment; and constraints on the Chief Executive.[68] *Polity III* extends the original database from 1982 to 1993.[69] I added data for 1993 to MID II to provide a Polity/MID set to 1993.

With the *Polity* data sets we can examine the effect of greater degrees of democracy on the propensity to use force in interstate disputes. Many recognized and respected Latin American democracies only gained a 6 in this data set (e.g., Chile in the 1960s, Uruguay in the 1920s) so when I discuss democracy in general, I consider all regimes falling within the 6–10 range.[70] In specific cases, I will examine whether thresholds appear at 7 or 8.

National-level Hypothesis

States at higher ranks of the relevant scales (institutionalized democracy or constraint on the executive) should participate in militarized interstate disputes significantly less frequently than those at a lower rank.[71]

Two probit estimations were analyzed in table 4.4, for South and Central America (including the Caribbean and Mexico). The dichotomous dependent variable was operationalized by whether or not a MID occurred during a regime year.

South American data do not support the hypothesis that domestic constraints make a difference in militarized dispute participation. Regressing level of democracy on the dependent variable proved statistically insignificant for South America (significance at 0.44). In Central America, however, the hypothesis was supported with statistically significant findings (at the 0.01 level) and coefficients in the hypothesized direction (implying a negative impact on the occurrence of a MID). Unfortunately, these findings largely reflect the paucity of high democratic scores outside of the Costa Rican experience. Costa Rica was democratic at a level of 10 for all but one year, while no other Central American or Caribbean country attained a 10 in this time period and rarely reached the level of 6 (table 4.5). We can't tell if it is the impact of democracy or something unique to Costa Rica which is correlating with diminished involvement in a MID in Central America.

From Table 4.5 we can see that the average number of MIDs per regime year up to 1988 does not exhibit a constant downward pattern as we move up the democracy scales. Even taking into account the relatively fewer

TABLE 4.4 Democracy and Participation in Militarized Interstate Disputes
(Probit Analysis)

Variable	Coefficient	Std Error	T-stat	Significance
South America 1884–1993				
Constant	− 0.6292	0.0669	− 9.40993	0.000
Democracy	0.0127	0.0165	0.76906	0.442
Central America 1908–1993				
Constant	− 0.7181	0.0652	− 11.0137	0.000
Democracy	− 0.0420	0.0172	− 2.4386	0.015

TABLE 4.5 Level of Democracy and MID Participation

Subregion	Number of MIDs/Regime Years at Level of Democracy										
	0	1	2	3	4	5	6	7	8	9	10
Central	43/2107	46/321	10/91	8/62	9/80	4/20	8/32	1/4	3/12	—	12/80
America	40%	14%	11%	13%	11%	20%	25%	25%	25%	—	15%
South	23/65	36/240	50/255	19/57	63/186	16/50	27/117	0/6	14/64	4/18	3/14
America	35%	15%	20%	33%	34%	32%	23%	0%	22%	22%	21%

regime years at the highest levels of democracy (9 and 10 in South America, 7–9 in Central America), there are still some regime years at low levels of democracy which are more peaceful than more democratic years. For example, in Central America the same number of MIDs occurred at level of democracy 3 as at 6, even though there were almost twice as many total regime years (62 compared with 32) at the lower level. In South America, MIDs at level 1 just exceeded those at level 6 (36 to 27) despite there being 123 more regime years at the lower level.

Dyadic-Level Hypothesis

The first section basically confirmed the results of other studies of the impact of democratic institutions on international behavior: for a country's foreign policy in general, they do not matter.[72] In this section we examine the proposition that it is not until democratic states confront each other that the peaceful impact of democracy on their behavior is felt.

Using the democracy level of 6 as the cutoff between democracy and nondemocracy there were 433 regime years of democracy in our time frame (1884–1993 in South America, 1907–1993 in Central America). Table 4.6 presents the MID behavior of democratic dyads (pairs of democracies).

From the table we note that democratic dyads were clearly less likely to experience MIDs than were mixed dyads (characterized by a combination of democratic and nondemocratic states). But, the same is true of nondemocratic dyads relative to mixed dyads. In fact, the proportion of total dyads that suffer MIDs is practically identical for both democratic and nondem-

TABLE 4.6 The Participation of Democracies in Latin American MIDs After the
National Period[a]

	Total Dyads	MID	% of Total
Democratic	1,699	19[b]	1.12%
Nondemocratic	13,217	157	1.19%
Mixed	8,082	154	1.91%

[a] South America 1884–1993 and Central America 1907–1993. Dyads include the U.S., but not European states for the relevant time period. For a discussion, see text.

[b] Includes five Ecuador-Peru MIDs not recorded in the MID data base. Carlos E. Scheggia Flores, *Origen del Pueblo Ecuatoriano y Sus Infundadas Pretensiones Amazónicas* Lima: Talleres de Linea, 1992 p. 61 reports a MID in 1983; Ministry of Foreign Affairs, Hacia la Solución, reports two MIDs in 1985, and one each in 1988 and 1989.

ocratic dyads: 1.12% compared with 1.19%, respectively. The slight difference would actually decrease if we were to incorporate my democracy rankings after 1993 given the prevalence of democratic dyad MIDs in the contemporary period (see Table 2.6).

Conclusion

The democratic peace argument states that the nature of democratic institutions makes it at best difficult for leaders of democracies to use force against each other. This argument assumes that voters will always prefer peaceful negotiations to the use of force, and that voters' ability to punish decisionmakers forces leaders to heed this preference. Two critical flaws limit this model. Variations among democratic institutions affect the immediacy and directness of voters' ability to punish or even observe decisionmakers. Specifically, electoral constraints, the structure of the voting process, the process of electoral accountability, and the existence of veto gates all have the potential to limit voters' power. In addition, the assumption that voters will always prefer peaceful negotiations is not borne out empirically.

In Latin America in the last two centuries, the use of force does not allow us to distinguish interactions between democracies from interactions between nondemocracies. Democratic status does not have a statistically significant impact on the decision to use military force, and democracies are nearly as likely to use military force against each other, as are nondemocracies. Mixed dyads of one democratic and one nondemocratic nation are most likely to use military force.

Democracy has many qualities in its favor and as a form of government is desirable. But the theoretical and empirical analysis in this chapter demonstrates that, in and of itself, guaranteeing peaceful relations among states in Latin America is not among those qualities. If we want to understand the pattern of interstate conflict in Latin America's security complex we need to look beyond domestic political systems.

We proceed in chapter 5 to examine the military distribution of power argument. There are two competing and mutually exclusive versions to this argument: that two nations with equivalent power will not have military conflict, and that a situation in which one nation has a preponderance of power will not lead to military conflict. After evaluating the contribution of this model, we assess whether the combination of the military distribution of power argument with the democratic peace model provides insight into the use of military force.

5   The Distribution of Power and Military Conflict

Does the distribution of power affect the likelihood of militarized conflict? The bumper sticker debate between "If you want peace, prepare for war" and "Arms are made for hugging" resonates in the halls of government as well as in the towers of academia. Yet there is another major debate on the issue. If power matters, is parity or preponderance more likely to lead to peaceful competition among states?

The claim that military power is a fundamental contributor to interstate stability is contentious, especially in the Latin American context. By the early twentieth century U.S. and British diplomats in South America ridiculed the "vanity" which led governments there to seek modern weapons and training. Yet the U.S. and British governments competed with Germany, France, and Italy to provide the weapons and training.[1] After World War II U.S. military arms policy changed and sought to control the flow of armaments into Latin America, both in terms of quantity and quality.[2] Militaries were encouraged through training and arms policy to focus on internal rather than external "enemies."

Yet there have always been advocates of "power brings regional peace" formulas in Latin America. European training before World War I emphasized traditional definitions of security and deterrence missions. During the Cold War Latin American militaries took the money and political power which internal missions provided, but also worried about their neighbors. Many Latin American citizens, legislators, and civilian military analysts also believed in the importance of the balance of power.[3]

In the wake of redemocratization after a period of authoritarian rule there is renewed vigor against thinking about Latin American defense establishments functioning as modern militaries. Anti-militarists in the U.S. and Latin America do not believe military power is stabilizing. Still others see no external threats in Latin America to which military preparedness would be an appropriate response. Both types of critics seek to turn Latin American militaries into police forces or development corps, denying them any legitimate role in traditional external defense scenarios.[4]

This chapter examines the theoretical rationale for the argument that the distribution of power matters for understanding the use of force in foreign policy and evaluates the empirical record of Latin America. The chapter has four sections. The first two lay out the theoretical argument. I begin with a discussion of the importance of relative military power in an anarchic international system. Next, I examine the two major schools of thought concerning the impact of power distribution and war. Balance of power analysts argue that parity drives peaceful management of conflict, while power transition theorists claim that preponderance and intent constitute the keys to international conduct.

The last two sections explore the empirical record in Latin America. Qualitative analyses of important enduring rivalries among Latin American states are followed by statistical analysis on the issue of power balancing. In this last section I also examine whether the combination of military power and democratic institutions helps us explain the patterns of the use of force. The chapter demonstrates that neither overall military balance nor preponderance is a necessary or sufficient condition for militarization of conflict.

The Importance and Relational Nature of Military Power

Power analysts are Realists. All analysts working in the Realist paradigm share some basic starting points. Anarchy is the fundamental condition of international relations as long as political units that interact wish to remain independent. The implications of anarchy are twofold: the use of violence to resolve disagreements may occur because there is no legitimate and effective authority to prevent its use and the units are forced to rely on self-help to survive and prosper. Self-help in an anarchic system in turn privileges power relations, thereby forcing states to consider the importance of relative over absolute gains. A Realist world is a world in which the use of military force cannot be eliminated, and at best is deterred by superior force.

Realists are divided, however, by the understanding of what drives state behavior under conditions of anarchy. Thucydides' focus on the innate drives for power in men, and therefore in the political institutions that they create, is echoed in Machiavelli, Morgenthau, and Mearsheimer.[5] Most modern analysts of the Realist school, however, reject the utility of the assumption that states are power seekers and maximizers, and instead focus upon the search for security.[6] The implications of this difference for understanding international behavior are fundamental.

If security concerns drive state behavior, under conditions of anarchy a security dilemma develops. In a self-help world, capabilities rather than intent matter; my attempt to safeguard myself worries you because you cannot be sure of my intentions. But the fact that you might sincerely be seeking security rather than power means that we may be foregoing cooperation that would be beneficial to both. The possibility of a cooperative security response that would not affect the relative distribution of power stimulates the search for ways to diminish the impact of the security dilemma.

If we substitute the assumption that states seek power rather than security, the relationship between states becomes stark. Make the drive for power innate and overriding and the security dilemma disappears: I *will* dominate you if I can; I know that and you know that. Cooperation is dramatically limited and short term in this Realist world. States do not even share a common interest in surviving, absent a situation of mutually assured destruction.

A focus on security rather than power is a more useful theoretical assumption to guide research in understanding foreign policy. Maximization of power does not follow logically from the assumption of anarchy, but a drive for security does.[7] Power maximization theorists are led, as were Thucydides and Morgenthau, to make assumptions about the nature of human behavior to sustain their argument. A security focus is more theoretically parsimonious and does a better job dealing with the issue of cooperation under anarchy.

The conditions under which the security dilemma may be mitigated and cooperation stimulated is answered in two different ways. The answers break down into two camps: those focusing on credibility and those on capability. While liberals devise many theoretical justifications for why credibility of pacific intent can be brought to levels which virtually eliminate the dilemma, Realists point to the cases where pacific intent did not carry the day to argue for the prudence of focusing on capabilities.[8] For these latter analysts the dilemma is diminished to the extent that the defense has the advantage over the offense, usually conceived of in terms of the technology of the weapons themselves or the strategies states implement to use them.[9] The basic point is that the cost of guessing wrong about intent will fall dramatically if the offensive capability of a potential offender is not sufficient to gain them advantage. Under these conditions it will be prudent to increase cooperation with states with which one has serious disagreements and perhaps even decrease one's defense budget.

Using either a technological or strategy-based offense-defense focus to explain militarized conflict in Latin America is problematic. With the exception of the 1941 war between Peru and Ecuador and any dyad in which a great power confronts a Latin American country, differences in the military arsenals of rival states are minimal. Military strategies (with the difference of the dyads just mentioned, as well as the El Salvador-Honduras war of 1969), also do not give one Latin American country an advantage over another.

Even when we consider that the offense-defense balance distinction is not usually an appropriate lens through which to think about the military balance of power in Latin America, the question of how much military power is enough remains relevant. Low absolute levels of military expenditures or arms arsenals are not in and of themselves sufficient to keep disputes from militarizing. Power is relative and what matters in a Realist paradigm is the distribution of military power between potential disputants. According to this line of reasoning, the absence of a MID is largely the result of a potential initiator being deterred by the existing distribution of power between herself and the potential target.

But what should we count to evaluate the distribution of power? Calculating the distribution is not a straightforward task, even if we limit ourselves to a Realist focus on which resources matter in the field of battle.[10] The debate largely breaks down into whether one should focus on overall or specific military capability. Advocates of the former assume that major skirmishes could escalate to a long drawn out war, thus resources that can be turned into military power in the medium term matter. In a major war a state is likely to have the time to mobilize and use all of its resources. Victory and defeat are expected to largely follow the distribution of resources. Consequently, when calculating whether to engage in military activity against another state, it is the overall distribution of military capability that matters. Analysts who focus on specific military capability assume that the decision to escalate a crisis is based on very short term considerations. This chapter focuses on overall military power, leaving the question of specific military capabilities for chapters 6 and 7.

This discussion may seem too abstract to analysts who believe that Latin American governments use international disputes to divert attention from domestic failings. As noted in chapter 2, Latin America's security challenges arise from both external and internal factors (power distribution among states, political weaknesses of governments domestically). Realists do not deny the existence of domestic problems, but argue that whether or not those domestic problems affect foreign policy is largely determined by the distribution of capabilities among states. Thus a government may wish to employ diversionary tactics to distract domestic opponents, but it will only do so against states that are not expected to respond by inflicting such great pain on the country that the government is held to account. The attempt to distinguish between nonmilitary proximate causes and underlying military causes[11] breaks down in this formulation. Realists argue that the underlying cause is anarchy and the security dilemma and the proximate cause is the distribution of power.

If the distribution of power argument is a powerful explanation of interstate conflict, we need to develop and examine hypotheses about what distributions make the use of military force in foreign policy more likely.

Parity or Preponderance?

Power analysts disagree about whether parity or preponderance diminishes the likelihood of military conflict. The theoretical literature on the distribution of power and war examines the question from a systemic perspective.[12] Yet, as will be seen below, policymakers in the region often focus on the regional or bilateral distribution of power to explain military conflict.

If balance of power theorists are correct, parity should mean both fewer wars and less violent militarization of disputes. Parity brings peace because neither side can be reasonably sure of winning a war at acceptable costs.

Hypothesis 5.1 Power Parity and War: When power is roughly equally distributed, states will be more likely to refrain from war.

Hypothesis 5.2 Power Parity and MIDs: When power is roughly equally distributed, states will be more likely to refrain from engaging in MIDs, in particular major crises.

The power preponderance argument takes a different tack. Rather than see peace resulting from powers of relatively equal military strength balancing each other, preponderance analysts perceive peace to result from one power deterring challengers through its significantly greater power. Predominance is usually defined as having 80 percent more power than the rival, but some analysts make the distinction at 3 to 1 (moderate preponderance) and again at 10 to 1.[13]

At the systemic level, the preponderant power organizes the international system to reflect its own interests, hence a rising power will wish to reorganize the system to its own advantage. If the status quo defenders have a preponderance of power, the costs of challenging the status quo will likely be higher than the benefits, hence the revisionist state will behave peacefully. But when power shifts in favor of the revisionists, the likelihood of war increases.[14] In particular, the speed of the transition matters. Fast transitions make war all the more likely.[15] Speed, however, is measured ambiguously: sometimes Organski calls change "within a lifetime" "fast" and "very fast."[16]

We can extrapolate from this discussion of rivalry between a preponderant power and its rising rival to the question of relations among smaller powers. Organski and Kugler do not believe that power preponderance is relevant to "peripheral" states, i.e., those who are not disputing leadership of the international system. They note that small-state wars may occur independently of the distribution of power at the systemic level, hence changes there may not affect small-state war.[17] The logic of revisionist states being unhappy with the status quo, however, suggests that we can utilize the insights from this approach for our analysis. To test this hypothesis we have an easily identifiable population of revisionist states in Latin America consisting of the enduring rivalries discussed in chapters 1 and 2.

Hypothesis 5.3 Power Preponderance and War. When power predominance exists in a dyad, war is unlikely. The likelihood increases if a power transition occurs, with a rapid transition increasing the likelihood of war even more and just before parity.

While the two approaches to power distribution differ about the specifics, they both argue that power distribution is a necessary, though not sufficient, factor accounting for war. Most quantitative studies argue that it is power preponderance, not parity which contributes to peace or war, though Organski and Kugler disagree.

If preponderance means less war because the challenger fears war with the defender more than vice versa, we should see more bullying with force by the defender to enforce the status quo. The revisionist state presumably will express its displeasure in some fashion short of those expected to provoke war. But the preponderant state can punish without fear of escalation to war. This may explain U.S. military intervention against weak Latin American states seen as anti-American.

Hypothesis 5.4 Power Preponderance and MIDs. Preponderant defenders of the status quo should bully by consistently using force in their disputes and the weaker revisionist state should not respond in kind.

Quantitative Analyses of Power Distribution

Historical analysis of relative military power in Latin America is difficult for anyone utilizing quantitative methodologies. Data on military budgets, arms expenditures, and imports are problematic until the 1970s[18] when they became merely debatable.[19] The combat readiness and skill of men and machines forms a basis for calculating strategic advantage yet is not quantifiable in any scientific way. Although this theoretically affects all nations, it is a particular problem in Latin America, where numerous armies have demonstrated their incompetence on the battlefield. Since not all the militaries are incompetent (the Chileans in particular are feared), and some evolve over time (e.g., the Peruvians in the late 1930s and the Ecuadorians in the late 1980s both became more efficient militaries), one cannot simply impose a general discount rate across all countries.[20]

These data limitations require that we proceed with caution in setting up and interpreting the analyses. The initial statistical analysis undertaken in this section relies on the widely used National Capabilities Database of the Correlates of War project.[21] I use measures of military expenditures in order to examine short-term shifts in the balance of overall military power and their potential effects on militarized conflict. The time period examined must also have some internal coherence, established by a major watershed which separates it from other time periods.

With these limitations in mind, for the statistical portion of the quantitative testing I begin with the Cold War and end in 1992.[22] In this time period there were only three wars, which are too few to carry out mean-ingful statistical analyses.[23] Hence, we cannot evaluate Hypotheses 5.1 and 5.3 in this initial test. Probit analyses are used to evaluate Hypotheses 5.2 and 5.4

The military relationship in the dyads was operationalized in two dif-ferent ways. The first, military, is the change (over the previous year) in military expenditures for side A, divided by the change (over the previous year) in military expenditures for side B. This variable assumes that military expenditures is a good proxy for measuring a change in the relative military capabilities in a dyad. In order to overcome distortions that resulted from ratios with extreme values over 1 (over a 100% change in the expenditure ratios) these extreme values were coded as 1. Likewise, those with ratios less than -1 were coded as -1. While the 1, -1 cutoffs for the ratios are somewhat arbitrary, coding a large change in the military ratio this way provides sufficient indication of a significant change in relative military capabilities

A second measure for relative military capability was created in the ex-pectation that there could be a military buildup to the crisis beginning as early as a year before. The variable LGMILLD is identical to MILITARY except that it captures the change in relative military capabilities in the year prior to the year analyzed for the occurrence of a MID. This variable may more accurately capture the dynamics of military imbalances that produce a militarization of a dispute in the short term.

The first models specified MID behavior as a function of changes in the military balance in the year of the dispute, in the year prior to the dispute, and utilizing both measures. If the coefficient is statistically significant and positive, it means that an increase in power preponderance is an important determinant of MID behavior. If the coefficient is negative, it means that the power relationship has become more equal. The results were statistically meaningless. Hypotheses 5.2 and 5.4 would seem, therefore, to lack any statistical support.

Before deciding that the variables were either irrelevant or too poorly measured to be useful, I looked for another variable which might be con-founding the impact of the military balance. Given the arguments in favor of the pacifying effects of democracy, and as a way of further testing the argument of the previous chapter, I incorporated democracy as another vari-able in the model. Democracy is measured as in chapter 4, using the *Polity* database.

New models were estimated, using changes in military expenditures both in the year of the MID and in the prior year as well as the democraticness (DEMDYAD) of the dyad. The results were again disappointing:

The statistical significance of the hypothesized causal variables in Model 1 were well above the standard cutoff (0.05): MILITARY (0.14), LGMILLD (0.37), and DEMDYAD (0.12). Thus the results could have happened by simple chance more often than is acceptable. Once again, neither power parity nor power preponderance seems to make a difference for the decision to use force in an interstate dispute.

Before abandoning the model, it is appropriate to consider whether we have measured the democracy variable adequately. The previous chapter argued that a 6 on the *Polity* database was an appropriate threshold for defining democracy in Latin American. Studies of other regions utilizing *Polity* find 6 to be a very low cutoff point. To evaluate whether too low a cutoff score was the problem in Model 1, Model 2 was developed, with the same military variables and a new democratic variable, consisting of countries with a *Polity* score of 7 or better. The results were more encouraging, though still inadequate.

The military variables improve marginally but remain statistically insignificant (same year from 0.14 to 0.13 and lagged from 0.37 to 0.36). The democracy variable (0.07) now approaches an acceptable level of statistical significance. Encouraged, another model was run with democracy levels raised to 8, but significance fell dramatically to 0.21. This outcome may be the result of having an inadequate number of democracies in Latin America that reached this level. Since the finding supported by Model 2 was sensitive to a change in level of democracy, the results might also be sensitive to the fact that the U.S. scored a 10 throughout the period and did not overtly use

TABLE 5.1 Model 1 of MID Behavior: U.S. and Latin America, 1948–1993

Variable	Coefficient	Standard Error	Significance
Constant	− 2.282	0.037	—
MILITARY	0.069	0.047	0.14
LGMILLD	− 0.040	0.045	0.37
DEMDYAD	− 0.185	0.118	0.12

TABLE 5.2 Model 2 of MID Behavior: U.S. and Latin America, 1948–1993

Variable	Coefficient	Standard Error	Significance
Constant	− 2.284	0.037	—
MILITARY	0.070	0.047	0.13
LGMILLD	− 0.041	0.045	0.36
DEMDYAD7	− 0.289	0.159	0.07

military force against a Latin American country scoring 7 or better. Models excluding the U.S. from the data were developed.

The variable for military expenditures in the year of the dispute experienced a slight deterioration in statistical significance, from 0.13 to 0.16. Democracy defined by level 6 became dramatically insignificant in intra–Latin American relations (0.77), falling below that for our military variable when lagged one year (0.64). As the insignificance corresponds to that found for U.S. and Latin American dyads at the 6 level, models were also run with democracy at 7 and then 8. In both cases the level of statistical significance remained abysmally low: Democracy 7 (coefficient -0.044; standard error 0.167; statistical significance 0.79) and Democracy 8 (coefficient 0.068; standard error 0.172; statistical significance 0.69).

The failure of these first models might reflect the problems already discussed with the data, rather than the actual impact of parity or preponderance. Unfortunately, I can't resolve that problem. But suggesting that the limited data we have do not support a simple power argument for MIDs, or

TABLE 5.3 Model 3 of MID Behavior: Intra-Latin America, 1948–1993

Variable	Coefficient	Standard Error	Significance
Constant	− 2.406	0.044	—
MILITARY	0.078	0.055	0.16
LGMILLD	− 0.025	0.053	0.64
DEMDYAD(6)	− 0.038	0.134	0.77

even one that takes democraticness of the dyad into consideration, represents progress on the issue.

We can now take a more modest approach to test the hypotheses about power distribution and war. Ideally we should examine the relative distribution over time of parity and preponderance, develop a ratio of war and MIDs to each particular power distribution, and determine whether a statistically significant difference exists between the two power distributions for the likelihood of war and the militarization of crises.

Given the limitations of the data, it is more appropriate to test for whether a particular distribution of power is *necessary* or *sufficient* for the hypothesized explanations concerning the use of military force. I examine variations on the use of military force by whether its use led to severe crises or war. Table 5.4 presents the major crises in the last 30 years, and Table 5.5 examines the wars of the twentieth century.

There were fourteen major crises in this period, defined by whether both sides perceived a possibility of escalation to war or one side utilized major military force against the other. Three crises escalated to wars (El Salvador-Honduras, Argentina-Great Britain, and Ecuador-Peru 1995). One crisis developed into a mini-war (Ecuador-Peru 1981, with up to 200 deaths) and one resulted in a major invasion (the U.S. sent more than 20,000 troops to Panama and there were 557 deaths.[24] Another crisis escalated to an undeclared war (the U.S. armed and trained the "Contras" against the government of Nicaragua and the CIA mined Nicaraguan harbors). I don't consider the Haitian crisis to have escalated because U.S. troops landed only after the Haitian government agreed to accept them.

The parity theses (Hypotheses 5.1 and 5.2) find strong support in the case of major crises and war in the last 26 years (Table 5.4). Only three of the fourteen disputes involved parity and none escalated. This means that none of the three overt and one covert wars occurred in a context of military parity.

The preponderant argument concerning war (Hypothesis 5.3) is rejected for the last 26 years because all three wars in the period involved preponderance. What is especially damning to this argument is that in all three cases it was the weaker state (Honduras, Argentina, and Ecuador), that engaged in provocative behavior. The same pattern holds when we examine major crises. Ten of the fourteen major crises were initiated by weaker powers refusing to back down in confrontations with preponderant rivals. Of those major crises which escalated in this period, five of the seven (Ecuador-

TABLE 5.4 Power Distribution and Major Crises[a] in Latin America (1969–1998)

Crisis	Countries	Escalation	Power Distribution
1969	El Salvador-Honduras	War	Preponderant
1976/77	Peru-Chile	No	Parity
1977/78	Peru-Ecuador	No	Preponderant
1978/79	Argentina-Chile	No	Preponderant
1981	Peru-Ecuador	Mini-war	Preponderant
1982	Great Britain-Argentina	War	Preponderant
1980s	U.S.-Nicaragua	Covert War*	Preponderant
1986	Colombia-Venezuela	No	Parity
1989	U.S.-Panama	Invasion	Preponderant
1991	Peru-Ecuador	No	Preponderant
1993	Venezuela-Colombia	No	Parity
1993/94	U.S.-Haiti	No	Preponderant
1995	Peru-Ecuador	War	Preponderant
1998	Peru-Ecuador	No	Preponderant

*The U.S. recruited, financed, armed and trained the Contras to fight against the Sandinista government.

[a] MIDs in which either both sides perceived a possibility of escalation to war or one side utilized major military force against the other. E.g., the 1980 mobilization of troops on both sides of the border, including a visit by the Venezuelan President, seems not to have been perceived as anything more than a show of force. Alfredo Vazquez Carrizosa, *Colombia y Venezuela: Una historia atormentada*. Bogotá: Tercer Mundo Editores, S.A. 1987, 2nd edition, revised p. 441; Earle Herrera, *¿Por qué se ha reducido el territorio venezolano?* Caracas: Alfadil/Trópicos, 1978 pp. 52–53

Sources: Power distribution for 1969 to 1981 Max G. Manwaring, "Monitoring Latin American Arms Control Agreements," in Morris and Millan, *Controlling Latin American Conflicts*. His figures begin in 1970, but we can easily assume that El Salvador's 145 to 1 advantage over Honduras does not represent a dramatic change from the previous year; for 1986 to 1998 rough calculations from ACDA, *World Military Expenditures* pp. 59, 61, 78, 88; *Keesing's*.

TABLE 5.5 Power Distribution and War in Latin America
(After the National Period)

War	Countries	Issue	Power Distribution
1932 Leticia	Peru attacks Colombia	territory	Parity
1928–35 Chaco	Bolivia attacks Paraguay	territory	Parity
1939–41 Zaarumilla	Peru attacks Ecuador	territory	Preponderant attack
1969 Soccer	El Salvador attacks Honduras	migration*	Preponderant attack Weaker
1982 Malvinas	Argentina seizes British territory	territory	Weaker attack Preponderant
1995 Cenapa	Ecuador provokes Peru	territory	Weaker provoke Preponderant

* Although there were underlying border issues, migration was the spark which ignited the crisis.

Peru thrice, Argentina-Great Britain, and Panama-U.S.), were initiated by the weaker state (only in El Salvador-Honduras and the U.S.-Nicaragua did the preponderant power initiate militarization). In addition, the only power transition occurred between the traditional rivals Argentina and Brazil, which went from a 4 to 1 Argentine advantage to a 3 to 1 Brazilian in a decade.[25] Despite the speed of the transition, no major crisis developed between them.

If we persist in letting data availability guide our analysis we would find some surprising results concerning the combination of military power and domestic institutions. Three of the fourteen crises occurred between states under military rule, but none escalated to even a mini-war (Peru-Chile, Ecuador-Peru 1977/78, and Argentina-Chile). Democratic regimes accounted for just under half the regime years in Latin America during this period, but were the first to use large-scale military force in five of the six which escalated (El Salvador v. Honduras; Peru v. Ecuador twice; the U.S. v. Nicaragua; and the U.S. v. Panama). Most escalated disputes were between democracies and authoritarian governments, but a war and a mini-war occurred between two democracies (Ecuador and Peru in 1995 and 1981). And in two of the three cases in which a preponderant power escalated its dispute with a weaker power, it was the democracy that escalated (the U.S. against Nicaragua and Panama). We could conclude from this analysis, therefore, that in Latin America military governments never fight each other, that large-scale use of violence correlates with democracy, that preponderant powers only bully if they are democracies, and that democracies are more likely to fight each other than are non-democracies.

The results of Table 5.4 are so counterintuitive that they should be highly suspect. Although many quantitative analysts use very short time frames to analyze their questions we should not be seduced by statistical requirements. The 30-year period was determined by the availability of our quantitative data, not by any watershed that could theoretically justify such a selection. What we know about the characteristics of war and MIDs in the previous 70 years (see chapter 2), confirms that such results are artifacts of the time period studied.

Table 5.5 presents the six Latin American wars that occurred after the National Period[26] along with the nature of the dispute and an impressionistic distribution of power at the time.[27]

There were two cases of parity and war (Peru v. Colombia and Bolivia v. Paraguay, both in 1932). Four wars occurred under conditions of preponderance, but in two the preponderant power attacked the weaker (Peru v. Ecuador in 1941 and El Salvador v. Honduras in 1969), and in two the weaker attacked or provoked the preponderant (Argentina v. Great Britain in 1982 and Ecuador v. Peru in 1995). We can also note that power preponderance has always been on the U.S. side and that in the twentieth century no Latin American country engaged in war with the U.S., although the U.S. repeatedly invaded Latin American nations with great force. Table 5.5 and the U.S. experience confirm that war is not peculiar to one type of power distribution, hence, Hypotheses 5.1 and 5.3 are both rejected for the period covering the 20th century.

In short, sophisticated quantitative studies to evaluate claims about the impact of power distribution on militarized interstate conflict are of questionable value. Using less rigorous methods suggests that military power by itself is not an important determinant. This result could arise because our quantitative indicators are weak, because military power matters in ways different from the dimension studied by quantitative analysis, or because it has no impact. Before accepting the latter conclusion we should take a historical and qualitative look at the distribution of power question in the specific context of a long-term rivalry.

Balance of Power Calculations in Latin America

For a number of reasons the measures of the distribution of power are even more ambiguous in Latin America than elsewhere. I have already mentioned the extreme variation in the region on the combat readiness of men. Equipment is also unevenly maintained and cannibalized. Even ammunition may be unusable, as the Argentines discovered when many of their bombs failed to detonate in the Malvinas War.[28] On the diplomatic front, formal alliances among one set of Latin American nations against another were rare in the twentieth century. Yet expectations of alliances developing in the event of an outbreak of war influence the calculations of statesmen and military planners throughout the region.

Despite the ambiguities of determining an appropriate balance of power, Latin American governments have long acted as if they understood its logic. The pattern of regional arms trading reflects these rivalries and possible alliances. Brazil exports arms to Chile, but not to Argentina. Argentina in turn exports arms to Peru and Bolivia, rivals of Chile, but not to Chile or Brazil. Meanwhile, Chile exports to Ecuador, a rival of Peru, but not to its neighbor Peru.[29] Indicative of the perception that unilateral arms reduction is potentially dangerous, when arms control and other confidence building measures have been pursued it is generally at the bilateral and multilateral levels.[30]

The analysis in this section does not seek to determine whether all weapons purchases are governed by power distribution considerations. Clearly they are not.[31] The relevant question for this analysis is whether militarization of conflict occurs repeatedly at any particular point in the evolution of the power relationship.

As the two most powerful Latin American countries, the relationship between Argentina and Brazil is an excellent case for evaluating the influence of power calculations upon dispute behavior. This dyad is particularly attractive because it represents the major power transition case in Latin America during the twentieth century. The Argentine-Brazilian relationship historically combined power projection issues with territorial disputes. Given the data limitations, I begin with a rough sense of the distribution of power at the beginning of the century and examine its evolution over the course of the century.

Brazil occupies a unique position in Latin America. It is Portuguese rather than Spanish, and thus in a cultural sense different. Until late in the nineteenth century it was also a monarchy, in a hemisphere in which monarchy was suspect. Brazil was also able to overcome the political fragmentation that broke up the early Spanish American states and thus physically loomed as a giant in the area. In contrast to Argentina, which stressed its links to Europe, Brazil attempted to create for itself an American identity, much as the U.S. had. Argentine wealth and European culture led it to perceive itself as the natural leader among the republics created out of the Spanish American Empire. No other Western Hemisphere state was, however, willing to concede that mantle to the Argentines.

The Argentine-Brazilian rivalry began early, with war in 1825–28 and continuous tensions leading to a war scare in 1873. Uruguay was created as a buffer state between the two, guaranteed by the British. As with all buffer states, the rivals each attempted to control it. The Argentines in particular utilized military threats to pressure Uruguay on issues of maritime boundaries and foreign policy. Brazil also provided military and diplomatic support for the successful overthrow of the Argentine dictator Rojas in 1852.[32]

In classic balance of power behavior Argentina and Brazil did not let their rivalry prevent cooperation to ensure that other potential rivals did not develop. They joined forces in the virtual obliteration of the once powerful Paraguay during the War of the Triple Alliance (1864–70).[33] But such collaboration did not produce lasting friendship, especially as many Brazilians felt that Argentina benefited greatly from the alliance.[34]

Brazil and Argentina were wary of each other, but unsure of the possibility and costs of an outright military resolution of their conflict. Each state also had territorial disputes with other neighbors, raising the prospect of another multifront war. Leaders in both countries studiously avoided war by utilizing international law and bilateral diplomacy to keep the level of distrust at peacefully manageable levels. But periodic arms buildups also served a deterrent function as they helped to keep the specter of a disastrous war alive if diplomacy failed. Because each had large tracts of unsettled land and perceived the likelihood that a war would escalate to one of attrition, defense policies became oriented to both professionalizing the military and building up total national resources via development.[35]

At the turn of the twentieth century Brazil was busily settling her borders in the west and southwest, while Argentina was professionalizing and modernizing its military in response to a war scare with Chile. Through the use of bilateral negotiations and arbitration Brazil peacefully gained territory the size of France. But Brazilian diplomacy was not invincible. Outmaneuvered by Bolivian diplomacy Brazil militarized the Acre dispute in 1902–3 against first Bolivia, and then Peru. The need to depend upon military threats strengthened Foreign Minister Baron Rio Branco's perception that the declining military capability of Brazil over the past 20–30 years, from its prior naval preeminence in the region, hurt its international respect.[36] The Baron and many military officers also worried that Brazil was becoming weaker relative to Argentina, and that war was a possibility.[37]

Rio Branco set out to improve Brazil's standing by professionalizing the training of its military and increasing its armaments. From 1906 to 1914 Brazil acquired ships, armaments, and professional training from the major European suppliers. Among the ships were three Dreadnought battleships from Britain, including the largest built to that day. Some of the ships were constructed with unusual draught requirements, which Argentines interpreted as indicating an intent to use them on the Rio Plata, presumably against Argentina.[38] At the same time the Baron attempted to bring Brazil into close diplomatic relations with the U.S. and ride its coattails to predominance in South America.

Brazil's diplomatic and military policies worried Argentina despite its naval superiority (table 5.6). Given Brazilian advantages in manpower (estimated at 3 to 1 in 1906[39]) and geographic depth, as well as the potential for a Brazilian-Chilean alliance to encircle Argentina, naval superiority was perceived as a necessary part of Argentina's defense policy. Argentina's response to Brazil's naval program was twofold: Argentina accelerated military professionalization and undertook its own naval program, including the purchase of two Dreadnoughts. On the diplomatic front, Argentina sought to be the interlocutor between Latin America and the Great Powers. This response, if successful, would have allowed Argentina to benefit from its own strategic resources as well as to have access to more resources through the favor Argentina would gain with the Great Powers; the strategy would also keep Argentina from becoming overly dependent on one Great Power.[40]

The competition between the two South American leaders became tense enough in 1908–10 that British diplomats in South America reported that

TABLE 5.6 Naval Balance, Argentina-Brazil 1906

	Argentina	Brazil
Battleships	5	3
Armoured Cruisers	4	0
Protected Cruisers	3	6
Torpedo Gun Boats	5	2
Torpedo Boats	22	4
Gunboats	4	0
Destroyers	4	0

Source: D.R. O'Sullivan-Beare, Acting Counsel General, British Mission in Brazil, to Sir Earl Grey, London; November 10, 1906; Public Records Office, Foreign Office 371.13 folio 40648 p. 291ff

the Rio Plata region was experiencing a war scare. The crisis was defused by the conjunction of three factors. Brazil's navy revolted and used a Dreadnought against Rio de Janeiro itself. In addition, two of the chief protagonists, Foreign Ministers Estanislao Zeballos and Rio Branco faded from the scene.[41]

Despite improved relations armaments purchases continued on both sides. After World War I, Argentine and Brazilian military establishments traveled in different directions, largely because of differences in domestic political and economic contexts. The Argentine military was deeply impressed by the unexpected direction in which the European war developed, worried that they had trained for the wrong war and embarked on an important rebuilding effort in the 1920s. Despite good relations with Brazil, in 1923 the Argentine Congress approved an armament program which, had it been implemented, would have made its armed forces the most powerful in Latin America. Manpower also increased significantly. In 1925 a naval buildup was authorized, which would have turned the Argentine navy into the world's sixth most powerful (on paper). The Depression was a brief challenge to Argentina, which dealt with it by tying itself closely to the British economic orbit with the Roca-Runciman Treaty; subsequently the economy prospered.[42]

Brazil tried to respond, but given its domestic economic and political turmoil through the 1920s and 30s, it postponed military increases in the 1920s, ostensibly until 1932, but in actuality to 1937–38.[43] The military was keenly aware of the power disparity and expected an Argentine, Paraguayan, and Uruguayan alliance, possibly even including Chile, against Brazil. They utilized a French military mission to prepare for battle in the southern part of the country.[44]

In the late 1930s the rivalry between the two nations began to heat up once again, although the two governments, now dictatorships, had been collaborating in tracking down communists.[45] Argentina's ascendancy reached its zenith in 1939. It accounted for 33 percent of all of South America's trade, 80 percent of all of Latin America's foreign exchange and gold reserves and its national income was 25 percent greater than Brazil's. The Argentine Navy was the premier of Latin America, with two modern battleships, three new Italian cruisers, and sixteen destroyers; by comparison, Brazil had two old battleships, one cruiser, and one destroyer. The Army, one half the size of Brazil's, was the region's best trained, equipped, and prepared, as was the Air Force, rumored to have between 161 and 600 aircraft.[46]

Yet the Argentines did not feel secure. Their military buildup provoked a reaction by Brazil, which once again sought closer ties with the U.S. as a way to offset Argentine advantages. In 1937 they requested the loan of a few destroyers; the U.S. denied the request because Brazil's neighbors were "very vehemently" opposed.[47] As the European war threatened, Brazil's diplomatic and geographic advantages began to tell. Both Argentina and Brazil attempted to develop security relations with the U.S. that would increase their national capabilities. But the U.S. was wary of Argentina's nationalism (which would keep the country neutral until the last days of the war) and Brazil willingly followed the U.S. lead. In addition, the U.S. wanted to safeguard Brazil's geographic bulge in the northeast opposite Nazi occupied Africa. Brazil became the beneficiary of a massive arms buildup and infrastructure development. Brazil, however, perceived its threats differently from the U.S. and chose instead to utilize much of its new military resources to fortify its border with Argentina in the southwest.[48]

Argentine neutrality had negative consequences. The U.S. attempted to isolate Argentina militarily, economically, and politically.[49] The Argentines feared that power was shifting to an alliance between Brazil and the U.S. Argentina informally pursued arms supplies in Germany and Italy. On the same day Brazil declared war against the Axis, Argentina formalized its arms request to Germany. But their own war needs prevented the Germans from meeting Argentine requests for "submarines, airplanes, anti-aircraft weapons and munitions of every sort."[50]

World War II turned the tide against Argentina and favored Brazil. It consolidated its position as the dominant U.S. ally in South America by actively participating in the European war.[51] Brazil's economy boomed after the war, as Argentina's fell into a stop-go pattern of growth, thereby dramatically increasing Brazil's national capabilities relative to Argentina's. Brazil's defense expenditures as a percentage of GNP grew significantly in the second half of the 1950s, just as Argentina's began a dramatic decline compared with that of the Peron years.[52]

By the 1960s the growth of Brazil's national capabilities relative to Argentina's gave it a sense of security even in the context of geopolitical doctrines which emphasized interstate competition.[53] Brazil was content to limit its military allocation to a small proportion of the national budget, while Argentina sought to balance the absolute level of expenditures in the much larger Brazilian economy. But Argentina had now lost the race with Brazil, which experienced a booming economy as well as internal peace even with a military government.[54] The Argentine economy virtually collapsed under the strains induced by domestic political battles, even under numerous authoritarian governments. Manwaring's relative military capability index shows Argentina turning a 4 to 1 advantage over Brazil in 1970 to a 3 to 1 disadvantage in 1981.[55]

The Argentine military government mobilized its forces against Brazil in 1977[56] but then made the fateful error of shifting its military focus from the long stalemated relationship with Brazil to the unstable situations with Great Britain and Chile. At the start of the Malvinas/Falklands war some Brazilian military analysts worried about the problems of having a successful and belligerent Argentina as a neighbor. The Beagle war scare, in which Argentina had to retreat after a great public fanfare, and the disastrous war with Britain in the Malvinas/Falklands Islands destroyed Argentine military resources and reputation. In addition, Argentine hopes for economic and political resources that could be used in the competition over strategic balances were dashed. Even with Argentine rearmament immediately after the war, Brazil remained unconcerned.[57]

Brazil and Argentina began, under military governments, broader cooperative relations. A multiparty agreement with Paraguay resolved issues around the Iguazo electrical project. Cooperation on nuclear issues defused an incipient nuclear arms race, and led to both countries ultimately signing the 1967 Treaty of Tlatelolco, which bans nuclear weapons in Latin America. The capstone to the new relationship was the Treaty of Asunción of 1991 that created a free trade zone among Argentina, Brazil, Uruguay, and Paraguay (Mercosur).[58]

The "new Argentina" of today has transformed its traditional rivalries into partnerships, decimated its military establishment, and become the South American country most in favor of the cooperative strategy. Still, Argentine Defense Ministers Oscar Camilión and Jorge Domínguez (both civilians), have said that the local balance of power must be maintained.[59] It successfully pursued formal status as a "major non-NATO ally" of the U.S. in 1997, though it was rejected by NATO itself when it solicited entry in 1999.[60] Although this is largely a symbolic payoff, it does give Argentina preferential access to surplus U.S. weapons.

Argentine rearmament produced parity concerns in Chile, but not in Brazil.[61] Still, Brazil has not discarded its military capabilities. Brazilian defense concerns have turned northward. The Amazon attracts attention because of international concern about the increasing destruction of the rainforest and the country's own concerns with illicit transborder activities (mainly drug trafficking and gold mining).[62]

The historical preoccupation with strategic balances, including their military components, is not limited to the Argentine-Brazilian relationships, nor those between military governments. The long-standing Colombia-Venezuela democratic dyad is one of the most conflictual in contemporary Latin America. The two countries dispute 34 points along their border, with the most serious being in the Gulf of Venezuela, while illegal immigration, transborder guerrilla activity, and smuggling heighten Venezuelan concerns about Colombian intentions. In 1987, the appearance of a Colombian navy vessel in Venezuelan claimed waters provoked a major interstate dispute. The *Caldas* incident kept military forces on alert for two weeks.[63] After the crisis Colombia dramatically increased the size of its armed forces, partly due to increased guerrilla activity, but also stimulated by Congressional concerns that during the crisis Venezuela's superior military standing put Colombia at a disadvantage. This decision to redress the military balance was made even though both countries were democracies and in the process of increasing their economic relations. Tensions again erupted such that in March 1995 a leading Venezuelan historian felt it necessary to appeal in the press for calm, lest war break out.[64]

The Chilean-Peruvian relationship provides another example of democracies perceiving the prudence of military security. Although Chile does not currently perceive an immediate threat from Peru, it is upgrading its Air Force with purchases of Mirages and perhaps F-16s. The Chilean Air Force commander in chief justified these additions by noting that they would keep the country's fleet on a par with the Peruvian, which was also renovating its Air Force.[65]

Conclusion

The admittedly limited and impressionistic evidence of this chapter suggests that the distribution of overall military power is not a major factor in Latin America's violent peace. The decision to use military force in an international dispute is not systematically affected by whether the dyad is characterized by power parity or preponderance, measured in terms of total national capabilities. There is still no relationship even when we consider the potentially confounding effects of democratic institutional constraints.

Although I had expected the lagged military variable to capture the dynamics which produce militarization of a dispute, it was the least significant of the variables examined, with the exception of intra-Latin American democratic MIDs at a *Polity* level of 6. Consequently, a change in the overall military balance is unlikely to be a factor in the decision to militarize a dispute, assuming that changes in the level of military expenditures is an adequate way to measure this variable.

The democracy variable in the intra-Latin American models for the post Cold War period is highly insignificant. The analysis in this chapter thus contributes more suggestive evidence that democracies in Latin America are unaffected in their decision to utilize force in their foreign policy by whether or not the country with which they have a dispute is democratic. This holds true even after the effects of military balances are taken into consideration.

The lack of availability and unreliability of quantitative data limit the conclusions in this chapter. Available data in combination with qualitative analysis suggest that the military distribution of power is of very limited utility for explaining the use of force in interstate conflict in Latin America. However, the quality of military power, the issues of alliances, and the question of economic and political development were all perceived by policymakers and publics to affect a state's relative power position, even though these factors did not determine whether force was used or not.

In the following two chapters we will explore the utility of the military bargaining model for explaining the decision to use force. First we will examine the case of two military governments, then turn to a democratic dyad. The democratic case is a contest of unequal powers, allowing us to further explore whether the perception that power matters is borne out in reality.

6 Military Leadership and the Use of Force: Illustrations from the Beagle Channel Dispute

The model of militarized bargaining developed in chapter 1 provides a fourth framework by which to analyze the use of force in interstate relations. Five factors related to the costs inherent to the use of force, the costs acceptable to the public, and the public's ability to hold its leaders accountable are hypothesized to determine whether the use of military force is a rational policy option. This chapter examines a military dyad to explore the utility of the militarized bargaining model.

Military governments are often seen as quick to utilize military force to resolve conflicts. Not only is the application of force their profession, but also, the very fact of controlling government means that force has been utilized against opponents at home. Military governments are thus seen as predisposed to address problems with the use of military force.

A few analysts see a tradeoff for the military between using military force at home and abroad because they conceptualize the use of force as "war" and therefore requiring a diversion of resources from domestic control to external aggression.[1] Yet some military governments are able to use the police and a special intelligence bureaucracy to maintain domestic control without affecting the military's fighting capacity; in Latin America, Chile is the best example.[2]

The chapter begins with a brief discussion of the Beagle Channel dispute between Argentina and Chile that produced a full mobilization on both sides, a declaration of war, yet no actual combat. We then turn to examining the factors hypothesized to affect the costs associated with the potential use of force: the politico-military strategy chosen (S), the strategic balance (SB), and the characteristics of the force used (CF). A third section examines the costs acceptable to the leader's constituency (CC) minus the slippage in accountability produced by the domestic means of selecting leaders (A). A subsequent section includes a brief discussion of the Argentine decision to use force in the Malvinas crisis to demonstrate the ability of my analytic framework to show how the same actor (the Argentine military government) can choose to use force in one crisis (Malvinas) but not in another (Beagle).

Brief History of the Dispute

The boundary treaty of 1881, in which Chile recognized Argentine sovereignty over Patagonia in return for Argentine neutrality during the War of the Pacific, provided some guidelines for future delimitation of the waterways south of the mainland. A specific reference to the Beagle Channel provided that the islands south of the Beagle Channel would belong to Chile. The treaty also sought to provide the basis for peaceful co-existence by establishing the principle of "Chile in the Pacific, Argentina in the Atlantic." This bi-oceanic principle was reaffirmed in the 1902 Pactos de Mayo, which also provided the mechanism for resolving border disputes: arbitration by the British monarch.[3]

Unfortunately, what appeared clear at the turn of the century became controversial. Over time the strategic importance of the islands increased dramatically. Latin American countries laid claim to, first, a 200 mile maritime conservation zone in 1952, then a 200 mile territorial sea in 1970. The discovery of petroleum and organic resources in the area, and the competition over future rights to the Antarctic, further increased the value of controlling the south Atlantic.[4] In 1952 the pair had their first MID since 1905, and seven more followed up to the crisis in 1978.

The controversy revolved initially around two issues: did Argentine sovereignty stop at the water's edge in the channel? And which path did the Beagle Channel follow in its eastern mouth? The importance of the former question lay in whether the Argentine military base of Ushuaia (inside the Channel but on the Patagonia mainland) would be accessible to the Navy via Argentine waters. The route of the channel in the east would determine the sovereignty of the islands of Picton, Nueva, and Lennox, thereby affecting territorial seas and claims on Antarctica. There were multiple attempts between 1902 and 1970 to resolve the issue, but the two countries could not agree on the bases for negotiations on this or any of the other 23 disputes on their borders. In 1960 Argentina had gone so far as to propose recognizing Lennox as Chilean in return for navigation rights along all of the southern waters and the submission of the question of the other two islands to arbitration by the International Court of Justice (ICJ) at the Hague. Chile's Congress, however, rejected the proposal because it considered the navigation issue too generous to Argentina.

In 1964 Argentina dropped its insistence on a navigation treaty, but bilateral talks failed to produce a proposal for the ICJ. The following year the Argentine Foreign Minister commissioned French and Italian jurists to prepare studies on the likely outcome of international arbitration. Both studies were optimistic about the likelihood of gaining a dividing line down the middle of the Channel and pessimistic concerning gaining any of the three islands. Foreign Minister Miguel Angel Zavalla Ortíz subsequently publicly rejected arbitration and called for direct bilateral talks to find a political solution to the Beagle dispute.

Chile took matters into its own hands in 1967, deciding under the treaty of 1902 to unilaterally submit the dispute to the British Monarch for arbitration. But Argentina, now with a military government, continued to reject arbitration and the British Foreign Office refused to act in the absence of a consensus of the two parties. The Argentine National Security Council (NSC) attempted to revive bilateral negotiations in 1969, but to no avail. The following year the NSC decided that, in light of the importance of resolving all of the border disputes between the two countries and Chile's refusal to negotiate the Beagle issue directly, Argentina would accept arbitration. The service branches were consulted, and gave their approval. This position was maintained during the next two military governments in 1970 and 1971. In July 1971 arbitration by the British Monarch and an international court was formally requested in London by the two nations.[5]

General Alejandro A. Lanusse, president of a government in transition to democracy, expected to lose one or two islands. The General wanted to promote regional integration with Chile and saw navigation rights as an obstacle. The question of Atlantic projection by Chile was not an issue for Argentina at this time, apparently for two reasons: Lanusse expected to retain at least one island,[6] which presumably would be the easternmost, and the bi-oceanic principle itself was a well-established part of the bilateral relationship.

Argentina re-democratized in 1973, just as Chile succumbed to a military coup. From 1973 to 1976 the two countries submitted their oral and written arguments to the court. But at the same time the new democratic government moved to stop the arbitration. The Foreign Minister queried Argentina's two representatives before the Court of Arbitration on the advisability of retiring from the proceedings, but was counseled against such action, apparently because they had no legitimate reason to withdraw. In January 1976, an MID occurred between Argentina and Great Britain in the Shackleton affair. One of the Argentine representatives suggested that either Argentina could withdraw from the proceedings on the grounds that the arbiter was no longer on friendly terms with one of the parties, or that the British could be privately convinced to withdraw in light of the deteriorating relations. In addition, Argentina's two houses of Congress voted unanimously for the process to be suspended while it reviewed the case and decided whether to continue or not. In March 1976, the President of the Senate scheduled a meeting with President María Estela Martínez de Perón to discuss the matter.[7]

The utter collapse of the government in the face of economic crisis and dramatic political violence, however, provoked a coup and the meeting never took place.[8] The new military government appointed a Rear Admiral to examine the proceedings and he consulted with the prior Foreign Minister as well as with the international jurists who had prepared the earlier studies on arbitration. The government decided to continue with the arbitration.[9]

On May 2, 1977 the Court rejected the bi-oceanic principle as a basis for delimitation in favor of an interpretation based closely on specific geographic details in the texts of the 1881 treaty. All three islands were found to lie south of the Beagle Channel and consequently awarded to Chile. The judges found that the issue of maritime boundaries was outside of their competency and should be negotiated between the parties. The award provided for a nine-month period to execute the treaty.

The Argentine government, stunned by the decision,[10] realized that the Court's refusal to recognize the bi-oceanic principle had potentially dire implications. If negotiations on maritime limits broke down, Chile had the internationally recognized right to draw its lines of sovereign extension from the islands into the sea. Not only could these lines project Chile into the Atlantic, but they could also dramatically reduce Argentine claims in the Antarctic because much of Chile's new limits would block Argentine projection south to Antarctica.[11] Therefore, under the new context of no bi-oceanic principle, Argentina needed at least one island to safeguard its interests in the region. On May 3 they issued a communiqué claiming that no nation was bound to accept decisions by an arbiter affecting national interests or those violating national sovereignty *when those issues had not been expressly part of the arbitration.*[12] The following day Argentina proposed to Chile that bilateral negotiations be undertaken to solve all 24 outstanding controversies, including the Beagle Channel and associated matters.[13]

The Chilean government recognized its windfall and quickly accepted the Arbitrator's decision. They agreed to discuss all issues not resolved by the Arbitral Award and on July 14, 1977 promulgated Supreme Decree 416, implementing its right to a territorial sea based on lineal projection from its newly conferred possessions. With this move, Chile effectively made a return to the status quo before the arbitration impossible. Thus Argentine inaction would mean *de facto* acceptance of the arbitration.

Seven possible points on which the parties could potentially agree characterized the structure of the bilateral bargaining situation between the two countries. These ranged from recognition of the bi-oceanic principle with 0–3 islands, through shared sovereignty in the territorial sea, to elimination of the bi-oceanic principle, with Chile gaining a broad or narrow projection into the Atlantic. In 1977 Chile's actions communicated that its preference curves extended out only to a limited projection into the Atlantic and had a steep slope (i.e., it would view anything less as a significant loss). Argentina's minimally acceptable outcome was a bi-oceanic principle without any islands, but accepting the *laudo* meant that Chile would have international legitimacy in unilaterally implementing its preferred outcome in the face of no agreement.

Figure 6.1 illustrates the bargaining situation. We can easily see that, under the conditions prevailing in 1977–84 there was no basis for a negotiated agreement. Argentina thus had only two options: capitulate to Chile's position or move Chile's preference curve outward, to at least include the bi-oceanic principle and all three islands as Chilean.

The challenge for Argentina became to broaden Chile's bargaining range to include discussions of the islands. Argentina might settle without the islands, but it needed the islands to be a topic of discussion to keep Chile from walking away from negotiations on the territorial sea corresponding to the islands. Having already lost on legal grounds, Argentina needed a political settlement that could appreciate the importance of the bi-oceanic principle for stability in the region; thus staying away from the International

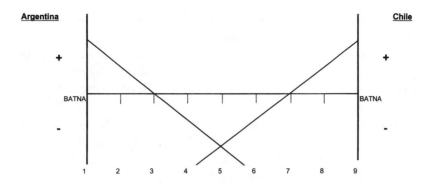

FIGURE 6.1 Bargaining Scenario Argentina-Chile 1977

1 = Bi-Oceanic Principle, 0 Islands to Chile
2 = Bi-Oceanic Principle, 1 Island to Chile
3 = Bi-Oceanic Principle, 2 Islands to Chile
4 = Bi-Oceanic Principle, 3 Islands to Chile
5 = Shared Sea, 1, 2, or 3 Islands to Chile
6 = No Bi-Oceanic Principle, 3 Islands to Chile

Court of Justice was paramount. For Chile, however, failed bilateral negotiations still left it with an internationally recognized new status quo that gave it the benefits of a South Atlantic power.

Informal discussions during the nine months provided for the Award to be executed failed to resolve the issue.[14] During these discussions Chile proposed territorial exchanges between the Beagle Channel and the Straits of Magellan. For the Argentine government such a proposal reinforced their view that Chile would protect its newly allocated projection into the Atlantic.[15]

On January 25, 1978 Argentina formally declared the arbitration award "null" because of "serious, repeated, and varied errors, omissions and excesses." Chile publicly rejected the Argentine action the next day, claiming that the arbitrators had acted correctly and Argentina was bound by treaty to accept it.[16] Formal bilateral negotiations began and continued until October 1978. Both sides demonstrated some interest in possible mediation, but failed to agree on neither who could mediate nor the basis for mediation.

In light of Argentina's overall weak bargaining position, it turned to military force as a signal of its commitment on the issue in hopes that it would broaden Chile's bargaining range. While Argentina did not prefer war, it was prepared to fight to keep Chile out of the Atlantic. Negotiations broke down in November and troops were deployed to strategic points. Argentina decided on December 12 to seize the islands, drafted a declaration of war on December 21, and gave the order to attack on December 22, 1978. The naval squadrons came as close to each other as 20 nautical miles.[17]

It is commonly believed that Papal mediation solved the issue, but this is a misleading oversimplification. Unfavorable weather led to the postponement of the seizure of the islands, and the next day the Pope notified both countries that he was sending a personal representative to sow the ground for a possible mediation effort. Argentina grasped at this new effort to find a negotiated settlement and put seizure of the islands on hold.[18] Chile, which would have fought only if attacked, accepted Papal intervention without prejudice to its position on the non-negotiability of the islands.[19]

Yet even as the Pope's mediation developed, militarized bargaining continued. Argentina remained steadfast in insisting that the bi-oceanic principle was the key to the deal and Chile continued to seek to preserve its gains in the Atlantic. Consequently, Argentina rejected a papal suggestion in 1980 that sought to make the waters in the area a common patrimony. Neither the Argentine defeat in the Malvinas War in 1982 nor redemocratization in 1984 led to changes in the Argentine position on the bi-oceanic principle (see Appendix). Resolution came only in 1984–85. In 1984, as part of a comprehensive agreement to resolve all 24 points in dispute, Chile desisted from contesting the bi-oceanic principle and Argentina recognized Chilean sovereignty over the Beagle Channel Islands. (Figure 6.2 illustrates the shift in bargaining positions.) Even then, the final agreement was opposed by the Commander-in-Chief of the Chilean Navy and passed the Argentine Senate by only one vote.[20]

Explaining the Use of Military Force

Foreign Policy Goods

Each leader seeks to deliver a foreign policy good to his constituency. The ability of each leader to deliver these goods depends on the evolution of the bilateral bargaining situation. Our interest lies in illuminating the

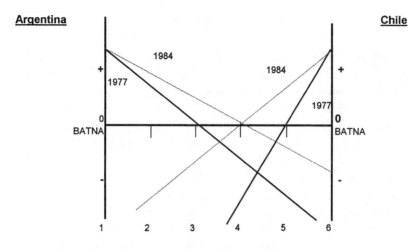

FIGURE 6.2 Bargaining Scenario Argentina-Chile 1977, 1984

1 = Bi-Oceanic Principle, 0 Islands to Chile
2 = Bi-Oceanic Principle, 1 Island to Chile
3 = Bi-Oceanic Principle, 2 Islands to Chile
4 = Bi-Oceanic Principle, 3 Islands to Chile
5 = Shared Sea, 1, 2, or 3 Islands to Chile
6 = No Bi-Oceanic Principle, 3 Islands to Chile

reasoning which made incorporating the use of force as a bargaining tactic rational for each side in its quest to deliver these foreign policy goods.

Argentine Presidents in the 1960s and 1970s, whether military or civilian, wanted to settle a long conflict with Chile, but not at the expense of the bi-oceanic principle, which had helped define the country relative to its neighbor Chile. As a result, the bi-oceanic principle was a public good. In addition, by 1976 Argentine relations with Great Britain were souring over the Malvinas dispute. Chile historically had good relations with Great Britain. Argentina's bargaining power with Great Britain over the sovereignty of these islands would be seriously diminished if Chile were to project itself into the south Atlantic.[21] Consequently, Argentina was in a bind in 1977. Accepting the Arbitral Award as handed down had potentially serious consequences.

Some Argentine leaders, especially in the Navy, were interested in a private good: sovereignty over one or all of the islands in the Beagle Channel. While Videla was willing to use the islands as a bargaining chip to gain acceptance of the bi-oceanic principle, these minority political voices wanted more.

The goods President General Pinochet wished to deliver were twofold. The Court had presented him with the opportunity to demand Chile get the full benefits of the *laudo,* which included unforeseen Chilean benefits in the Atlantic. The public good consisted of the sanctity of international treaties and laws concerning territorial sovereignty.[22] Chile had reasons to fear the implications of renegotiating treaties recognized by international law. As noted in chapter 3, Chile's current dispute with Bolivia over a sovereign outlet to the sea was rekindled at this time. Tensions produced a war scare, with Peru potentially joining Bolivia.[23]

The Award did not explicitly reject the bi-oceanic principle, but it did make it possible for Chile to project itself into the Atlantic. This projection would be a private good for ultranationalists. Since the turn of the century Chileans had largely accepted that they were a Pacific rather than Atlantic power. Maritime projection does not seem to have had the same support as defending sovereignty over the islands.

Expected Costs

Political-military Strategy

Argentina sought to break the link between possession of the islands and the right to project into the territorial sea via bilateral negotiations. Argentina could not accept Chile's offer to submit the arbitration award to the World Court. The only solution Argentina could countenance required either bilateral negotiations from scratch or mediation by someone who could not only recognize the strategic necessity of the bi-oceanic principle, but also convince the Chileans to accept these terms for mediation. In the absence of either solution Argentina was prepared to defend its Atlantic interests by force of arms.

Argentina needed to convince Chile that Chile's own interests would be better served by reopening negotiations on both islands and territorial seas and resurrecting the bi-oceanic principle. Given Chilean intransigence, Argentina's bargaining was essentially limited to raising the specter of a costly military confrontation with Chile.

Chile's international security had been based on maintaining the status quo after its conquests of the nineteenth century.[24] The credibility of Chile's refusal to be coerced into making concessions would be severely diminished if it accepted Argentina's proposal to ignore the results of an international arbitration. Chile thus offered in 1978 to discuss issues not addressed by the Arbitration and to take the dispute over the arbitration to the International Court of Justice. But it could not agree to renegotiate that which it had already been granted, unless the costs of not renegotiating increased dramatically beyond Argentine irritation.

Past MID experiences with unhappy neighbors suggested that Chile could expect some saber rattling by Argentina. In the Beagle case, Chile would need to demonstrate that it had the military capacity to make an Argentine seizure of the islands extremely costly. This would entail either thwarting an Argentina attack in the Channel or convincing them that a successful attack in the south would mean full-scale war. This strategy was complicated by three factors. First was the possibility of an Argentine-Bolivian-Peruvian alliance against Chile. Chilean military strategists believed they could easily defeat Bolivia and inflict heavy damage upon one of the other two adversaries. The task was to make one hesitate long enough before joining the other that Chile could defeat the first invader before the second joined in.[25] Second, Chile needed to maintain a strong military presence in both the north and south. Finally, Chile needed to avoid provoking Argentina by overreacting to its use of force as a signaling device.

Strategic Balance

Both governments were international pariahs because of their human rights records. Ideally, Chile could count on diplomatic support from all countries that opposed the use of force in settling disputes. Even the U.S. administration of Jimmy Carter, which had extremely poor relations with both countries, told Argentine representatives in no uncertain terms that the use of force to regain the islands was unacceptable.[26] Chile and Argentina were both confident of Chile's ability to win in the diplomatic and legal halls around the world if war broke out.

The military situation was complex. An analyst might be tempted to simplify by counting numbers of weapons and people, even including Peruvian forces in the balance, and geography.[27] Argentina's population is more than 2.5 times that of Chile's, with Peru adding another 1.5 times Chile's population. Argentine GNP was a little over four times Chile's, although Peru's was only roughly two-thirds that of Chile's.[28] The difference in troop strength is not as overwhelming, but still large: in 1976 estimated figures were Chile 83,000 troops total (50,000 Army, 23,000 Navy and 10,000 Air Force); Argentina 137,000 total (83,000 Army, 33,000 Navy and 21,000 Air Force); and Peru 69,000 total (46,000 Army, 14,000 Navy, and 9,000 Air Force). Chile also fell behind in terms of naval and air equipment at the time.[29] The geographic disadvantages for Chile are little strategic depth east to west and vast distances between north and south (roughly 4,000 miles). By this reckoning, a war with Chile would have produced a quick and cheap Argentine victory.

Chile, however, had very important advantages that rendered war with it costly and risky for Argentina as well. As a status quo power, Chile would be fighting a defensive war on its own territory rather than invading someone else's. The northern deserts were heavily mined, making invasion here costly and difficult. The Chilean armed forces had extensive supply and transport equipment, ensuring that their lines of communication would hold up well. The quality of the Chilean soldier was generally recognized as excellent.[30] The qualitative differences relative to Peru mean that Chile could count on a defensive advantage far greater than the traditional 3–1 force ratio generally perceived necessary for an attacker to count on success. And even if one were to grant Argentina equal quality on the ground, it only had a 1.6–1 advantage. Finally, there is no history of Argentine-Peruvian military cooperation. During the War of the Pacific, Argentina preferred to negotiate its own deal with Chile rather than aid Peru. In the tense negotiations leading up to the 1929 treaty there is no evidence of Argentine pledges of aid to Peru. And when the 1976–78 period of tension between Peru and Chile began, the Argentines were again silent even as the Peruvians mobilized their forces. Since Argentina had never been a credible ally for the Peruvians, they could hardly have a high degree of confidence in Peru's willingness to become involved in a war with Chile when it was advantageous for Argentina.[31] There is no record of discussions between Argentina and Peru concerning joint military action, and none of the interviews provided by Argentine military and diplomatic actors of the day mention such discussions.

These Chilean advantages do not imply that it could have won a war against Argentina, but that is not the relevant point. To deter their neighbors the Chileans do not have to demonstrate a capability to win. They need, instead, to make a credible case that a military adventure against Chile would not be cheap. In 1978, the Argentine Junta could not be very confident that war would produce a low-cost victory against Chile.

Characteristics of Force Used

Chile's desire to demonstrate resolve but not escalate unnecessarily meant that it was unlikely to use force early in a dispute. Instead, its actions would be geared toward credibly communicating their determination and capability to defend via declarations of resolve, mobilizations of units, and deployments in defensive positions. Because Chile's military was already mobilized to run the country and its internal security missions had already demobilized the democratic opposition, the domestic costs of signaling military resolve to Argentina were low. Chile's politico-military strategy required force to be actively used only to repel an Argentine invasion of the country or seizure of an island. Full-scale war would entail use of the Army and Air Force in the center and north and the Navy and Air Force in the south. Thwarting an Argentine military operation against the islands required naval and air actions in the south. In either case, the costs could be expected to be high for Chile.

Argentina's politico-military strategy provided for the use of force in three ways: to coerce Chile into broadening its negotiating stance before violence escalated; to seize an island and negotiate from a position of strength; and to fight a war if necessary. If Argentina were successful in coercing Chilean negotiators via demonstrations of Argentine military capabilities and will, the costs of such use of force would be minor. Argentina thus engaged in domestic mobilizations, overflights of Chilean airspace, and naval bombardment of uninhabited islands. Seizing and holding an island for negotiating purposes would be cheap only if done by surprise and without provoking a Chilean escalation. Surprise however, would be difficult since the preferred strategy was to initially use force to communicate the seriousness with which Argentina perceived the Beagle dispute. Chile's Navy would consequently be on the alert in the region lest the signaling escalate into an attempt to seize territory. Thus, if the islands were not seized at the beginning of the militarized bargaining strategy, seizure later likely meant war, at least in the south.

A military stalemate in the south would bring Argentina international condemnation for using force and provide Chileans with little incentive to broaden their negotiating range. In fact, it would probably narrow it, since Chile had international law on its side as well, and would presumably result in Chile's refusal to negotiate on the other 23 outstanding disputes. Taking the islands in the south would thus mean having to pursue victory if Chile resisted. Victory required moving into Chile in the north at the same time, and hence full-scale war. And again, high costs.

To summarize the total expected costs associated with the use of force: Militarized bargaining costs were low for Argentina, since Chile was not likely to attack; and it was low for Chile as long as Argentina did not decide to escalate from threats and demonstrations to seize the islands by force. As for the cost of war, it was likely to be high on both sides since Chile was on the alert in the south.

Restraints on Costs

Constituencies' Cost Acceptance/Aversion

Argentina

Generals Videla, Viola, and Galtieri had three constituencies to whom each had to deliver goods at acceptable costs if he were to remain in office for his specified term and choose his successor. These were the Junta, the Army's high command, and those in civil society whose support was necessary for a leader's political project to advance. Alfonsín, the first president in the transition to democracy, had a constituency consisting of the traditional Radical Party voters, voters who had abandoned the traditionally majority Peronist Party in 1984, and those officers in the military who had supported democratization.

Within the Junta during 1977 Videla represented only 1 out of 3 votes and was in danger of being outvoted. This appears to have occurred early in the dispute. Videla had accepted the recommendations of an Inter-ministerial Commission concerning maximum and minimum negotiating positions, including the possibility of "joint sovereignty" over water and land. but the Junta rejected any consideration of Chilean sovereign access to the Atlantic.[32] On this point the 1977 Junta did not waiver, even when it was renewed with a new cast in 1978, and neither Junta differed from the democratic government of Raúl Alfonsín in 1984.[33] Videla, Viola, Galtieri, and Alfonsín all confronted this limit to the Argentine position.

The Junta preferred a negotiated solution to fighting, but also preferred fighting to losing on the bi-oceanic principle. It thus paid close attention to the informal negotiating sessions carried on by the Foreign Ministries in July and October 1977. When those failed, the Junta turned to direct military contacts. After rejecting the Award in January 1978, the Junta sent a military mission to Chile to confirm that Argentina wished to commence formal bilateral negotiations.

In the Junta, only Admiral Emilio Massera was anxious for a military resolution. Admiral Massera sought to use military successes in restoring the economy, combating subversion, and reaffirming Argentine sovereignty in the South Atlantic (Beagle and Malvinas) to win a Presidential election.[34] His constituency comprised nationalist forces within the military and he courted the Peronists, even talking to the remnants of the urban guerrilla Montoneros living in exile as well as with Estela Perón, whom the Junta had overthrown in 1976.[35] After the second meeting of Presidents on February 20, 1978 and in response to Pinochet's declaration that Chile respected international law and would defend the Arbitral Award, Admiral Massera ended a speech in Buenos Aires with "the time for words has ended!"[36] But Massera's opposition to Videla and his own political project lost him support within the Navy. He retired in September 1978 and his successor in the Junta became more cautious.[37]

The Junta's caution did not mean that it was unwilling to decide upon war if necessary. They authorized the Foreign Minister to meet the Chilean Foreign Minister on December 12, 1978 and agree to the Pope as mediator, as long as the issue included items covered by the Arbitral Award, i.e., land from which Chile could project into the Atlantic. After this effort failed to persuade Chile, Army Chief Viola, under stiff pressure from the service's High Command, pressed for a quick resolution of the issue. While the Navy and Air Force believed the moment was not ripe for a military solution, they acceded to the Army's position.[38] The decision was thus made in the Junta on December 14 to seize the islands in order to force Chile to negotiate on Argentine terms.

The Junta still held out for a modification in the Chilean bargaining range right up to the perceived last moment. Although the U.S. government proposed on the 12th that the disagreement be submitted to the Organization of American States dispute resolution mechanisms, Argentina insisted on pursuing the bilateral route (as did Chile).[39] The Junta dispatched a high-level military mission on December 17 to meet with their counterparts in Chile, but to no avail. When informed of the Pope's mediation offer on the 22nd the Junta grabbed this last opportunity to avoid war, and immediately suspended their plan for seizing the islands, withdrew their fleet, and re-opened the borders.[40]

Cardinal Samore met multiple times with the Junta. The sticking point was Chile's refusal to accept a wording of the mediation process that did not foreclose the possibility of discussing issues seemingly settled in the Arbitral Award. Chile finally acquiesced and on January 5, 1979 the Argentine Junta agreed to have the Pope mediate the dispute. Presidents Videla, Viola, and Galtieri were now able to proceed with the negotiations with little day-to-day interference from the Junta.[41]

Although it had backed down from war, the Junta never gave up on the use of military force to pressure Chile. There were MIDs in 1980, 1981, and 1983 with the last military government embarking on a transition to democracy in the wake of the defeat in the Malvinas. The Junta also rejected the Pope's suggestion of a shared sea with Chile in 1980 and supported Galtieri's decision in 1982 not to renew the bilateral treaty with Chile which called for the juridical resolution of disputes.

Videla had initially been able to contain the hardliners in the Army while he was both President and Commander-in-Chief of the Army. After Videla lost control of the Army in the middle of 1978 the High Command wanted to seize the islands as a negotiating ploy. Army Chief Viola was unable to assert his control over the institution either and it was the Army which pushed through seizure of the islands in December 1978. While Viola was President, Army Chief Galtieri appears to have acted upon his own authority and closed border crossings between the two countries.[42] The military was too divided to accept the Pope's proposal of joint sovereignty over the seas, preferring to risk military escalation once again.[43] They were focused enough on fighting Chile that even during the Malvinas War against Great Britain in 1982 the Army left its best troops on the borders with Chile, rather than shift them to the Malvinas.

The Army thus emerges as quite belligerent after mid 1978. The officer corps was willing to assume the military costs of confronting Chile. It is not clear, however, that they expected to face the full costs of any engagement. If the war remained limited to the islands, the Army would bear little of the direct costs since seizure would be largely in the hands of the Navy and Air Force. Since a land war would escalate only if Chile provoked it in the north, and Chile was well known to have a defensive posture, the chances of a major land engagement must have seemed minimal.[44]

Although Argentina lived under a military government during the Beagle dispute, the major political issues of the day, including the Beagle, were discussed in the newspapers. In addition, newspapers were often linked to one or another military faction, and would report on intra-military government discussions and feuds. There was evidence that major political forces wanted to retain the islands and to keep Chile out of the Atlantic. In October 1977 high-profile writers, businessmen, retired military officers, and politicians (including the leader of the Radical Party and the man who would become President after the collapse of the military regime in 1984, Raúl Alfonsín) published a declaration in the major Buenos Aires daily. This diverse group demanded that "not one meter of our air, sea or territorial space could be negotiated away without a manifestation of the national will, whether that be via the reestablishment of constitutional government or by a national referendum."[45] The latter clause indicates that defending Argentine sovereignty took precedence over redemocratization.

The public at large was not in the dark on the issues at stake, or on the alternatives to the use of force. Pinochet's telegram of November 3, 1978 suggesting that a friendly government be asked to mediate the dispute, rather than renew bilateral negotiations that had already proven fruitless, was published in a major Buenos Aires daily. In addition, the text of the Pope's telegram to both Videla and Pinochet encouraging a peaceful settlement was also published the day it was received, December 12, 1978.[46]

The return of democracy in 1984 made the public more important in policy decisions. The nationalist fervor that had produced massive demonstrations in support of the Junta's military seizure of the Malvinas Islands in 1982 had been dampened by the defeat at the hands of the British. The public clearly demanded no wars, but it was not clear how much nationalism in the country's foreign policy they were willing to give up to avoid war.

The Peronist Party perceived that negotiations with Chile were a platform on which they could regain the loyalty of those voters that had supported Alfonsín in 1984. Alfonsín sought to mitigate this attack by publicly defending the bi-oceanic principle and Argentine claims to the Antarctic. In a telling pronouncement, Interior Minister Antonio Troccoli noted that good relations with Chile were a priority that needed to be addressed immediately, "defending, of course, the bi-oceanic principle."[47] Although the Peronists attempted to strike at Alfonsín by opposing the 1984 Treaty of Peace and Friendship in the plebiscite, the electorate supported it overwhelmingly. The Treaty passed the Senate by a narrow 23–22 margin, with one abstention.[48]

Chile

General Pinochet's constituencies in the relevant years of 1977–84 were the Army and right wing political forces and individuals, many of whom assumed positions in his government. Although even leftist political forces in exile believed that Chile should not renegotiate what it had won in international arbitration,[49] Pinochet was certainly not paying attention to their desires.

There seemed to be unanimous agreement among Pinochet's constituencies on two points. First, that Chile had international law on its side (the irony of being an international pariah on human rights issues escaped them). Second, that Chile could not succumb to intimidation by the Argentine military government. Because Argentina was demanding that Chile give up what it had gained through a legal process or face war, the idea that Chile should defend itself against military aggression even if war ensued seems not to have been disputed within these military and political forces.

To summarize constituency cost acceptance/aversion: In Argentina from 1977 to the outbreak of the Malvinas War of 1982 using military force *if necessary to defend the bi-oceanic principle* appeared acceptable not only to the military Junta, but also to the reemerging political forces. In the absence of a specific discussion of those costs it would have been extremely risky for an Argentine leader to assume that the public would have accepted high costs. Pinochet's constituency also supported the use of military force if necessary. Because they would have been responding to an Argentine attack and were right wing nationalists, Pinochet likely assumed they would offer all to defend the country.

As for the accountability of the leader to constituencies, Argentina and Chile in 1977–78 both had military governments. Yet because the structure of the military governments and the events leading up to the coups which brought them to power differed dramatically, the Argentine and Chilean Presidents had distinct vulnerabilities to their key constituencies in the armed forces and society.

Argentina

Argentina had significantly greater internal armed conflict than Chile in the period leading up to the coup in 1976. The Argentine military coup was welcomed by virtually everyone and, since the scale of the Dirty War within Argentina was unknown at the time, the government faced little domestic opposition from traditional political forces in 1977–78. In Chile, the 1973 coup had been a traumatic experience and there was a large, though cowed opposition. Still, the Chilean military government retained the allegiance of the center and right who feared a return to the polarized politics of the Allende years if the military relinquished power. Although the economies of the two countries were in states of collapse at the beginning of the MID, both began short-lived recoveries at the height of the crisis, and saw their economies collapse again beginning in 1981, with the Chilean economy recovering in 1984.

In Argentina, the military coup of 1976 was designed to restructure Argentine politics, society, and the economy. The military leadership recognized the enormity of the task and designed an institutional form of government to maintain unity within the armed forces during the process. The supreme organ of the state was the Military Junta, in which each of the three services' Commanders in Chief would have equal standing. While the Commanders represented their services, they were not autonomous of their officer corps. The high commands of each branch met separately to discuss and assess the issues of the day. In this fashion power was intended to reside only in the military and would be exercised only jointly.

The Presidency was an executive office, officially subordinate to the Junta, and to be occupied by a retired officer so as not to disrupt the division of power within the Junta. General Videla had been named President although he was not retired because the military believed that the fight against domestic enemies required the leader to be an active duty officer. A formal document recognized this situation as temporary, to be remedied once domestic order had been secured. In August 1978 the period of exception was ended and the Presidency separated from the Junta, with General Videla retiring and General Roberto Viola taking his place on the Junta as Commander-in-Chief of the Army. The Junta could veto presidential decisions by a two-thirds vote, except that deposing the President required unanimity.

The functions of government were initially divided into thirds, and military officers dominated the cabinet. The Navy received responsibility for foreign affairs, among other assignments. In 1976, a rear admiral carried out the evaluation for the Navy-supported Foreign Minister which approved continuing the arbitration. Upon retiring as Army chief in August 1978, Videla convinced the Junta to allow half the cabinet to be composed of civilians and the other half of retired officers.

General Videla was a moderate within the military. Unlike hardliners, he sought to maintain a dialogue with forces within civil society, particularly political parties. At the end of November 1978, just as the Beagle Channel dispute was entering its most dangerous phase, the General attended two significant civilian events along with half of the leadership of one of the leading parties, the Unión Cívica Radical (UCR). This action signaled the beginning of a serious political opening, which picked up steam in 1979.[50] Army Chief and soon to be successor to Videla, General Viola had always advocated a dialogue with the political parties. Videla and Viola, however, would have to deal with forces within the military that sought either no transition at all or to drag out the transition.

The limitations on Videla's policy choices were in evidence as the end date of the formal negotiations with Chile neared. Videla and his Foreign Minister, Air Force General Carlos Washington Pastor (who was also Videla's brother-in-law), discussed possible mediators. With the collapse of formal negotiations on November 2, 1978 the Military Committee went into per-manent session to plan Argentina's next move. This committee was com-posed of the President, the Junta, and the secretaries of the three service branches; in mid-November two generals from the Army General Staff joined.[51] In December 1978, Chile was willing to accept the Pope as me-diator, but insisted on the Award being one of the issues to be mediated. Videla decided to expand his bargaining range in light of Chilean intransi-gence, but the Junta intervened and forced him to retract such modifica-tions.[52]

Videla and Pastor attempted to pursue a diplomatic route without the Junta's knowledge. They sent representatives to the U.S., the USSR, France, Germany, and the Vatican, as well as to the UN in an attempt to bring international pressure to bear on Chile to modify its stance. But the Argen-tines found no allies because no one was willing to back the use of force and Chile was defending the Arbitral Award. On December 15 and 16, during meetings at the U.S. State Department, the White House and Con-gress made it clear that any use of force would be condemned by the U.S. and its allies. The U.S. government did offer, however, to ask the Vatican to act quickly to try and defuse the crisis.[53]

Videla tried another maneuver to get around the Junta's tight rein. He met with the Papal Nuncio on December 14 and informed him that he had given the orders to seize the islands the following week. Videla reportedly expressed his personal desire to avoid the use of force, but feared that the Junta would remove him if he backed down now. This surprising revelation of Argentine war plans must have been designed to spur the Vatican into immediate action to persuade Chile to make the necessary concessions to get negotiations back on track. Videla seemed to understand that the Junta would allow him to negotiate only if Chile modified its negotiating stance.

Viola found himself with even less freedom of action upon assuming the Presidency. The debate over terminating Videla's dual role as President and member of the Junta thrust the high command into playing increasingly active roles in determining major policy. The Army high command was able to extract a commitment from Videla's ally and heir apparent, General Viola, that he would retire after serving only half a term as Commander-in-Chief and not modify the high command while Army leader.[54] The latter would prove a severe constraint. His successor as Army chief, General Leopoldo Galtieri, proved to be a rival rather than ally, ultimately toppling and replacing him as President.

As long as the Junta wanted to govern the country itself and was willing to use repression to guarantee its rule, the number of domestic allies it would need would be small. But as soon as they contemplated opening up the political process, even short of holding elections, and ruling through a civil-military alliance, their need for allies increased. Such needs would provide these civilian allies with informal and weak, but very real, abilities to constrain policy choices.

By 1978 the liberal economic program was providing fruits and urban guerrillas were defeated (both had enormous costs for the losers, but many of these were still unknown to society). The liberal economic program would serve to ally policy technocrats and internationally competitive business with the military. In 1979 business groups began to anticipate the change in the presidency set for 1981 and pressured different "candidates" to pay more attention to their needs.[55]

The Junta publicly declared that the new president would be its "legal representative," thereby warning potential candidates and political parties that it was not willing to share power.[56] Intense discussion and politicking within the armed forces eventually led to General Viola's selection in October 1980 and he became President in March 1981. But Viola could not count on the support of his successor as Army Chief. General Galtieri represented the hardline faction within the Army and wanted to become President himself. Within the Junta Galtieri allied himself with the Navy's representative, Admiral Jorge Isaac Anaya, a supporter of Admiral Massera's willingness to use force quickly to resolve disputes.

Viola's short reign in 1981 was characterized by increasing tension from walking the tightrope between the moderates and hardliners.[57] Viola changed the orientation of economic policy, made overtures to the Argentine Industrial Association, and selected leaders of the agricultural and mining sectors to head the respective ministries. The new Minister of Labor was a general who opened a dialogue with the unions, while the new Interior Minister announced the priority of the "political dialogue." On July 14, 1981 the political parties formed the Multipartidaria and entered into discussions with the Minister.[58]

General Galtieri forced Viola out in December 1981. He became President yet retained his position as Commander-in-Chief of the Army, thereby altering the relationship between the Presidency and the Junta in his favor. Galtieri had to promise Navy Chief Admiral Jorge Isaac Anaya that he would support an invasion of the Falklands Islands in order to get his support for the Presidency.[59] Three factors suggest that Anaya's influence over Galtieri would have diminished upon his becoming President. First, Galtieri's own political program gave him personal reasons for wanting to seize the Falklands (see below). Second, Anaya could not topple Galtieri on his own. The third member of the Junta, Air Force General Basilio Lami Dozo, not an enthusiastic supporter of the Falklands invasion, would have been unlikely to support toppling Galtieri over this issue. Finally, Galtieri was firmly in control of the Army and the Navy had less political weight, as demonstrated previously in the disputes between General Videla and Admiral Massera.

While Galtieri had significantly diminished the Junta's ability to constrain him, he began developing new constraints on his freedom of action. Although a hardliner, Galtieri realized that the Junta's days were numbered. The economy was slipping into chaos and the political parties were increasingly active. His political project, consequently, was to create a new civil-military alliance that would guide the transition back to democracy and lead him to victory in the elections. He publicized his net worth to demonstrate that he was not corrupt, promised to return his presidential salary to the Treasury, and began making public appearances "shaking hands with the elderly and kissing babies."[60] The Multipartidaria demand in February 1982 for "the immediate restitution of the Malvinas"[61] made defending sovereignty of Argentine territory an important issue in any upcoming electoral campaign. Compromising on the bi-oceanic principle would have been a poor political move in 1982.

Once Raúl Alfonsín became President the constraints upon the Executive shifted to the Congressional and electoral arena. Alfonsín was the first presidential candidate to defeat the Peronist party in free elections since 1948, but the Peronists claimed control of the Congress. Alfonsín perceived that no politician could concede the bi-oceanic principle to Chile. When Alfonsín lobbied politicians at home to support the Pope's suggestions for a solution, he insisted that any agreement would defend both the bi-oceanic principle as well as Argentine claims in the Antarctic. This formula paid off, as the plebiscite on the Treaty was a major success. Although the Peronist-controlled Senate passed the Treaty by only one vote, Alfonsín had already made his point with the electorate.

Chile

In Chile, the military coup of 1973 was carried out as a collegial affair, but Army Commander-in-Chief General Augusto Pinochet soon consolidated control over the Junta. During the early years the Junta came to believe that the country needed to undergo radical changes in the social, political, and economic spheres and that these changes would be possible only under their "guidance." Unlike their Argentine counterparts, Chile's military feared that the politicization of the military that was inevitable under direct rule would undermine its professional capabilities. The ruling Junta was, therefore, made up of the commanders of the four service branches (Army, Navy, Air Force, and National Police) who were directly accountable only to themselves.

Pinochet retained his position as both a member of the Junta and President. This combination gave him enormous policymaking leeway because Junta decisions had to be unanimous. In January 1978 Pinochet increased his independence from the Junta by overwhelmingly winning a symbolic referendum endorsing his government. The Air Force and Navy Commanders in the Junta attempted to prevent the referendum because they understood that it would give the President an additional basis of legitimacy, but Pinochet held it under executive order.[62]

Pinochet developed a secret police that were directly answerable to him as President and they instilled fear even within the military. He also promulgated a decree that allowed him to purge the ranks of the Army officer corps of any potential competitors, including virtually everyone from his generation. There was thus little opposition to Pinochet within the government or the Army.

General Pinochet had a rival in the Junta, Air Force General Gustavo Leigh. But Leigh's political project sought to create a civil-military alliance to run the country and this prospect clashed with the general desire of the armed forces and police to "stay out of politics." Leigh and his top generals became isolated within the military and could not build important alliances in civil society. When Pinochet mobilized paratroopers, the other members of the Junta, and his cabinet to depose General Leigh and 18 high ranking Air Force officers in July 1978, Leigh had little alternative but to back down from a confrontation.

In 1979–80 Pinochet moved further to legitimize his government outside of the Junta. A new constitution was written and passed overwhelmingly in another plebiscite. Although opponents of the regime denounced the voting process, he now had a "popularly legitimated" mandate to remain as President for another ten years, with a possibility for "reelection." The perception of the business elite and right wing political forces that only Pinochet stood in the way of a resurgence of the Socialist-Communist alliance gave him great autonomy on policy matters. The support of most of this sector even survived the short-lived but dramatic economic collapse of 1982–83.[63]

Pinochet had more independence from the Junta than his Argentine counterpart because Chile's Junta saw his continuity as fundamental to their legitimacy and the institutional structure of the authoritarian government provided no justifiable way for the Junta to constrain him. If the Junta were to depose General Pinochet it would have to confront the government (staffed largely by Pinochet loyalists) and the Army (under direct control of Pinochet and a handpicked group of Generals), and to call into question their own legitimacy. It was not until the Junta decided that a transition to democracy was desirable that they were willing to risk a major confrontation with Pinochet.[64]

General Pinochet thus had great political leeway in structuring a package to resolve the Beagle dispute, *as long as he did not give up islands*. The arbiters had found in Chile's favor on the question of islands and had left maritime projection to be negotiated between the two countries. Once Pinochet decided that a deal with Argentina was in Chile's best interests, he was willing to give up the private good of maritime projection for the public good of the sanctity of international treaties regarding territorial sovereignty.

Although the Navy Commander-in-Chief wanted to hold out for the private good, Pinochet seems to have paid no costs in overruling him.

In sum, regarding restraints on costs, Chile's leader confronted an ideal situation. Chilean society, even those in exile, perceived the Argentines as the aggressors and supported defending Chilean sovereignty, as defined by the arbiters. Since war would result only if Argentina attacked, Pinochet could count on his constituencies' support of Chile's defense. Not only did he have their support, he had great leeway on the specifics of policy because of the polarized political environment within Chile. Argentina's military and democratic leaders were greatly constrained by their military and civilian constituencies. Although the identities of the constituencies varied by leader, all were defenders of the bi-oceanic principle. The challenge for Argentine leaders was to deliver the foreign policy good, but avoid large-scale war.

If Not Beagle, Why Malvinas?

In the Beagle Channel dispute the Argentine Junta demonstrated a willingness to use the threat of force to bargain and an eagerness to grasp at an exit strategy when it was offered. Why did the same Junta fail to draw back from the confrontation with Britain over the Malvinas? Exploration of Galtieri's decision to seize the disputed Malvinas Islands provides further suggestive evidence for my model of militarized bargaining.

Although I argued above that Galtieri was more secure within the Junta than other analysts claim, everyone agrees that he was seeking public support for a run for the presidency in a transition government. Thus *Galtieri's political future was very accountable to Argentine political forces*. So why did he embark on a foreign policy which turned into such a disaster for him?

The answer lies in the high benefits and low costs that he expected to pay for bringing home this foreign policy good. Restitution of the Malvinas was clearly a public good in Argentina. The political parties themselves recognized the drawing power of the Malvinas issue. In February 1982, as part of their program for a transition to democracy, through the Multipartidaria they had demanded "the immediate restitution of the Malvinas." The massive street demonstrations in support of seizing the islands and the lack of such demonstrations against war when it became clear that Britain would fight demonstrate that Galtieri's potential public constituencies favored the effort and were willing to pay an unspecified price of war to achieve it.[65]

The political-military strategy was clearly to seize the islands and then negotiate, not fight. Argentina had previously taken the issue to the UN and in 1964 the General Assembly included the islands on a list of territories to be decolonized. Following a UN resolution the British and Argentines initiated negotiations in 1966. After initial progress, talks stalled in 1968 when the 1,200 inhabitants of the islands were given effective veto power over any agreement. Originally hailing from Great Britain, the islanders preferred the status of British subjects to becoming Argentine citizens.

Negotiations took on a new life after 1977, when the Conservative government of Margaret Thatcher began cutting state expenditures. Funds for supplying and defending islands located 8,000 miles away and with little economic or strategic value, seemed like a good item to strike from the budget. Galtieri and his advisers also believed that Britain's government would calculate the international cost of fighting for the islands to be greater than the domestic costs of standing up to the islanders and Parliament. The Argentines believed that world opinion and the U.S. government would see this as a decolonization issue and support Argentine claims.[66]

The strategic balance seemed to favor Argentina. The Argentine leadership studied previous episodes in which military force was used to develop scenarios about likely responses to an Argentine seizure. From the Suez Crisis of 1956, the Argentines noticed that the U.S. had sanctioned British, French, and Israeli use of military force to regain control over the Suez Canal after Egypt had nationalized it. Egypt's attack on Israel in 1973 demonstrated not only that militarizing a dispute could draw international attention, but also confirmed the willingness of the U.S. to pressure a close ally (Israel) to make concessions in order to gain a peaceful solution. The Argentine decisionmakers also noticed that India's seizure of Portuguese Goa in 1961 was initially condemned by the international community, and then accepted as a *fait accompli*. Finally, the British decision to come to terms with their renegade former colony Rhodesia in 1981 was seen as a harbinger of likely British response to a "peaceful" Argentina occupation of the Malvinas.[67]

Although the Junta did not believe Britain would fight, they also assumed that if Britain did react militarily Argentina could defend the islands. The British were 8,000 miles away, with a weak capability to project military power into the south Atlantic. The Junta certainly overestimated Argentine capabilities, but even more important were calculations about the weather and U.S. behavior. The seizure of the islands had been planned for May 15 when winter would make naval operations to expel the Argentines extremely treacherous. And the U.S. was expected to remain neutral.[68]

The characteristics of force used (a surprise landing with an overwhelming number of troops) were designed to permit seizing the islands while avoiding British casualties. A bloodless takeover was expected to dampen the emotional response of British nationalism, thereby making it less likely that a military response would be forthcoming. Peaceful occupation was also designed to mitigate the Junta's poor international reputation on human rights. In addition, the Junta expected that the international community would see the "peaceful" occupation as a restrained response to British intransigence in negotiations over an issue that the UN had already declared ripe for decolonization.[69]

Argentine calculations were thus that likely costs associated with seizure of the Malvinas Islands were very acceptable: $S + SB + CF < CC - A$.

The problems began when the seizures had to be carried out earlier in the year because the British were becoming suspicious. Since the idea was to carry out a bloodless seizure, a British alert would require a change to more costly action, both militarily and diplomatically.[70] The British, who had decided to fight rather than commit to negotiating sovereignty,[71] now had ample time to put a task force in place before winter *if they had the aid of the U.S.*

The U.S. government, despite U.S. Ambassador Jeane Kirkpatrick's efforts and communications to the Argentine government, opted to see this issue as one of international aggression rather than decolonization. The U.S. provided the British task force with access to a naval base along the route, as well as fuel, munitions, and satellite intelligence that tracked Argentine military moves. By the time Galtieri realized that the military costs of keeping the islands would be far greater than he had calculated, his domestic political costs of backing down were clearly high enough to oust him from office and, if the Junta fell with him, to threaten prosecution for human rights violations. Thus pressed, he gambled on winning the war.[72]

Militarizing the Malvinas dispute can thus be understood as a rational policy decision by the Argentine leadership, not simply an attempt to divert attention from problems at home. Winning the Malvinas would have provided a policy good to a constituency that held tremendous influence over General Galtieri's political future. The miscalculations of the Argentine Junta were not the result of irrational military bravado, but largely due to

British and U.S. failures to take the Argentines seriously and signal deterrence credibly. In the Beagle Channel Dispute with Chile, the Argentine Junta had demonstrated their rationality, as well as prudence, when Chile signaled deterrence credibly. In this case the Argentines understood that the costs of a war would be high and grasped at the last straw offered, even when it was not clear that the Pope's mediation would work.

Conclusion

Exploration of the Argentina/Chile dyad demonstrates the utility of the militarized bargaining model for understanding a military government's decision to use force. Viewing the Beagle Channel dispute through the lens of costs of force, constituencies' tolerance of costs, and their ability to punish decisionmakers makes the Argentine and Chilean decisions to bargain militarily, yet stay away from war, understandable, rational, and even prudent within their contexts.

Ultimately, Chile had a great advantage in being able to keep the military from governing as an institution. This meant that political decisions were subject to less pressure from the officer corps and that the fighting ability of the institution was never seriously undermined. General Pinochet could make decisions and expect them to stick and have a high degree of confidence in his military's ability to defend the country. Hence, in the model's terms, the constituencies' inability to punish Pinochet increased his freedom to bargain. Further, the strategic situation in which Argentina was necessarily the aggressor if war occurred virtually guaranteed popular support for fighting a war.

Argentina's military governments were vehicles by which the officer corps of the three service branches became intimately involved in policy choices. Videla, Viola, and Galtieri (though less so the latter) were severely constrained by the politicization of the officer corps. At the same time, these leaders were also limited by the need for civilian support for their political projects. Hence, consistent with the model, the greater constraints on the Argentine president limited his bargaining options. Faced with intransigent adversaries and constituencies eager for foreign policy goods, Argentine policymakers chose the political-military strategy of rattling sabers. In the Beagle dispute, the President's constituency preferred a costly war to the new status quo; in the Malvinas, where Argentina had intended to present the British with a fait accompli and move directly to negotiation, war was preferable to capitulation for both the Junta and the public.

Given the common assumption that military governments are more willing than other regime types to consider the use of force, explaining a military government's use of force does not necessarily demonstrate a model's power for understanding the behavior of other regime types. The following chapter explores the usefulness of the militarized bargaining model for understanding decisions around the use of force in a democratic dyad composed of unequal partners.

7 Democracies and the Use of Force: Suggestions from the Ecuador–Peru Dispute*

Can democracies fight against each other? Chapters 2 and 5 demonstrated that in Latin America democracies use force against one an-

---

* The democratic status of both countries, especially Peru, was in question in 2000. In February a coup failed in Ecuador, though President Jamil Mahuad was forced to abdicate in favor of his vice-president. In May Peruvian President Alberto Fujimori insisted on holding elections whose fairness was questioned domestically and internationally. The opposition candidate withdrew, the vote was held anyway and Fujimori was declared the winner. The U.S. government and the Organization of American States officially recognized Fujimori as the winner, despite "irregularities." Michael McCaughan, "US accepts 'illegitimate' election of Fujimori" *The Irish Times* June 21, 2000, p.12; "American Nations Press Peru for More Democratic Reforms" *The Toronto Star* June 29, 2000. In September 2000, faced with a scandal involving his intelligence chief and mounting protests, Fujimori disbanded the intelligence service, called for new presidential elections, and declared that he would not be a candidate. Latin America Data Base, *NotiSur–Latin American Affairs*, "Peru: President Alberto Fujimori Announces New Elections" Volume 10, Number 34, September 22, 2000. In November 2000, during a trip to Japan, Fujimori announced his resignation from the presidency, effective immediately, and there is speculation that he will try to stay in Japan indefinitely. Sebastian Rotella, "Peruvian Congress Rejects Fujimori's Resignation and Fires Him Instead," *Los Angeles Times*, A:13, November 22, 2000.

Because these events happened after the 1995 war and the 1998 peace agreement, the case is still relevant for the democratic peace argument. One should also note that throughout those tumultuous first six months of 2000, there were no reports that the peace agreement was called into question in either country.

other and with increasing frequency as their numbers increase. This chapter explains the decision to use force among democracies through the framework of the militarized bargaining model. In doing so it sheds light not only on why democracies can fight, but also demonstrates that a focus on the costs of using force is a useful way of thinking about militarizing disputes even when decisionmakers are not military dictators.

The chapter begins with a brief discussion of the territorial dispute between Ecuador and Peru that produced 32 militarized disputes in the twentieth century, including two wars (1941 and 1995) and two other full mobilizations (1910 and 1981).[1] This case is particularly interesting because Peru was significantly more powerful than Ecuador during most of this period. This power disparity allows us to explore under what circumstances a smaller power will confront a larger power with military force. Following a summary of the dispute, we examine the factors affecting the costs associated with the potential use of force: the politico-military strategy chosen (S), the strategic balance (SB), and the characteristics of the force used (CF). A third section examines the costs acceptable to the leader's constituency (CC) minus the slippage in accountability produced by the domestic means of selecting a leader (A). A subsequent section considers why a democratic public can be a stimulus for the use of force even against another democracy.

Brief History of the Ecuador-Peru Dispute

The Amazon River offers access to the potentially rich Amazon basin, and a potential trade route to the Atlantic for South American countries on the Pacific coast. During the Independence wars some areas ostensibly controlled by Quito joined the Peruvian armies, rather than those fighting farther north.[2] Peruvian authorities claimed such acts represented self-determination to constitute part of Peru. After Independence Peru attempted to seize further areas, including the major port city of Guayaquil, but was defeated by the forces of Gran Colombia (which at the time included Colombia, Venezuela, and Ecuador). Peru renounced some territorial claims in the Pedemonte-Mosquera Protocol, but the Congress of Gran Colombia did not ratify it. Gran Colombia subsequently dissolved into three countries and Ecuador sought to make the peace treaty effective. Peru rejected the treaty and Ecuador's claim to the boundaries of a now defunct state. The dispute was papered over by the 1832 Treaty of Friendship, with both sides interpreting the phrase "present limits" according to their own interests.

The area in dispute was remote, with no infrastructure and largely inhabited by indigenous peoples. In 1860 Ecuador attempted to compensate European creditors with land in the Amazon. Peru attacked, forcing one defeated leader to recognize Peruvian claims, but other Ecuadorian leaders repudiated the treaty. Interestingly, although Chile sought Ecuadorian assistance during its two wars with Peru (1837 and 1879), Ecuador maintained strict neutrality.[3] Since Chile won both wars, Ecuador may have lost an important opportunity to resolve the territorial issue in its favor.

Ecuador attempted to cede land for debts again in 1887. This time Peru (recently defeated by Chile in the War of the Pacific)[4] and Ecuador agreed to negotiate their differences, with unresolved issues submitted to the King of Spain for binding arbitration. In 1890 the Peruvian Executive granted Ecuador access to the Marañón River; the Ecuadorian Congress quickly ratified the Treaty but Peru's Congress demanded a renegotiation. Between 1900 and 1904 a series of military clashes occurred in the region due to the expansion of rubber and gold exploitation, as well as Peru's increasing integration of the region into the national economy. Diplomatic relations between Ecuador and Peru were severed for a time. In 1905 Ecuador signed a secret treaty with another of Peru's territorial rivals, Colombia, in which each guaranteed the other's territorial integrity.[5] There was also an informal understanding in both Ecuador and Peru that Chile might help Ecuador in any conflict with Peru.[6]

In an effort to avoid war, the parties turned to the King. In 1910 rumors that the King's advisers found Peruvian legal arguments compelling produced riots in Ecuador.[7] President General Eloy Alfaro rejected the arbitration, called for new bilateral negotiations, and declared Ecuador's willingness to fight to preserve its Amazonian character. Both countries mobilized troops and an arms buildup ensued. Argentina, Brazil, and the U.S. mediated, suggesting that the dispute be taken to the Permanent Court of Arbitration at the Hague. Peru accepted, but Ecuador called for direct negotiations.[8]

Although the King did not render his judgment, its basic outline now defined the issue. Any juridical examination would most likely reproduce the King's judgment. Peru adopted arbitration as a fallback position if direct negotiations failed, while Ecuador sought to avoid juridical settlement. Of course, Peru would have no incentive to concede anything in bilateral negotiations, preferring the status quo (in which it occupied large sections of the disputed territory). Ecuador kept the level of tension on the border high in hopes that other Latin American states and the U.S. would insist that Peru accommodate Ecuador (in the 20 years prior to 1910 there were only 3 MIDs; for the next 8 years they were constant).

Despairing, Ecuador modified its strategy in 1916. It settled a dispute with Colombia in the Amazon to gain an ally against Peru. New attention centered on the U.S. in the wake of Word War I.[9] Both Ecuador and Peru hoped the U.S. could obtain a "just" settlement in territorial conflicts in which they were the weaker party. (In these cases a "just" settlement was defined as one that would give the weaker party a better deal than could be garnered in bilateral negotiations; i.e., Ecuador vis-à-vis Peru and Peru vis-à-vis Chile). Because the U.S. stridently advocated peaceful resolution of conflict (even to the point of using its own military might to impose it on Central America and the Caribbean![10]), Peru and Ecuador avoided militarized disputes through the 1920s.

The promise of diplomacy proved ephemeral. Peru, facing a new war scare with its powerful nemesis Chile, enticed Colombia to abandon Ecuador with a better deal in 1922: sovereignty in the disputed area north of the Amazon river in exchange for the territory previously ceded by Ecuador to Colombia. Ecuador severed relations with Colombia.[11]

But in 1932 Peru escalated a minor border incident in the Leticia region into a major conflict with Colombia.[12] Colombia's military success encouraged Ecuadorian diplomatic and military posturing. As an "Amazonian" nation, Ecuador tried inserting itself into the Leticia cease-fire negotiations, but Peru blocked it. Military confrontations between Ecuador and Peru revived in 1932. Ecuador and Peru resumed diplomatic negotiations in 1933 but increased border clashes in 1938 ended them.

Ecuador's internal political situation continued to be unstable in the 1930s and its military languished in domestic political struggles. In contrast, Peru began to climb out of the era of dictatorship. Peruvian officers blamed the politicization of their institution during the days of authoritarianism for the Colombian defeat. They resolved to professionalize themselves for their proper mission: the defense of national territory. This asymmetry would have dramatic consequences.[13]

In the late 1930s the Peruvian military saw an opportunity to resolve a territorial issue and end a history of defeat. Ecuador responded by establishing small frontier outposts in the disputed territory to serve as tripwires, hoping to trigger international intervention.

In 1941 Peruvian troops, tanks, and planes swept across the disputed regions, penetrating deep into Ecuador itself.[14] Ecuador confronted a U.S. and Latin America preoccupied with the war in Europe and the Pacific. Peru threatened to occupy the territory until Ecuador recognized Peruvian claims in the Amazon. Bowing to pressure for inter-American solidarity, Ecuador accepted the Rio Protocol in January 1942. Argentina, Brazil, Chile, and the U.S. became guarantors of the treaty. The Protocol denied Ecuador sovereign access to the Amazon River.[15]

The territorial dispute between Ecuador and Peru appeared settled. The government that signed the Protocol, the military leaders of the 1944 coup and the subsequent democratic government of President José María Velasco Ibarra all accepted the Protocol.[16] Border demarcation proceeded without serious controversies, with Brazilian arbitration resolving a number of issues in 1944, until 95 percent of the area had been resolved.

In 1947 a 78-kilometer section to be divided by the *divortium aquarum* between the Zamora and Santiago rivers, proved problematic. The Cenepa River was discovered to flow through the expected *divortium aquarum*, making demarcation by the letter of the Protocol impossible. Ecuador suggested in 1949 and 1950 that the Amazon issue constitute part of a renegotiation.[17] Peru attempted to deter Ecuador's developing challenge to the status quo by asserting the primacy of the Rio Protocol, which denied Ecuador sovereign access. Peru proposed that a natural division existed in the Condor mountain range farther to the northwest (i.e., into Ecuador).

The bargaining challenge for Ecuador was to get Peru to move its position out toward Ecuador's. Figure 7.1 illustrates the preference curves of the two parties in 1950 by solid dark black lines. There were seven points around which agreements could be constructed, and which break into two major distinctions: those that accept the fundamental terms of the Rio Protocol and those that would take a new look at the entire controversy. Ecuador preferred the latter type situations, beginning with multilateral renegotiations because Peru's bargaining power would be decreased in a multilateral forum. Arbitration within this context would be Ecuador's next best solution, followed by bilateral negotiations with Peru, but still in the context of a discarded Rio Protocol. If the Protocol had to be accepted, multilateral negotiations were to be preferred over arbitration, followed by direct bilateral negotiations with Peru. The least acceptable outcome to Ecuador was to accept Peruvian interpretations of the Protocol.

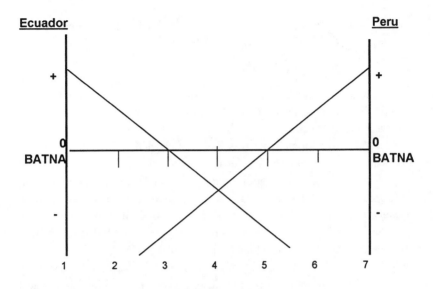

FIGURE 7.1 Bargaining Scenario Ecuador-Peru, 1950–1995

1 = Multilateral renegotiation outside the Rio Protocol
2 = Arbitrate outside the Rio Protocol
3 = Bilateral renegotiation outside the Rio Protocol
4 = Multilateral negotiation within the Rio Protocol
5 = Arbitration within the Rio Protocol
6 = Bilateral negotiation within the Rio Protocol
7 = Accept Peruvian interpretation of the Rio Protocol

The problem for Ecuador was that Peru had no reason to stray beyond the negotiating positions while accepting the Rio Protocol. It had already accepted Brazilian arbitration on a disputed point, as called for in the Protocol. But the internationally recognized treaty safeguarded Peru's fundamental interests in the Amazon and Peruvians saw no advantage in modifying that position. Ecuador would have to create a situation in which Peru would find it to be in its own interest to modify its position. Given Ecuador's relative weakness vis-à-vis Peru, it could not succeed alone.

Ecuador rejected Peru's proposed solution and began building its legal case for the *inapplicability* of the Protocol in the Cordillera del Condor region, as well as developing a diplomatic offensive for international support. In 1950 President Galo Plaza withdrew Ecuador from the border demarcation commission. At the 1951 OAS meeting to consider the hemispheric response to extracontinental aggression, Ecuador's Foreign Minister raised the issue of intracontinental aggression to no avail.[18] The 1959 OAS conference of foreign ministers, scheduled for Quito, was postponed when Peru refused to attend because the host country included the dispute on the agenda. The return to international diplomacy was also accompanied by renewed border clashes.

In 1960 President-elect Velasco Ibarra responded to Ecuador's inability to create a coalition around the idea of inapplicability by raising the stakes further: he declared that, in addition to being inapplicable, the Protocol was *null* because it was the result of Peruvian military aggression. Ecuador attempted to build a coalition around this idea in both the OAS (1959, 1965, 1980, and 1981) and the UN (1976, 1980, and 1991) but failed completely. By questioning a treaty negotiated after a war, the Ecuadorians touched a sensitive nerve in the international community, which reacted by asserting the sanctity of international treaties. In response, Velasco Ibarra in his next term declared that "an honorable transaction" (i.e., sovereign access somewhere to the Amazon) could allow Ecuador to accept the Protocol.[19]

Despite Ecuador's push on the diplomatic front in the 1960s it joined Peru as allies in general foreign policy. They were on the same side in the "Tuna Wars" with the U.S. concerning the 200-mile jurisdiction. A dramatic shift in Peruvian foreign policy after the leftist military coup of 1968 produced a new possibility for resolution. Under General Juan Velasco Alvarado Peru sought to build a Third World oriented foreign policy, supported by a Latin American bloc of nations. The Andean Pact, created in 1969, promoted economic integration, and trade between the two countries expanded.[20]

Although the Andean Pact began to lose momentum in 1976 Peru rejected Ecuador's contention that progress on the border could provide the impetus for renewed progress among Pact members.[21] Brazil's initiative for Amazonian cooperation and development seemed to offer Ecuador a de facto presence in the Amazon, but Peru short-circuited this effort in the final Treaty signed in 1978.[22]

International diplomacy and economic cooperation did little to resolve Ecuador's Amazon problem. This failure led to a renewal of the latest phase of militarized clashes in 1977, just as democracy was returning to both countries. The first of Ecuador's newly democratic Presidents, Jaime Roldós, proclaimed in his inaugural address that his government would continue to pursue "recognition of the historic and inalienable Amazonian rights" of Ecuador.[23] Roldós died in 1981 as the plane in which he was traveling to inspect Ecuadorian outposts in the disputed zone crashed.

Thirteen MIDs occurred between 1981 and 1998, which represents the most intense period for the rivalry in the twentieth century (table 7.1). Two of these clashes developed into major crises. In 1981 up to 200 people died in the confrontation and Peru threatened to invade Ecuador in a repetition of 1941. Ecuador had to appeal to the guarantors of a treaty it did not recognize by the euphemism of "the four friendly countries" to halt the fighting and reportedly paid reparations to Peru.[24] Skirmishing among patrols almost escalated in 1991, but was papered over by a "Gentleman's Agree-

TABLE 7.1 Militarized Interstate Conflicts: Peru-Ecuador 1910–1998*

Year	Year	Year	Year
1910	1932	1950	1977–78
1911	1934–36	1951	1981
1912–13	1937	1953	1983
1914–16	1938	1954	1984
1917–18	1939–42	1955	1985
	1942	1956	1985
	1943	1960	1988
			1989
			1991
			1993
			1994
			1995
			1995
			1998

* MID database; Loftus, *Latin American Defense Expenditures*, pp. 27–29; *Hoy* December 29,1995, and "Peru and Ecuador Hold Fresh Talks" *Financial Times* September 8, 1998 p. 9; Scheggia Flores, *Origen del Pueblo Ecuatoriano*, p. 61; Ministry of Foreign Affairs, *Hacia la Solución*, pp. 194–195

ment." Short of building confidence, the agreement provided more grievances as the Peruvians later refused to abandon the outpost in question.[25]

Relations between the two countries did not deteriorate despite the MIDs.
Economic cooperation accelerated after 1985. President Alberto Fujimori
became the first Peruvian President to travel to Ecuador in 1991, and he
offered various economic development proposals, as well as the possibility
of a free port for Ecuador on the Peruvian Amazon.[26]

For 34 days in early 1995 Ecuador and Peru sustained their most serious
military confrontation since 1941, with reliable unofficial estimates putting
the dead at more than 1,000. Both sides deployed sophisticated aircraft and
Ecuador used modern intelligence technology. Armed forces mobilized in
the jungle region of the actual fighting, and along the west coast, where the
navies also gathered. Ecuador called up its reserves.[27] To avoid escalation,
Ecuadorian President Sixto Durán Ballén abandoned the nullification thesis
and publicly asked for the guarantors' mediation.[28]

The guarantors brokered a cease-fire, separated the two military forces,
and called for negotiations. In December 1995 Peru mobilized 6,000 troops
on the border in response to Ecuador's purchase of four Kfir fighter-bombers
from Israel. Although military confidence-building measures occurred in the
disputed sector during January and February 1996, the Peruvian negotiator
arrived in Quito with copies of his book supporting Peru's interpretation of
the 1947 negotiations.[29]

Negotiations stalled after dealing with nonterritorial issues. After a war
scare in August 1998 the two presidents agreed to allow the four guarantor
countries to devise a settlement. (The shift in preference curves is represented in figure 7.2 by the dotted lines.)

The guarantors insisted that before taking up the task, both Congresses
had to agree to abide by their decision. Within a week of getting such approval, the guarantors had their decision, along with a sweetener: a pledge
of $3 billion in development aid. Peru achieved a major aim as the border
was determined to lie along the Cordillera del Condor. Yet Peru had to pay
a high price for its victory. Ecuador was granted perpetual sovereignty over
a square kilometer in Peruvian territory to build a monument to its soldiers
who defended Tiwintza, the outpost that came to symbolize the 1995 war.
Ecuador also gained sovereignty over port facilities in a Peruvian site on the
Amazon River. (Fujimori had simply offered access to a port in 1991.) And
Peru was required to pay for and build roads connecting those facilities to
the Ecuadorian, rather than Peruvian, Pacific coast.

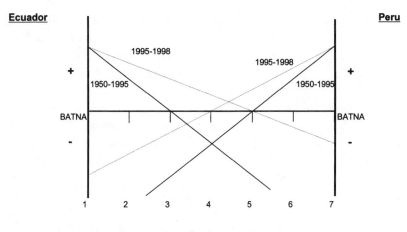

FIGURE 7.2 Bargaining Scenario Ecuador-Peru, 1950–1998

1 = Multilateral renegotiation outside the Rio Protocol
2 = Arbitrate outside the Rio Protocol
3 = Bilateral renegotiation outside the Rio Protocol
4 = Multilateral negotiation within the Rio Protocol
5 = Arbitration within the Rio Protocol
6 = Bilateral negotiation within the Rio Protocol
7 = Accept Peruvian interpretation of the Rio Protocol

Peruvian Foreign Minister Eduardo Ferrero Costa resigned once he suspected that these were the terms to be offered by the guarantors.[30] After the terms were made public riots broke out in the chief Peruvian city in the Amazon, Iquitos. But Fujimori stood his ground. In Ecuador, people accepted the trade of a sovereign outlet to the Amazon they never had for guaranteed access and the promise of development aid.

Explaining the Use of Military Force

Foreign Policy Goods

Ecuadorian Presidents since 1947 have wanted to settle the dispute with Peru, but not at the expense of the country's claim to sovereignty in the Amazon. The foreign policy good was not settlement per se, but rather a sovereign outlet to the Amazon. Achieving this goal would enable the President to recover some of the national pride and self-respect that most Ecuadorians believed Peru had trampled on with its "aggression" in 1941. It thus constituted a "public good." Ecuadorian leaders did not pursue any private goods in this rivalry.

Peruvian Presidents had a different foreign policy goal that reflected the country's diplomatic and military advantages over Ecuador. Peru's leaders had to avoid delivering a "public bad": getting caught in a diplomatic renegotiation which would give Ecuador sovereign access to the Amazon. In essence, therefore, Peruvian leaders had to deliver the defense of the gains of the 1941 war. Since virtually all Peruvians accepted the Rio Protocol (see below) defending it was a "public good."

Once President Fujimori embarked on his neoliberal development program for Peru the creation of economic linkages with neighboring countries became an important factor in Peruvian foreign policy. These potential economic links would constitute a public good to the degree that their benefits were widely distributed. If these economic benefits were limited to groups in the border area, however, they would be private goods. Fujimori certainly saw them in the broader context, and hence, as public goods.

Expected Costs

Political-Military Strategy

Ecuador first challenged the Protocol settlement in the diplomatic arena, declaring it "inapplicable" in 1950 and null in 1960. In the mid 1970s the U.S. signaled that this strategy was appropriate when it said that Peru's position was too intransigent.[31] The democratic governments after 1979 followed their predecessor's leads. Appeals were made in the UN (1980 and 1991) and OAS (1980 and 1981) to take up the issue and the Pope was suggested as a possible mediator in 1991.

A purely diplomatic strategy could not propel Peru to renegotiate. International actors were reluctant to reopen issues that had been legitimated in an international treaty and Ecuador did not have the capability by itself to pressure Peru into discussing the issue. In the face of Peru's rejection of third-party involvement outside the parameters of the Rio Protocol, Ecuador's democratic governments followed a strategy of using military force to keep the issue alive and induce third parties to intervene. Ecuador did not attempt to seize and control the disputed territory.

Ecuador's strategy required not provoking Peru into escalating a conflict as long as Ecuador's armed forces could not hold out long enough for third parties to intervene diplomatically. The debacle in 1981 demonstrated the continued weakness of Ecuador's armed forces. Over the next decade they developed their military capabilities and lulled the Peruvians with confidence-building measures among military personnel in the Cordillera del Condor zone.[32]

Ecuador's strategy after 1981 also monitored the Peruvian institutional context. Ecuador's military command believed that the Peruvian military became demoralized and corrupted after a decade of fighting a civil war against both guerrillas and the drug trade (during which the institution was heavily criticized for human rights abuses and in which officers succumbed to narcodollars). Fujimori's interference with the military chain of command in order to assure personal loyalty was also believed to have hurt Peru's military. Peru was expected to be surprised by Ecuadorian defensive capabilities, waste significant resources in trying to overwhelm them, and be unable to adjust its local strategy before the costs of the war forced Peru to either escalate or negotiate a cease-fire. Faced with significant losses in the Amazon, aware that Ecuador's Navy had already left port, and observing the mobilized Army in the south, Peru was expected to negotiate.[33]

The Ecuadorians patiently waited for the right moment. In 1987 they discovered a new Peruvian outpost, Paquisha, in territory recognized as Ecuadorian during the demarcation which occurred in the 1940s. Rather than denounce it, they waited until 1991 to make it an issue.[34] During the 1991 controversy they did not back down and conflict was avoided by a gentleman's agreement establishing a security zone and the mutual withdrawal of forces from two outposts. Neither side withdrew, producing a stalemate unchanged by minor MIDs in 1993 and 1994. These events suggest that Ecuador was ready to militarily contest Peru by 1991, but needed Peru to initiate the fighting.

Peru's political-military strategy, based on the sanctity of international treaties, did not change with the return of democracy in 1980. Peru argued that the Protocol called for the four guarantors to resolve any disagreement within the parameters of the treaty. Under the terms of the treaty, Ecuador had a right to transit through Peruvian waters to the Amazon, but not to a sovereign outlet. Hence Peruvian leaders could ignore, if not explicitly re-ject, Ecuadorian calls for outside parties to intervene.

Within this Peruvian strategy, the use of military force was guided by two goals. The first was to keep Ecuador from effectively establishing outposts in remote disputed areas. The second was to resolve any military confron-tation quickly, so as to avoid international pressure for a new basis for settling the dispute.

Diplomacy could produce economic benefits via increased cooperation. Both sides were aware that economic diplomacy might be a lever with which to induce the other side to make concessions. When the two countries were under military rule, Ecuador's attempt to tie reviving the Andean Pact to discussing the territorial issue was quickly and clearly rejected by Peru. In the early 1990s, when newly elected President Fujimori traveled to Ecuador offering economic cooperation as a means of developing a new bilateral relationship, Ecuador's democratic Presidents refused to accept any linkages with the Amazonian dispute.[35]

Strategic Balance

The balance of capabilities became more complex after 1980 for reasons partly having to do with democratization. As long as the dispute remained bilateral and the potential for escalation great, the *military balance* appeared to favor Peru. Ecuadorian decisionmakers understood the fundamental dis-parity in military power.[36] Dramatic defeat in 1941 propelled the military to support democratization to free itself from domestic politics and profession-alize. Fitch's detailed analysis of military perceptions and justifications for supporting or threatening Ecuadorian democratic governments in the period 1948 to 1966 does not uncover disagreements between civilians and military officers over the Amazonian issue.[37]

Ecuador's leaders did not believe that the balance of *diplomatic capabil-ities* favored Peru. Ecuador had demonstrated good faith in accepting the delimitation of 95 percent of the border along the terms of the Protocol. Everyone could recognize that the strong trampled the weak in 1941. With World War II over, the international community could remedy the injustice suffered by Ecuador by insisting that Peru negotiate a relatively small (com-pared to what had been "lost") sovereign access to the Amazon. Although Peru repeatedly argued for the sanctity of international treaties, the decla-ration of inapplicability in 1950 did not question the treaty itself. Ecuador argued that the failure of the Protocol to incorporate the real geographic situation made negotiations necessary.

Ecuadorian leaders recognized that "justice" would not attract sufficient international attention. Ecuador needed, therefore, to keep the issue alive in order to persuade the international community to pressure Peru. The military skirmishes, renewed in 1950, thus were directed at the international community, not Peru. The U.S. raised Ecuadorian expectations that the international community might favor a "just" solution to the conflict in the mid-1970s when it critiqued Peru's position.[38] The active role of the guarantors in terminating the 1981 mini-war indicated that Ecuador was on the right track, if they could survive Peru's initial military response.

Peru enjoyed diplomatic successes for almost fifty years, as neither the OAS, the UN, nor the Pope would mediate the dispute since the Protocol gave this task to the four guarantors of the treaty. The 1981 experience convinced the Peruvians that they continued to have the military and diplomatic advantage. The quick military victory meant that the guarantors interpreted their role simply as one of helping to evacuate the Ecuadorians safely.

The ability of Ecuador's armed forces to resist Peruvian attacks in 1995 shifted the diplomatic balance. This time the guarantors worried that the conflict might escalate to large-scale war, especially as Peru kept committing more resources to the battleground in the Amazon. Ecuador seized upon this new opportunity, recognizing the Protocol and committing itself to work with the guarantors for a resolution of the conflict. Nevertheless, Peru maintained an advantage in that the mediators in the negotiation were the guarantors of the Rio Protocol, thereby ensuring that the negotiations would not stray far from the 1941 agreement.

Characteristics of Force Used

In the latest flare-up of the rivalry there were twelve minor MIDs (1977–78, 83, 84, 85, 85, 88, 89, 91, 93, 94, 95 and 98; see table 7.1), and two major ones (1981 and 1995). From the 1950s to the 1980s Ecuador structured its penetration of disputed territory with only small units in isolated jungle outposts. In 1981 Ecuador constructed outposts on the eastern side of the mountain range, with poor lines of communication to Ecuador in the west. This was a quick and cheap incursion into disputed territory. Any direct confrontations with Peruvian troops would produce quick retreats or at worst a low number of casualties. Ecuador did not expect a strong response by Peru, especially not an invasion into Ecuador proper.

After the 1981 defeat, Ecuador's military redesigned the manner in which they used force.[39] The emphasis was still on using minimum force, only more efficiently and successfully. They chose terrain that would limit the maneuverability of aircraft (with the mountains at their back and steep mountains on each side Peruvian aircraft had to come from one direction). Triple canopy jungle made it difficult to detect Ecuadorian defenses, thereby allowing soldiers to sit hidden in trees with surface to air missiles. Planting cheap Chinese plastic anti-personnel mines made it difficult for Peruvian paratroopers to penetrate the area on foot. Weapons purchases seem to have been secret, ensuring that the Peruvian military would be unable to take effective countermeasures.[40] Effective lines of communication (a system of footpaths leading back to Ecuadorian base camps and villages) were developed. They also contracted Israeli and Chilean intelligence and communication experts to create a system to intercept Peruvian communications. Finally, they prepared national defenses in case of escalation, including getting the Navy out of port quickly.[41]

The characteristics of force used by Peru for confronting Ecuador did not change between 1981 and 1995. The expectation remained that Peru had military dominance both in the region and overall. Modern fighter-bombers, attack helicopters and well-trained paratroopers were expected to give Peru the ability to inflict a quick and cheap defeat on any Ecuadorian incursions. The military build-up of the 1970s in preparation for war with Chile also meant that the country had significant equipment in reserve to sustain initial losses, if they occurred.[42]

Because Ecuadorian positions were exposed in 1981, victory came quickly and cheaply. At that time Peru had enough confidence in its military superiority to threaten an invasion of Ecuador. Its hesitation to pursue victory in 1995, however, indicates that Peru understood that the military costs of large-scale war were now significantly higher than before.

Summary of Costs

MIDs were cheap for Peru as long as it could overwhelm Ecuadorian outposts easily. War had been cheap in 1941, looked cheap in 1981, but its potential military and diplomatic costs had increased greatly by 1995, especially if the international community became involved. MIDs were cheap for Ecuador as long as Peru did not escalate. 1981 had been an expensive defeat without advancing Ecuador's political-military strategy. By 1991 a defensive war looked possible, though still costly. If the international community intervened quickly as a result of war, they would likely pressure Peru to make some concessions to resolve the dispute.

Constituency Cost Acceptability

Ecuador

Democratic politicians after 1979 could draw on past experience to evaluate what their constituencies wanted and what costs they were inclined to accept. Ecuador remained democratic throughout the period during which its strategy to challenge was conceived and implemented, 1948–1960. The distinct constituencies of the three presidents elected in the period suggest that this represented a broad national consensus. Plaza was a moderate, with good relations with the U.S., Velasco Ibarra won the presidency in 1952 behind a conservative and populist alliance, as did Camilo Ponce in 1956 and Velasco Ibarra again in 1960. Plaza had little internal opposition when he declared the Protocol "inapplicable." Velasco Ibarra had just been elected President with more votes than the combined total of all his opponents, when he declared the treaty "null."

After the country's poor performance on the battlefield and in the OAS during the mini-war of 1981, Ecuador's Foreign Ministry undertook a national opinion survey on the issue to update the government's evaluation of national sentiment. The diplomatic corps perceived Ecuador's strategy as fundamentally flawed because it contested the principle of the sanctity of treaties and sacrificed national development to a vague territorial issue. But the opinion poll confirmed the popularity of the strategy of nullification and sovereign access.[43] In 1983 the Ecuadorian Congress reiterated the country's claim that the Protocol was null and void.[44]

Another poll carried out in 1992 provided further evidence of Ecuadorian feeling on the issue. The overwhelming majority of Ecuadorians believed the border issue obstructed development (79 percent yes, 15 percent no) and a majority believed the country should engage in free trade with Peru (55 percent yes, 39 percent no). Nevertheless, since 49 percent believed Peru to be an "enemy" country, compared with only 39 percent who perceived it to be friendly, Ecuadorians expected Peru to make the concession that would improve relations.[45]

Following the 1995 war, public opinion seemed to demand greater concessions in order to settle. During the war an opinion poll asked "Do you believe that it is possible for Ecuador to recover all the territory lost in 1941?" In Quito 27.5 percent and in Guayaquil 32.8 percent responded yes. When provided with the statement in 1996 "There are people who say that Ecuador should recover the territory which it lost in the 1941 war and that it should be done no matter the cost," 44.3 percent of Quiteños and 56.5 percent of Guayaquileños agreed! On the issue of a sovereign access to the Amazon, a vast majority believed it was possible despite the conflict (75.3 percent in Quito, 83.5 percent in Guayaquil; 1995 poll).[46]

Ecuadorians were not ignorant of the costs of continuing the conflict: 53 percent of Quiteños and 38.5 percent of Guayaquil respondents in a 1996 poll believed that Ecuador was more affected economically by the war than was Peru and a whopping 80 percent believed that armed confrontations would recur. In addition, while most believed that Ecuador had "won" in 1995 there was a dramatically increased pessimism over the country's ability to prevail in a new confrontation. In Quito 55 percent believed Ecuador had won but only 39.5 percent saw a possibility of future victories; in Guayaquil the corresponding results were 74.3 percent and 52.0 percent.[47]

Polling questions that examine the border issue in isolation do not provide a sense of the importance of this issue in relation to others. A poll carried out in June 1996, just before the final round of the Presidential election, asked potential voters in both Quito and Guayaquil if the candidate for whom they planned to vote would do better than his competitor on seven issues. One of the issues was negotiating with Peru, a particularly timely item given that the two countries had been negotiating a number of issues for more than a year.

Poll results indicate that for voters likely to support Bucaram, the difference between the two candidates on negotiating with Peru was less important than controlling inflation, stabilizing the economy, decreasing poverty, combating corruption or diminishing the number of strikes. For likely Nebot voters, however, negotiating with Peru and stabilizing the economy were the two issues on which they saw the greatest difference between the two candidates. The polling responses in table 7.2 and Bucaram's landslide victory suggest that while the border dispute with Peru is an important issue, it is not the defining issue in Ecuadorian politics.

The border issue can contribute, however, to a President's political troubles. Bucaram became the first Ecuadorian President to travel to Peru, for which some groups criticized him. But when, in a speech before the Peruvian Congress, he called for both sides to apologize, the uproar at home was nearly unanimous. Ecuadorians felt that they had no need to apologize, given that it was Peruvian "aggression" which had produced the problem in the first place. This *faux pas* contributed to Bucaram's impeachment a month later.[48]

Ecuadorian Presidents have military as well as civilian constituents. The military, while not interested in governing after 1976, did have an interest in the territorial issue. Civilians wanted the military to professionalize not only in order to implement the country's political-military strategy on the border but also as a means of ensuring the continuation of democracy. Since the return of democracy to Ecuador in 1979 four presidents oversaw the expansion of military capability. Thus even as the military's share of GNP declined dramatically under democracy, their capacity increased greatly.[49] Ecuador's military learned the lessons of their embarrassing defeat in 1981 and looked for the government to support its efforts to reverse the tables next time.[50]

After 1995 the Ecuadorian military became more amenable to an agreement even without sovereign access. The victory of 1995, after 150 years of defeats, helped the military regain its self-respect and made them heroes in the eyes of the public. The consensus within Ecuador, however, was that Peru would not accept a low-level stalemate or defeat the next time. The Ecuadorian military was not anxious for a large-scale war, both because the outcome was uncertain at best and the economic costs to the country would be disastrous. Continuation of the border tensions thus put the Ecuadorian military's hard-won prestige and national development at risk.[51] An agreement that conveyed a respect toward Ecuador could be accepted by the military as the fruits of its successful defense of Tiwintza.

Peru

Since redemocratization Peru has had three elected Presidents: Fernando Belaúnde 1980–85, Alán García (1985–90), and Alberto Fujimori (1990–present). Fujimori was also the leader during the authoritarian interlude between the dissolution of Congress in 1992 and the plebiscite in 1993 confirming the new constitution. While each leader had distinct constitu-

TABLE 7.2 Performance Expectations Among Likely Voters
(Percent)

Among Those Likely to Vote for Bucaram

Question #18	Jaime Nebot	Abdalá Bucaram	Both	Neither	Doesn't Know/No Response
There would be fewer poor	3.2	70.3	6.0	17.6	2.9
Prices would increase less	2.2	79.7	4.1	11.1	2.9
Would negotiate better w/Peru	20.4	55.7	8.5	7.6	7.7
Economy would be more stable	7.3	74.9	4.2	9.3	4.3
There would be less corruption	5.3	71.0	8.7	11.7	3.3
There would be fewer strikes and work stoppages	6.1	68.1	7.3	11.2	7.3
Public employees would be let go	34.5	43.3	8.1	5.9	8.4

Among Those Likely to Vote for Nebot

Question #18	Jaime Nebot	Abdalá Bucaram	Both	Neither	Doesn't Know/No Response
There would be fewer poor	63.4	5.1	3.9	24.2	3.4
Prices would increase less	65.3	8.6	6.1	15.2	4.8
Would negotiate better w/Peru	86.6	4.2	1.2	3.9	3.9
Economy would be more stable	84.3	4.3	2.0	5.6	3.7
There would be less corruption	74.9	5.3	4.0	13.4	2.4

TABLE 7.2 *(continued)*

Among Those Likely to Vote for Nebot

Question #18	Jaime Nebot	Abdalá Bucaram	Both	Neither	Doesn't Know/No Response
There would be fewer strikes and work stoppages	70.8	4.7	6.2	13.4	4.9
Public employees would be let go	47.0	30.0	9.2	6.3	7.4

Source: *Perfiles de Opinion* (Perfiles de Opinion, Cia. Ltda., Quito) #22, June 1996, 49–50

encies, no group expressed interest in resolving the dispute with Ecuador by renegotiating the Rio Protocol.

Belaúnde, elected by a broad national coalition, received 45 percent of the presidential vote, compared to the runner up's 27 percent. Since this was the first government in the transition to democracy, the military constituted an indirect constituency as well. Belaúnde's electoral coalition would collapse in protest over economic and social policy, as well as corruption.[52] Yet there was no pressure to change traditional policy toward Peru. The military wanted a convincing response in 1981 to deter future incursions by Ecuador, and Belaúnde worked closely with them. There were strong expressions of public sentiment in favor of expelling Ecuador from the area.[53]

García's populist coalition of center-left parties also controlled Congress with 105 of the 180 deputies and half of the 60 senators (the other half were distributed among 15 parties).[54] The leading constituencies in this multi-class alliance were nationally oriented business, the middle class and the urban working class. The promise of resources distributed by the state and nationalist ideology brought the alliance together. An economic crisis after 1987, partly the result of the populist program itself, split the alliance and led to García's dramatic fall in his approval ratings from more than 90% at the beginning of his term to just over 10% at the end.[55]

Fujimori's electoral coalition was not based on a traditional party and did not control congress from 1990–92 but did control the Democratic Constituent Congress (which also wrote the new constitution) from 1992–95 and the regular congress after the 1995 elections.[56] He won the 1990 elections in the second round with 62.4 percent of the vote, despite being outspent by runner up Mario Vargas Llosa by 60 to 1.[57] The success of his neoliberal reforms in controlling inflation and promoting growth, as well as his achievements in combating guerrilla violence made Fujimori extremely popular within Peru.[58]

In general Peruvians had a positive disposition toward Ecuador. In a poll conducted in January 1994, a year before the 1995 war, 63 percent of respondents perceived Ecuador as a "friendly country" and only 23 percent as an "enemy." (Peruvians, however, do refer derogatorily to Ecuadorians as "monos" [monkeys]. This may help explain why 49 percent of Ecuadorians saw Peru as an enemy.) In April of 1994 41 percent of Peruvians believed that "no problem" existed between the two countries because the Protocol had resolved it. Of those who saw a problem, more than half believed that the Guarantor Countries of the Protocol should arbitrate it. 73 percent believed that demarcation should proceed along the lines of the Protocol.[59]

Peruvians believed that Ecuador had been progressively intruding on Peruvian territory: 65 percent believed the troops had been there before 1994, and another 16 percent that they had arrived in 1994. During the 1995 war two opinion polls found overwhelming support for the actions of the armed forces (86.5% and 88.4%) and a bare majority approving of the behavior of the guarantor countries (54% and 57%). Fujimori's behavior during the war was supported by 59.2 percent. His chief rival Javier Pérez de Cuéllar, who advocated a more forceful response, received the approval of only 46.6 percent. Peruvians were aware that this conflict would not be a repeat of the mini-war of 1981: 34 percent thought it would take one or two months to expel the invaders and another 29 percent believed that it would take more than two months. The war was important enough that 55 percent believed that presidential elections should be postponed if the war continued.[60]

Peruvian opinion polarized around the manner in which the conflict could be resolved. A small majority in the two February 1995 polls (59% and 54%) supported mutual concessions but 27 percent in one poll and 40 percent in the other were opposed to any concessions. At the end of the war, 61 percent believed that no one had won and 25 percent that Peru had won. Another war was seen as very likely by 27 percent and likely by 40 percent. Only 13 percent thought it highly unlikely ("nada probable").[61]

In short, Peruvians generally supported the war effort, although they desired peace. A significant minority were unwilling to make concessions to Ecuador for peace, but the majority favored accommodation *as long as it was within the parameters of the Rio Protocol.*

Accountability of Leader to Constituencies

Ecuador

Ecuador's democratic polity is a presidential system. The president is elected every four years in national elections under a runoff system, in which a second round is held among the top two candidates if none receives at least 50 percent in the first round. The constitution was amended in the 1990s to allow reelection once, but not consecutively. The president selects his own cabinet, can propose legislation to the Congress, and can veto legislation; Congress can override his veto of nonbudgetary bills only by calling for a binding national plebiscite. The President can also go over Congress' head and propose a referendum on his proposals if Congress does not approve them.[62] In addition, he manages a "reserve fund" which is not subject to Congressional authorization or oversight, except in the case of corruption.

The legislature consists of one chamber, with 77 deputies. They cannot be reelected to consecutive terms. Twelve deputies are elected in national elections, with four-year terms. The remaining 65 are elected at the provincial level for two-year terms. Voters choose among "closed lists," that is, they choose parties rather than candidates themselves. Seats are allocated on a proportional representation basis. The electoral system has produced a weak and fragmented party system, in which parties multiply and elected officials switch parties easily.[63] One result is that the President's party never has control over Congress and legislation requires a coalition among parties.

Congress has significant leverage over the Executive in that it can censure cabinet members for political as well as criminal reasons; Ministers are frequently called to defend themselves and censure is commonplace. While the Constitution is ambiguous on whether the President must dismiss the censured minister, in practice he has always done so.[64] In 1997 Congress cynically utilized Constitutional provisions to drive out controversial President Bucaram on the unsubstantiated grounds of "mental incompetence." The political nature of the action was clearly evident, especially when Congress considered a constitutional amendment to bar any President removed from office for mental incompetence from ever running for office again![65]

Congress appoints the Supreme Court with parties receiving positions in proportion to their representation in the legislature. Justices are appointed for six-year terms, but are routinely replaced when a new Congress is elected.[66] The judiciary's dependence upon the Legislature further constrains the Executive in its relationship with the Legislature.

Ecuadorian civil society is well organized and willing to engage in pressure group activity independently from their representatives in Congress. In 1990 a newly organized group of indigenous communities, *Confederacion Nacionalidades Indígenas del Ecuador* (CONAIE), went on a national strike to demand attention to their economic and political plight; by 1996 they had become an important political party. Student groups, business associations, and unions went on a national strike in 1997 to protest against President Bucaram's administration. Mass demonstrations in the main plaza are a common occurrence.

The President of the Congress that impeached him succeeded Bucaram, but the new Interim President also quickly confronted strong opposition in Congress and from the public. His elected successor in 1998, Jamil Mahuad, was challenged with a national strike and demonstrations in the main plaza within six months of his landslide victory. In response to this pressure, Mahuad modified a number of the economic policies of his administration.[67]

The armed forces are the most respected institution in the country, far outdistancing the Congress or the Presidency.[68] Popular support is the basis for military influence in politics. Civil-military relations in Ecuador provide the military with considerable formal and informal autonomy. The Constitution gives the military a role in the social and economic development of the country, linking these to national security. Civilian expertise on defense matters is underdeveloped, thereby making it difficult for Congress to exercise significant oversight over defense policy. The military are guaranteed a share of revenue from petroleum exports, thus further reducing civilian control of the military budget. It is a treasonable act to defame the armed forces. A dependence upon the military for expertise, the weakness of Congressional oversight of military affairs, and the lack of a civilian as Minister of Defense suggest that the civil-military relationship is best characterized as one of weak civilian domination.[69]

The decision to move Ecuadorian troops into the disputed territory was at the very least known to the civilian leadership, and President Roldós even visited the outposts in August 1980.[70] Once the fighting began it is possible that the civilian government had little control over military operations,[71] but Roldós made the decision to ask the OAS and the "four friendly countries" to mediate. The military was not consulted and they did not seek to overturn the request.[72] The one coup attempt since the return to democracy was put down quickly by the Army in 1987.[73] Although the military may not have entirely agreed with President Durán Ballén's decision on how to terminate the military conflicts in 1995, they did not oppose it.[74]

The military can clearly weigh into a dispute and affect the outcome, therefore, a President has to consider their views. Since the military is not interested in governing,[75] the accountability of presidents to the military is indirect and depends more on the military's influence with sectors of civil society. Should politicians fail to resolve the political and economic crisis that confronted the country in the 1990s, public clamor for a more direct military role in governing is possible.[76]

Peru

Since redemocratization Peru has had two constitutions, one in 1979 and another in 1993 after President Fujimori closed Congress in 1992 and a Constituent Assembly was elected. Under the 1979 Constitution the legislature was bicameral but the 1993 Constitution responded to popular sentiment and made it unicameral.[77] Under the new constitution, the Congress elects a Permanent Commission of the Chamber, with members distributed proportionately among the parties represented in the legislature. The Permanent Commission has the power of impeachment, with Congress functioning as the jury.

Both Constitutions strengthened presidential power because stalemates between the legislature and executive were perceived by the respective Constituent Assemblies to have produced the coups of 1968 and 1992.[78] Both constitutions also stipulate five-year terms which coincide with presidential mandates; thus there is no possibility of a midterm check on the President. Legislative constraints on the Executive, nevertheless, continue to be important in Peru. Consequently, the 1993 Constitution should be seen as building upon a trend rather than as a break with the past.

Congress can censure a Minister for noncriminal reasons and he must resign. Under the 1979 Constitution if the Congress censured three Ministers the President could close the lower chamber and call for new elections within 30 days and under the existing electoral rules. Dissolution could not be invoked in the last year of a President's term or during a state of siege. If elections were not held within the allotted time, the dissolved Chamber reconstituted itself and the President's cabinet (Council of Ministers) was dismissed, with no member able to resume a cabinet position during the presidential tenure. The Senate could not be dissolved.[79] Since 1993 similar constraints on the Executive during the process of congressional dissolution prevail. Because there is now only one chamber in the legislature, it is the Permanent Commission of the Chamber that cannot be dissolved. The Permanent Commission, as well as the new Congress, are empowered to examine any decrees issued by the Executive during the intervening period.[80] Under both constitutions, a simple majority can overturn a presidential veto of legislation.[81]

The decree power of the executive was strengthened somewhat in 1993, although both Belaúnde and García utilized their decree powers extensively: they issued 2,086 and 2,290 decrees, respectively.[82] Under both Constitutions Congress can delegate decree power to the President for specified matters and time periods and Congress can overturn a decree.[83] Since 1993 the Executive can decree during a state of emergency or siege, but not on those matters "the Permanent Commission cannot delegate." States of emergency (during periods of internal disorder) only require notification of Congress and may not exceed 60 days without a new decree. States of siege (during periods of foreign and civil wars) may not exceed 45 days, Congress has the right to convene and any extension of the state of siege requires the approval of Congress.[84]

Electoral constraints on the President may have increased slightly under the 1993 Constitution. Previously, a president could be reelected, but only after one term held by another had transpired. Since parties are very centralized, and the President is leader of his party, presidents were unconcerned about subsequent elections. Since 1993 a president can be reelected for one immediate term, whereupon he must sit out a term before running for a new set of terms. Since Fujimori was first elected under the old constitution, he claimed that he could run for two terms under the new constitution.

Given decree powers, the structure of political parties, and the proscription against immediate re-election, Belaúnde and García may even have been under fewer institutionalized constraints than Fujimori, either from 1990–92 or under the new constitution until the electoral controversy of

June 2000. Although Belaúnde's coalition of center-right parties did not control Congress he pursued his agenda via decrees and knew that at his age (he would be over 80 at the end of his term), reelection after an intervening term was out of the question. García's party had control over Congress and he still made extensive use of his decree powers. Neither President made important changes in his governing program even after approval ratings fell precipitously. Belaúnde ended his term with a rating in the low 20 percent range and García with a rating in the teens. Fujimori had to avoid a fall in his ratings after the war, especially since his most likely rival for reelection at the time had a very high approval rating himself.

The institutional constraints proved utterly incapable of preventing Fujimori from closing Congress and purging the judiciary in 1992. His ability to override these constitutional constraints was fundamentally a result of the decline in the legitimacy of Congress and the Judiciary in the eyes of the public, the willingness of the military to support it, and the public's preoccupation with hyperinflation and Sendero Luminoso's guerrilla war. Immediately after the coup in 1992, 71 percent of those polled approved of closing Congress, 89 percent of restructuring the judiciary and 85.5 percent believed Fujimori should remain president.[85]

The new constitution enhanced a president's public policy prerogatives, but at a cost. The accountability of Fujimori to the new constitution, and therefore to his constituencies, increased after 1993. The constraints were not immediately apparent because his coalition won the congressional elections in 1995, giving him a majority with which to work in Congress.

The political dynamics of Peru changed in mid-2000, but the constitution still sets the parameters within which Fujimori has to function. Unable to annul elections and govern by decree, he had to hold the vote. Fujimori also had to engage in sufficiently marginal "irregularities" that the U.S. and Latin American governments, who have threatened sanctions against Guatemala, Paraguay and Ecuador when democracy was at risk, would recognize his victory. In addition, his party did not win a majority in Congress and he is actively seeking to convince some members of other parties to join his rather than close Congress.

We can gauge some of this accountability to the people and Congress at work during the 1995 war, which coincided with the presidential campaign. Fujimori's major opponent, former UN Secretary General Javier Pérez de Cuéllar and his military advisers, publicly wondered about Fujimori's ability to defend Peruvian interests and called for more severe action against Ecuador. In response, Fujimori claimed that his conciliatory policies had been designed to deceive Ecuador, and increased efforts to win on the battle-field.[86] Since Fujimori was not planning on ceding a sovereign access to Ecuador and regional economic development fits in with his neoliberal outlook (he sought similar programs with Chile), one should take this claim to be defensive campaign rhetoric. In March he offered Ecuador the carrot of a possible free zone in the Amazon, but as a result of congressional op-position, he retracted it.[87] Fujimori won in a landslide in April, although his victory probably had more to do with his success in bringing down inflation and curbing the Sendero Luminoso guerrillas, than with the war.

The question of the accountability of the president to the military is complex. Peruvian civil-military relations are best characterized as one of parallel spheres of influence, not civilian dominance.[88] The President has the initiative on national security policy, but operational control is largely in the hands of the military. Belaúnde first tried to use special police forces to deal with Sendero Luminoso. After Sendero defeated them in 1982, he, with the acquiescence of Congress, declared emergency zones which af-forded the military dramatically increased autonomy to deal with the guer-rillas. García initially attempted to strengthen civilian control over the armed forces by creating a Ministry of Defense and developing his own paramilitary and intelligence agents operating out of the Interior Ministry. But his deci-sion to rely on the Army to put down a prison revolt by Senderistas in 1987 and his attempt to promote APRA sympathizers within the officer corps short-circuited that effort.[89]

Fujimori made a bargain with one of the competing groups of officers to garner the institution's support for his government.[90] Some analysts see the military as severely constraining Fujimori. Purported evidence for this view is that he granted amnesty to the military for human rights violations carried out in the performance of their fight against internal subversion and nar-cotrafficking and military courts were given jurisdiction over civilians ac-cused of crimes against national security.[91] But Argentine President Carlos Menem (whose anti-militarist credentials are widely acknowledged[92]) also extended an amnesty to the military in an effort to end the human rights debate.[93] Fujimori himself prefers the bias of the military courts, and he kept General Nicolás de Bari Hermoza as chief of the Joint Command of the Armed Forces although the officer corps believed the General should have left his post upon retirement. During the war, and against military advice, Fujimori decided to go to Tiwintza, accompanied by the press.[94] Fujimori also removed Hermoza after the General claimed credit for the successful operation against the guerrillas holding the Japanese Ambassador and others hostage, as well as opposing a diplomatic settlement with Ecuador. In short, Fujimori retains the initiative with the military, makes a clear distinction between operational and policy questions, and is willing to intervene in operational questions when it affects his political program.[95]

President Fujimori made a number of public decisions that implied great domestic political risks for him[96] and his own personal authoritarian traits demonstrated his commitment to impose high costs on those who opposed his major projects. Fujimori seized upon the 1991 dispute to push for a definitive settlement, although he was criticized in the Congress for not dealing harshly with Ecuador.[97] In 1991, 92, and 93 he offered Ecuador a package linking economic development projects, a free port on the Amazon, reciprocal security measures, and arms limitations along the border in exchange for a border demarcation linked to the Protocol. His trip to Ecuador to offer details on the proposals represented the first by a Peruvian President; he would go three times.

At the same time Fujimori extended the olive branch (on Peruvian terms), he demonstrated his unwillingness to compromise on fundamental points. In early 1991 Ecuador asked privately that Peru abandon the disputed outpost. Peru's initial threats and subsequent refusal to abide by the agreement to mutually withdraw forces dramatically increased tensions and spiraled into the war in 1995. In 1992 Fujimori presented another indication of his refusal to bargain on major points in general when he responded to congressional opposition to his domestic policies by closing Congress.[98]

Summary of Constituent Cost Acceptance and Decision-Maker Accountability

Constituencies in both countries were knowledgeable about the dispute and favored a resolution, but with the other side making the greatest concessions. They repeatedly demonstrated a willingness to accept the costs of war *if it were necessary to defend their interests* in the Amazon. As long as Peru refused to recognize the legitimacy of their claims for renegotiation, Ecuadorians supported the militarized bargaining strategy even at the expense of the economic benefits they expected from better relations with

Peru. For their part, Peruvians supported using military force to defend the Rio Protocol.

Redemocratization did not imply great accountability of Presidents to either the legislature or the electorate. In Ecuador, this slippage after election was largely the result of the prohibition on reelection and the weakness of the party system, especially in Congress. In Peru, Presidents were theoretically slightly more accountable because they only had to sit out one term before competing for the Presidency again. But Belaúnde had no expectations of winning another term because he was already in his 80s. And García felt little accountability to the electorate, apparently miscalculating that the APRA party could survive voter disapproval in the 1980s.

Conclusion

What does the analysis of the Ecuador and Peru enduring rivalry suggest about the utility of the militarized bargaining framework for explaining the use of military force among democracies? Ecuador's consistent use of military force to challenge the Rio Protocol made little sense in a hegemonic management, democratic peace, or balance of power analysis. But it becomes comprehensible in a militarized bargaining framework.

Ecuador's population disputed the terms of the treaty ending the 1941 war. Ecuador's leaders consistently sought the means to challenge the status quo not as a diversionary tactic, but because their constituencies wanted a favorable resolution of the Amazon issue. The geographic error in the Protocol provided Ecuador with an opportunity to devise a political-military strategy to achieve an outlet to the Amazon. But it initially had neither the diplomatic nor the military ability to persuade third parties to pressure Peru into negotiating a new settlement. Changes in the characteristics of the force used, as well as in planning its use, were implemented across four different presidencies. These changes produced a shift in the strategic balance by 1995 at a cost acceptable to the majority of the population and to the military. Seizing the diplomatic initiative as peacemaker for the first time ever in its conflict, it forced the Guarantor Countries into an active role for the first time since the 1941 war.

Peru was the defender of the post-1941 status quo that granted Ecuador no sovereign access to the Amazon. Whereas Ecuador had an appreciation for the complexity of militarized bargaining, Peru did not. Fujimori's economic carrots were not linked to military policies that could have deterred Ecuador's strategy. Peru adopted a straightforward political-military strategy for defending the Protocol. As a defender of an internationally recognized status quo, Peru refused to reopen the question. Coercive diplomacy was promised at the local level to dissuade incursions, and another blitzkrieg into southern Ecuador was threatened if the first approach failed. While these military policies were an appropriate response in 1941 and 1981, when Peru's military capability diminished, its strategy became vulnerable to third party influence.

Because Peru did not have a dynamic sense of the strategic balance, it found itself forced to escalate the fighting. Not only did it fail to dislodge the Ecuadorians, in the eyes of many of its traditional international supporters Peru transformed itself from a defender of the status quo into a threat to the regional peace.

Ironically, the Ecuador/Peru dyad presents a case in which the transition to democracy actually increased the likelihood of violence. Popular sentiment opposed acceptance of the treaty at least since 1979 and across regime types. The Ecuadorian diplomatic corps opposed the principle of treaty abrogation at least since 1981. The key variable that changed by 1995 was the balance of military capability. In the transition to democracy, civilians supported "professionalization" of the military as a means of ensuring the continuation of democracy. No longer burdened by governing, the Ecuadorian military could focus on "professionalizing," which meant preparation to defend against its most likely foreign adversary, Peru. The resulting shift in the balance of military capabilities allowed Ecuador to pursue a strategy reminiscent of the early 1950s: diplomatic appeals to the international community underpinned by a level of military tension in the zone of conflict. In this context, Peru's resoluteness in defending its gains in the 1941 war, far from deterring Ecuador, ensured that militarization of disputes would plague the enduring rivalry until a definitive settlement could be obtained.

Part 3

Conclusion

8 Militarized Bargaining in Latin America: Prospects for Diminishing Its Use

This book proposed that thinking about international politics as a bargaining situation and the use of military force as a policy option available to decisionmakers gives insight into the dynamics of militarized conflict. As one of numerous options, the decision to use force was hypothesized to respond to a cost-benefit analysis. The factors considered in the analysis were identified as the political-military strategy for using force (S), the strategic balance (SB), the characteristics of force to be used (CF), the willingness of constituencies to accept costs (CC), and the level of accountability of the decisionmaker to her constituency (A). The relationship among these five variables was postulated as

$$S + SB + CF \leq CC - A: \quad \text{force might be used}$$
$$S + SB + CF < CC - A: \quad \text{force will not be used}$$

Chapters 2, 6, and 7 provided the evidence for the plausibility of this approach to understanding the use of military force. The historical data in chapter 2 indicated that militarized interstate conflict in Latin America was prevalent enough for the region to serve as a data set for analyzing the use of force. The historical record includes not only Latin American countries using force against each other, but also great powers, especially the U.S., adopting militarized bargaining tactics in their relations with Latin American nations.

I first illustrated the need for a model like militarized bargaining by demonstrating that the three major arguments purporting to explain the use of military force in this security complex failed to stand up to empirical evaluation. Chapter 3 presented a strong case that the U.S. could not provide hegemonic management of conflict in this security complex. Though the U.S. was paramount in the region, conflict among individual states had a security dynamic that escaped U.S. control, for good or ill. There was evidence that during the Cold War the U.S. aggravated the tendency to engage in militarized bargaining, but even during this period the U.S. was not the sole reason for states utilizing military force.

Chapter 4 examined evidence for the democratic peace argument, and established that the conflict behavior of democratic governments does not differ from that of nondemocratic regimes. Democracy was a weak variable even when the distribution of power was taken into consideration, as in chapter 5. Chapter 7 confirmed that democratic politics could keep an interstate dispute alive between two democracies, even to the point of war.

The third argument, that the distribution of power explains the use of force, fared no better in explaining militarized interstate disputes in Latin America. Chapter 5 demonstrated that neither parity nor preponderance correlated strongly with the decision to use force. In the particular case of war, an interesting finding was that the weaker power was likely to initiate it.

In this concluding chapter I move beyond Latin America's historical experience to think about how the occurrence of militarized disputes can be reduced in the future. First I review the negotiating situation and performance of the five factors of militarized bargaining in the case studies. Then we turn to some speculation about how one might affect the calculus of militarized bargaining and decrease its frequency.

Evaluating the Contribution of the Militarized Bargaining Model

Militarized bargaining proved to be a powerful analytical framework for examining the conflict dynamics within the Latin American security complex. Each of the disputes examined in detail evolved over time. Negotiations were proposed by at least one party, but either the other did not respond (Peru between 1950–1995) or had a bargaining range which produced a stalemate (Peru and Ecuador from 1995–1998; Chile and Argentina from 1977–1984; and Argentina and Britain from the 1960s to 1982). In each of the cases the initiating state sought to affect the negotiations by engaging in some military activity.

Statements of the actors, interviews and an analysis of actual behavior allow us to reconstruct the situation for each of the variables in the case studies. The structured and focused analyses in Chapters 6 and 7 demonstrated the utility of examining the five variables for understanding the decision to militarize a dispute. The following sections review the performance of the variables of the model in the cases under discussion.

Political-Military Strategy

I argued that the utility of force as a policy instrument has to be evaluated in the first instance in terms of its contribution to the policymaker's ability to advance her constituencies' interests. Advancing those interests can occur in different ways, depending upon the state of the relationship between the contending parties. These alternatives were summarized in five political-military strategies.

- keep the issue alive
- affect bilateral negotiations
- defend the status quo
- attract the support of third parties
- impose a solution

The case studies provided evidence of each of these strategies. After 1950 Ecuador had no diplomatic possibility of persuading Peru to reconsider its battlefield victories or of inducing the guarantor countries of the Rio Protocol to demand a rewrite of the treaty. Neither could it militarily force Peru to broaden its bargaining range to even discuss the issue. Multiple third parties were interested in promoting a peaceful final settlement, but they would not intervene without the acquiescence of Peru. Yet Peru had no incentive to bring third parties into the dispute outside of the Rio Protocol framework. The decision by Ecuadorian presidents to first declare the Protocol inapplicable and later null, and to provoke incidents on the border were reminders by policymakers to Peru, the international community, and their domestic constituencies that the issue was still alive.

The use of force by the Argentine military governments in the two cases examined was designed to affect bilateral negotiations. Argentine leaders responded to the Arbitral Award in 1977 proposing new negotiations with Chile. When Chile was amenable to discussing all matters not covered in the Award, Argentina used force to first communicate its commitment to the bi-oceanic principle and subsequently to attempt to bully Chile into broadening its bargaining range. In the Malvinas case, Argentina and Britain had been negotiating the issue of the islands for almost twenty years. To the Argentines' chagrin, the British government refused to discuss the issue of sovereignty. The Argentine leaders expected the British to be isolated in their efforts to regain the islands once Argentina controlled them. Under these conditions, British leaders were expected to negotiate a settlement recognizing Argentine sovereignty.

Peru and Chile both confronted adversaries who wished to change a status quo that was favorable to Peru vis-à-vis Ecuador (1950–1998) and Chile vis-à-vis Argentina (1977–1984). Their use of force was clearly defensive, which worked to their international advantage. The British response to the Argentine seizure of the Malvinas Islands was also couched in terms of defending the status quo from aggression.

In 1941 Peru sought to impose a solution on its rival. Peru's political-military strategy was to drive deep into undisputed Ecuadorian territory and hold it until Ecuador agreed to Peruvian terms. In the Malvinas case it was the British who refused to negotiate before a return to the *status quo ante* and insisted on militarily imposing those conditions.

Strategic Balance

The strategic balance referred to the factors outside the battlefield which influence the likely costs produced by the strategies that each actor can use in particular disputes. It was hypothesized that the appropriateness of a means of assessing the strategic balance depended upon the particular political-military strategy one was utilizing and the political-military strategy one was confronting. The strategic balance was defined by the resources that are relevant to those strategies; it thus helps us understand the bargaining situation between the actors.

Three broad categories of resources were hypothesized as useful in considering the strategic balance: diplomatic, economic, and military. Diplomatic resources were clearly important in the Ecuadorian militarized bargaining. Although Peru would likely win any all out war, inter-American diplomatic pressure *combined with* Ecuador's newly augmented defensive capabilities to convince President Fujimori that he should permit the Guarantors of the Rio Protocol to oversee bilateral negotiations. When negotiations stalled, Ecuador's diplomatic advantages enabled it to persuade the Guarantors to compensate it with the unique monument in Tiwintza. Peru received the minimum from the Guarantors (a border demarcation in accordance with generally accepted interpretations of the Protocol) and had to accept a monument to soldiers who died defending an outpost against Peruvian soldiers, as well as financing most of the joint economic development projects.

In the Beagle dispute, the overall military balance was fundamental. The rough military equivalence between the two countries, once we consider quality of soldier and defensive advantages, limited militarized bargaining between the two countries. Argentine military planners could not expect a short war with Chile if they seized the islands. In the Amazon dispute, the overall military balance always favored Peru and the local military balance long favored Peru. But when the local military balance shifted away from Peru, the dispute dynamics changed dramatically.

Economic resources were not a particularly useful negotiating tool in the two case studies examined. The parties certainly wanted economic benefits, but not at the expense of the particular issue in question. Examples include the Ecuadorian responses to Fujimori's offers in 1991–93. In addition, Argentina had initially accepted arbitration of the Beagle dispute precisely because it wanted better economic relations with Chile. Trade between the two did increase through the mid-1970s. But the decline in trade after 1977 did not deter Argentine dictators or democrats from insisting on the bioceanic principle as part of any settlement.

When decisionmakers determined that the costs of continued militarized bargaining were too high and looked for a way out of the dispute, economic side payments seemed to make a difference. Ecuador lost on the border demarcation, but gained in the economic realm with sovereign port facilities on the Peruvian Amazon, physical infrastructure linking those facilities to Ecuadorian ports in the Pacific, and the promise of international aid for joint economic development programs. The Treaty of Peace and Friendship, in which Chileans gave up the windfall of projection into the Atlantic, contains a section on economic development projects.

Characteristics of Force to be Used

The countries involved in the case studies all used different levels of force in their militarized bargaining. In the Beagle dispute, reserves were called up, airspace was violated, forces engaged in provocative maneuvers, and the Argentines even shelled uninhabited islands. Both states were engaged in signaling and sought to avoid physical contact right up to the day the order for seizing the islands was given. Victory, although expected, would likely have been costly to the Argentines because it would have entailed the use of all of its military assets.

Argentina began its MID with Britain expecting to avoid an actual military clash. The seizure of the Malvinas Islands was carried out with extreme care and with such overwhelming force as to ensure that British casualties would be nonexistent or minimal. In a clear indication that they expected the costs of the war to be high, the Argentine Junta refused to commit its full forces even after the war began. The Army left its best troops on the troubled border with Chile, while the Navy bottled up its ships after the sinking of the *Belgrano* by a British nuclear submarine. Only the Air Force committed its major resources. The Argentine Army and Naval leadership preferred to face the domestic political costs of defeat with their organization's resources largely intact.

Peruvian perceptions of Ecuadorian capabilities led them to believe that they could use limited but superior land, air, and sea forces to quickly defeat Ecuador. Before 1981 Ecuadorian decisionmakers recognized this power disparity, but believed that Peru would not overreact to minor incursions with escalation to war and that the international community would intervene to avoid future incidents, however small. By 1981 the international community had repeatedly demonstrated an unwillingness to become involved over Peru's objection and Peru had responded with a major use of force. As a result, the Ecuadorians altered their equipment and tactics in the late 1980s. By 1995 they could defend their outposts with a small land force. Peru was denied a quick victory in 1995, even after escalating its response at the local level. President Fujimori backed down from dramatically increasing the level and quantity of force used.

Constituency Costs Acceptability

The willingness of constituencies to accept the costs of militarization was expected to play an important role in leaders' decisions to use force. In the cases examined, acceptance of these costs did not break down by political regime type. Constituencies of authoritarian governments showed no greater willingness to pay costs than the constituencies of democratic governments. Nor did democrats demonstrate an unwillingness to use force against other democrats, at either low MID levels or even in war. Although it was difficult to calculate with any precision the level of costs constituencies were willing to accept, their general attitudes, and even eagerness, were expressed in a variety of ways and influenced decisionmakers.

During the Beagle crisis Pinochet's constituencies in the military and Chilean society were in accord with the decision to defend Chilean territory if the Argentines attempted to seize the islands. There were even indications that the opposition in exile believed that Chile was correct in defending the Arbitral Award. From 1977–1984 Pinochet was willing to negotiate on issues other than the islands, and this was a stance supported by his constituency. The option of defending the Award militarily rather than capitulating to Argentine military threats was clearly popular. When Pinochet finally accepted the bi-oceanic principle, among his constituency only the Air Force Commander in Chief continued to prefer the possibility of war with Argentina.

The Argentine constituencies of the Videla, Viola, Galtieri, and Alfonsín governments were distinct, yet all supported the bi-oceanic principle. Videla and Viola had clear demonstrations from the military branches that they preferred to keep the option of war open as long as Chile did not cede on the bi-oceanic principle. By December 1978 the Army officer corps, led by their Commander in Chief Galtieri, was willing to pay the costs of war rather than drag the status quo of disagreement on longer; the other services followed their lead. But the military did grab at the straw handed them by the Pope's intercession once Chile agreed not to limit the scope of the negotiations. This was a clear demonstration that even these military officers preferred to continue talking if there were a possibility of success rather than to pay the high cost of a war which they believed they could win.

It was difficult to find evidence for the Argentine electorate's views on the bi-oceanic principle after the ignominious defeat in the Malvinas. Alfonsín and the opposition Peronists believed that the public favored no deal over concessions to Chile. Alfonsín's government campaigned for an agreement with an explicit promise that the bi-oceanic principle would be included. The Peronist opposition was willing to keep the dispute alive rather than recognize Chilean sovereignty over the islands and voted against the treaty. But even the Peronists did not call for outright seizure rather than negotiations. In the wake of Malvinas, militarized conflict with Chile was unlikely to be popular.

In the Malvinas case the Argentine public expressed its pleasure in massive demonstrations when the islands were seized. The political parties themselves made regaining sovereignty in 1982 a component of their own platform calling for a return to democracy. Despite reports that the British were preparing a task force to regain the islands, there were neither public demonstrations nor political parties calling for peacefully returning the islands to the British. Civil society turned against the war only after it became clear that they were losing. The Argentine public appeared willing to pay the cost of 1,000 dead soldiers if the British had not recovered the islands.[1] Once the war was lost, however, massive demonstrations did occur against Galtieri's government.

Prime Minister Thatcher's constituencies all clamored for using military force if necessary to regain the islands. The Labour opposition believed it could gain support among the British electorate by attacking the Thatcher government for its inability to dissuade the Argentines from acting. The military build-up took weeks and was well reported in the press. Yet few voices were raised against the potential use of force. After the sinking of the *Belgrano* public opposition to the war increased, but still remained insignificant among the Conservative government's constituency.[2]

The Peruvian and Ecuadorian publics indicated a willingness to pay unspecified costs. The Ecuadorian polls after the 1981 debacle and the 1995 war were particularly revealing of both nationalist fervor and support for Ecuador's use of force. War on the scale of 1995 was certainly acceptable to the constituencies of both Durán Ballén and Fujimori. There is not enough evidence to know why Fujimori refused to escalate to all-out war. One could speculate that he feared the public would rebel once the costs became clear, though his constituency in the military seemed willing to escalate. Alternatively, he may have feared that his own political-economic program for modernizing Peru could not absorb the cost. The important factor for our purposes is that his decision to initially respond with force was made after his electoral opponents criticized him for weakness and that the decision to escalate was supported in the polls taken at the time.

Leadership Accountability

The accountability of leaders, as indicated by the ability of constituencies to affect whether or not the leader remains in office, ranged across the full spectrum, from highly accountable to very weakly so (table 8.1). Curiously, the most accountable from our cases included a military dictatorship as well as a parliamentary democracy. As the militarized bargaining model postulates, and the prior section underscores, the key factor is not accountability *per se*, but the junction of accountability with constituencies' willingness to bear costs. Thus we have the seemingly paradoxical scenario of a military junta first pushing its leader into declaring war, then pulling him back at the last minute (Argentina in the Beagle crisis), and a parliamentary democracy eager to support its leader's decision to wage war (Britain in the Malvinas).

Generals Videla and Viola and Prime Minister Thatcher were the most accountable to their constituencies because they could be removed at a moment's notice by the Junta and Parliament, respectively. Videla was so constrained that he lost decisionmaking power at the most critical point of the Beagle crisis. He chose to go along with the decision to seize the islands, fully expecting it to lead to a war that he did not want, because to oppose it would mean falling from office and failure of his political project. Viola fell from office in less than a year. Thatcher scapegoated a Cabinet Minister and would likely have fallen from office herself if the task force had not regained the Malvinas islands.

Velasco Ibarra was the most accountable of the democratic Presidents, but nevertheless was less so than the Junta leaders or prime ministers. During his time Ecuador allowed unlimited reelection, and he was in fact elected President five times and overthrown by the military four times. I am assuming that a military coup against an elected leader is more difficult for the military to undertake than to replace the head of a military junta. Velasco Ibarra took a dramatic step that significantly complicated future interactions between Ecuador and Peru when he declared the Rio Protocol null and void.

TABLE 8.1 Leadership Accountability in Chapters Six and Seven

Degree of Accountability	Reason	Leaders	Type of Government
Severe	Could fall at a moment's notice	Videla, Viola, Thatcher	Military junta—parliamentary democracy
Great	Future terms at risk (Leader himself or party)	Velasco Ibarra, Fujimori, Alfonsín, Galtieri	Presidential democracy military government seeking transition to electoral regime
Moderately accountable	One term reelection and weak party	Ecuadorian presidents after reelection	Presidential democracy
Not very	No reelection and weak party/one term non-consecutive reelection with decree powers	Ecuadorian presidents 1979–96, Alan García	Presidential democracy
Slight	Military leader controls junta/octogenarian leader of a weak party with decree powers	Pinochet, Belaúnde	Military government—presidential democracy

Within this same degree of accountability are Fujimori and Alfonsín. Fujimori was expecting to compete for reelection after 1992, and the 1995 war occurred during the presidential campaign. Since the 1993 Constitution allows unlimited reelection following a pattern of two consecutive terms in, one term out, Fujimori would feel his vulnerability to both the electorate and the military should he seek to carry out another coup. During the last stages of the Beagle negotiations, Alfonsín, even after the Malvinas defeat, did not believe he could accept Chilean projection into the Atlantic and still retain popular support for his government. Although under the constitutional rules of 1984 he could not be re-elected, as leader of the Radical Party Alfonsín feared electoral punishment for his party, especially since the Peronists had been the majority party since World War II. Galtieri was also quite vulnerable to the constituency he was attempting to create in order to achieve an electoral victory in the transition from a military government to a minimally democratic one.

The leaders who were at best moderately accountable were those from weak parties with reelection possibilities after sitting out a term. Ecuador's presidents after the 1996 reform of the 1979 Constitution fit this description. With weak and personalist parties, they could not expect, nor did they particularly care, if someone from their party succeeded them in office. The possibility of reelection is the main mechanism holding these leaders accountable. The successful impeachment of President Bucaram of Ecuador in 1998 on questionable legal grounds will most likely haunt his successors for a few years, but repeated use of this process would undoubtedly produce a transition to a different type of government. Consequently, it is unlikely to be used again.

The weakest accountability of democratically elected leaders occurred in situations when reelection was prohibited and weak party structure minimized the chances of succession by a party member. Such was the case in Ecuador between 1979–1996. In Peru, Alan García's term represented the anomalous case of a president who could not succeed himself, but could be re-elected, and whose strong APRA party controlled Congress. In this situation García assumed a lack of accountability which was not borne out by history: he made extensive use of decree power to govern, leaving office with an approval rating barely over 10 percent. Partly in response to this maverick behavior, the party system collapsed in Peru and García seems unlikely to ever be re-elected.

At the opposite end of the regime spectrum from democracy, Pinochet was very unaccountable to his constituencies because of the peculiarities of the 1973 coup. Chile's right wing forces and military feared a return of the radical left to a degree unknown in Argentina, where the Dirty War had eliminated the radical left. Pinochet played this card extremely well in the years of the Beagle dispute as he consolidated personal control over the government and marginalized the Junta. Belaúnde enjoyed a great degree of autonomy from his constituencies because he was too old to run for reelection (he died shortly after leaving office), he made frequent use of decree powers to govern, and his party was a personalist organization unlikely to win without his candidacy.

In summary, available data confirm that the five factors in the militarized bargaining model play significant roles in the cases examined.

Although constituency cost was difficult to ascertain with great precision in both Latin American democracies and military governments, we have sufficient indications that leaders considered some general parameters and avoided making decisions against their constituencies' wishes. These cases should provide sufficient plausibility for the model of militarized bargaining to stimulate further case study work on these and other cases.

Minimizing the Incentives to Militarize Disputes

In the wake of the recent experience of militarized disputes in Latin America, discussion of new schemes for "managing" regional security is widespread within diplomatic and academic circles.[3] Many policymakers and analysts believe that redemocratization, economic restructuring, and the end of the Cold War represent a watershed in the security environment of Latin America and will be sufficient to produce peace. This book clearly demonstrates, however, that the use of force in Latin America's interstate relations will not be banished so easily.

The militarized bargaining model suggests that the costs of initiating force need to be increased on either side of the inequality. Thus $S + SB + CF$ must be greater than $CC - A$. This can be accomplished either by increasing the costs of the use of force, or diminishing the acceptable level of costs for the leader. The following section will evaluate current proposals to limit the use of force in terms of the militarized bargaining model to discover their strengths and weaknesses.

Strengthening Democratic Institutions

Much of the focus of inter-American security policy has been to increase the accountability of leaders by strengthening democratic institutions.[4] These discussions at the level of governments assume that all Latin American countries except Cuba are democratic. Chapters 4 and 7 addressed some problems with the democratic peace approach. Here our focus is on how strengthening democratic accountability can operate in conjunction with the four other factors in the militarized bargaining model in order to minimize the probability of the use of force.

A number of problems arise with this approach to a less violent peace in the region. The first is definitional. Mexico certainly does not meet the criteria for democracy that democratic peace advocates have in mind. Second, merely having democratic institutions, even those ranking high on the Polity scale, does not guarantee tight accountability. Third, if the willingness of democratic constituencies to accept the costs of militarized bargaining is not diminished, increasing the leadership's accountability might still yield an equation favoring the use of force in a dispute. Fourth, the characteristics of force to be used in a particular situation might produce few economic, diplomatic, or personnel costs, and therefore fall within the range of cost acceptance of the democratic public. Finally, the model indicates that addressing one variable in isolation from the others may not produce the desired outcome since it is the interaction among the five that matters.

Strengthening democratic institutions not only affects leadership accountability, but may also serve to increase the size and breadth of the leader's constituency. Democratic peace advocates expect that having a larger and more diverse electorate will make it more difficult to gain support for utilizing force. Yet this book has demonstrated that democratic publics are willing to pay the costs associated with military force in order to achieve what they believe is a just settlement, even against another democracy. And Pinochet's ability to negotiate away Chile's projection into the Atlantic demonstrates that it is not always bad for policy outcomes when a leader is less constrained.

Economic Integration of the Americas

The idea that trade brings peace is an old one, in both Europe and the Americas.[5] Its contemporary manifestation adds the circulation of capital to the movement of goods. The basic point is the same: if people stand to lose economically from conflict, they will be more likely to resolve or peacefully manage their disagreements.

Many analysts and policymakers perceive the historically rapid rates of economic integration among various groups of Latin American nations as indicative of a decreased security threat environment.[6] New economic relationships are springing up even among states that in the past saw each other as rivals. These relationships are becoming institutionalized into organizations that perceive positive security payoffs as well: Mercosur, the Andean Group, and the Central American Integration System.[7]

Yet some governments, democratic as well as authoritarian, have demonstrated a willingness to forego the advantages of economic integration in order to pursue other national goals. Democratic El Salvador attacked Honduras in 1969 even though the war helped to destroy the Central American Common Market that had brought it significant economic benefits.[8] Ecuador and Peru in the late 1970s and early 1990s were willing to forego current and future economic benefits rather than accept its adversary's solution to the dispute. Despite a free trade agreement, Colombia and Venezuela tried to isolate economic integration from territorial issues in the 1990s rather than use the former to solve the latter. And Cuba to date has preferred national independence to participation in the U.S. schemes for economic development in the Caribbean Basin.

Clearly, the material benefits of economic integration by themselves have not been sufficient to ameliorate the region's violent peace. Once again, the model of militarized bargaining helps us understand why. Economic costs per se do not matter; rather one needs to assess their impact on political-military strategies, the strategic balance, the characteristics of force used, the willingness of constituencies to pay costs and the accountability of the leader to her constituencies. It is these factors which determine whether militarizing a disagreement is beneficial or not.

Arms Control and Other Confidence Building Measures

The purpose of arms control is twofold: to mitigate the security dilemma and to limit damage if an armed confrontation should occur. The underlying assumptions of this approach to conflict management are that disarmament is not feasible, at least in the short term, and that there is a possibility that states will utilize their military force against each other, either purposefully or inadvertently.[9] If rival states work together to control armaments, they build confidence in each other's willingness to avoid the use of force; consequently, the security dilemma is mitigated. And if force should be used, prior arms control can mean that the more destructive types of weapons are not available for use.

As Chapters 2 and 5 indicate, arms control is not a new subject in Latin America. Arms control and CBMs are not simple issues, dependent solely upon political will and an unmitigated good. Rather they are complex, with potential spillovers that are not often considered. The model of militarized bargaining provides a way to think about the conditions under which arms control and CBMs may be stabilizing or destabilizing factors in a rivalry.

OAS resolutions frequently refer to "legitimate defense requirements" when discussing curbing arms proliferation, but what does the phrase mean in practice? Arms registries in principle contribute to confidence building, but are less meaningful in the absence of agreement on what constitutes stable force levels. The strategic balance and characteristics of force to be used will affect the costs that constituencies are asked to pay in the different political-military strategies. The lower the costs associated with the use of force, the more likely that its use will be accepted by the constituencies.

Arms control and CBM efforts may be directed toward diminishing capabilities to attack another country. Nonoffensive defense appears ideal in that if everyone had strictly defensive capabilities, offense would be impossible. But geography (as in the case of the long narrow terrain of Chile) and technology can facilitate turning a defensive capability into an offensive one with a shift in military doctrine.[10] For example, Ecuador's increased defensive capabilities gave it an ability to militarily contest its border with Peru, resulting in the 1995 border war.

The two most conflictual democratic dyads, Colombia-Venezuela and Ecuador-Peru, were characterized in the 1980s-1990s by asymmetrical force behavior. Colombia and Ecuador both increased the size of their armed forces while rivals Venezuela increased slightly and ended with roughly the same size, and Peru decreased its armed forces significantly. Differences in internal threats are not sufficient to explain this contrasting behavior. Peru faced dramatically increased guerrilla activity from Sendero Luminoso in this period, but still steadily decreased its armed forces by almost 50 percent (from 8.9 per 1,000 inhabitants to 4.8). Ecuador had no internal guerrilla threat yet increased its military personnel. Colombia faced an internal threat but also began its military build-up in 1987, when the Caldas incident with Venezuela precipitated putting its military forces on alert.[11]

Many Latin American civilian leaders do not feel secure with a unilaterally and significantly diminished military presence, even in the absence of immediate security threats. Contemporary Argentina, democratic for 10 years and with clear civilian control of a dramatically downsized and politically weakened military, argues that the level of air power attained by the military government before the Malvinas fiasco is the norm to which it must rebuild to be secure.[12] In fact, Argentina has significantly increased its radar capabilities in the most recent purchases, even threatening to buy the radar from Israel if the U.S. continues to respect British desires for a weakened Argentine air force.[13] Although Chile does not perceive an immediate threat from Peru, it is also upgrading its Air Force with purchases of Mirages that will be renovated to be, as the Air Force commander in chief said, on a par with the Peruvian air fleet.[14] The performance of Ecuador's SAMs against Peruvian fighter bombers and helicopters will also fuel the perception across Latin America that future defense tasks will require more sophisticated equipment on both the ground and in the air.

The need for a deterrent military force is not simply a perception of the military and political leadership in Latin America. After the 1995 war more than 70 percent of the respondents in Ecuador believed that Peru would attack again. In Chile 46 percent of respondents in a 1992 survey believed that an attack by Argentina was possible and an equal percentage believed that an outlet to the Pacific for Bolivia constituted a threat for Chile.[15] The nationalist rhetoric in both Ecuador and Peru during the recent border war was very high and acrimonious, again despite the fact that both countries are democracies.

In short, arms control and CBMs, even in conjunction with democratization and economic integration, do not provide sufficient reason to expect a violent peace to become less violent. They are merely policies and structures; what matters is their impact on the factors which make the decision to use force rational.

The Importance of Mutually Reinforcing Incentives for Peace

The contemporary challenge for a more peaceful means of managing conflict in Latin America's security complex is to push the military threshold farther back, rather than to search for its elimination. The militarized bargaining model ultimately suggests that we may be best off with a combination of policies that affect power and values. Decreasing the military costs of confrontation without changing the values of the constituencies in each rival state can merely make violent clashes more likely as those who wish to bargain militarily find it cheap to do so. And even if society's values change and the good in question is devalued, if the military costs associated with using force are not altered the strong can still find it rational to intimidate, coerce and even invade the weak. The weak, in turn, can continue to irritate the strong in hopes of attracting third party attention.

Rather than blame strategic balancing and military weapons for undermining peace in the region, we should instead recognize their contribution to keeping the violent peace from escalating to reproduce the European experience until its occupation by the U.S. and Soviet Union after 1945. We should also note that economic growth and democratization in the absence of a stable and credible balance of power are more likely to be recipes for increased conflict, rather than the first steps toward integration or a pluralist security community. Prudence and cautious optimism promise to deliver more security to Latin America than euphoric idealism.

Appendix

Argentine and Chilean Behavior in the Beagle
Dispute 1977–1984

- 1977: Sends early signals to Chile that military force was an option.
- September 1977: mobilizes part of its fleet and increases movements in the south
- December 1977: troops deployed, munitions shipped, and air force activity intensified in the south
- January 1978: declares the decision by the arbiter, Queen Elizabeth II, null and void.
- January–February 1978: Argentine Third Army Corps undertakes major maneuvers in the north
- January–September 1978: Argentine economic harassment under guise of national security: law is passed which allows delaying trucks at border; some border passes are closed; transshipments from Brazil are impeded; Chilean trucks are charged up to $1,000 for "escorts" and "security goods" and are taxed going into Chile; Argentina also begins expelling Chilean citizens
- September 1978: Argentina commences blackout and air raid drills in provincial cities
- May 1978: Argentine Junta attends an unusually large air force display
- June 1978: Argentine army and air force engage in war games in the south
- October 1978: 500,000 Argentine reservists are called up

- October 24, 1978: Buenos Aires has blackout drill with sirens and alarms
- November 2, 1978: both countries begin total mobilization, troops to borders, and navies move south
- December 14, 1978: President Videla gives orders to invade the islands
- December 21, 1978: Argentina drafts declaration of war; both armed forces at full state of alert
- December 22, 1978: bad weather postpones seizure of islands
- December 23, 1978: Papal message; Argentina calls off the invasion
- January 5, 1979: Argentine Junta agrees to submit dispute to papal mediation
- January 8, 1979: Chile and Argentina agree to force withdrawals and renounce use of force; Chile drops objection to including islands in discussion
- March 4, 1979: mediation begins in Rome, ignoring islands and sea issues, focusing on other issues in the relationship to build trust first
- May 1980: after 200 meetings, a turn to territorial and maritime boundaries issue
- Chile changes mind and cedes on Cape Horn as overflight boundary
- December 12, 1980: Papal proposal for limited Chilean offshore rights and creation of Sea of Peace
- January 1981: Chile accepts Papal proposal; March 1981: Argentina rejects it
- April 1981: borders are closed and citizens of both are harassed
- January 21, 1982: Argentina terminates 1972 bilateral General Treaty on the Judicial Settlement
- April 23 1982: negotiations resume in the midst of Malvinas crisis
- April–June 1982: Argentina keeps best troops on border with Chile even while losing the Malvinas War
- September 15, 1982: both sides agree to accept Pope's proposal to renew 1972 Treaty
- March 1983: Pope proposes declaration of peace and nonaggression, Argentina rejects it, preferring a comprehensive agreement
- January 23, 1984: agreement of peace and friendship signed in Rome

- February–June 1984: subsequent negotiations establish: no common zone; specific navigational rights to certain islands; system for the resolution of future disputes that excludes outside tribunals; use of Cape Horn meridian as a point of boundary division
- June 11, 1984: Vatican mediator offers final suggestion for a solution; includes a bi-national commission to deal with all the economic issues
- October 18, 1984: full text of treaty ready
- November 25, 1984: Argentine referendum 77% yes, with 70% participation; Chile gets islands, but bi-oceanic principle safeguarded; no common zone; permanent bi-national commission to promote economic integration

Notes

Preface

1. Christian Parenti, "Making Prison Pay: Business Finds the Cheapest Labor of All" *Nation* 262(4) (January 29, 1996): 11–15

2. Cf., Kalevi J. Holsti, *Peace and War: Armed Conflicts and International Order 1648–1989* (Cambridge: Cambridge University Press), 1991; Geoffery Blainey, *The Causes of War* (New York: Free Press, 1973).

3. Thus studies are constantly "refining" the definition of which states are (or are perceived to be—which is a different argument altogether!), liberal and democratic and what constitutes the dependent variable. My review of the literature (discussed at length in chapter 4), found five operationalizations of the dependent variable and 13 variations on what constitutes a "democracy" for the purposes of the democratic peace argument.

4. There has been much attention to the need to create "conflict management systems" to deal with militarized conflict after the end of the Cold War. But most of this focus excludes interstate conflict in Latin America, as well as the use of military force by the U.S. See Max G. Manwaring and William J. Olson, eds., *Managing Contemporary Conflict* (Boulder: Westview, 1996); Edward J. Kolodziej and Roger E. Kanet, eds., *Coping with Conflict after the Cold War* (Baltimore: Johns Hopkins University Press, 1996).

5. Kenneth A. Oye, ed., *Cooperation Under Anarchy* (Princeton: Princeton University Press, 1986); Arthur Stein, *Why Nations Cooperate: Circumstance and Choice in International Relations* (Ithaca: Cornell University Press, 1990).

6. Barry Buzan, *People, States and Fear* (Boulder: Lynne Rienner, 1991, 2nd ed.), pp. 187–201.

7.   David A. Lake, "Regional Security Complexes: A Systems Approach" in David
      A. Lake and Patrick Morgan, eds., *Regional Orders: Building Security in a New
      World* (University Park, PA: Pennsylvania State University Press, 1997), pp. 45–
      67.
8.   Frank D. McCann, Jr. "The Brazilian General Staff and Brazil's Military Sit-
      uation, 1900–1945" *Journal of Inter-American Studies and World Affairs* 25(3)
      (August 1983): 299–324.

1. The Origins of Violent Peace

1.   Cf. Arie Kacowicz, *Zones of Peace in the Third World: South America and West
      Africa in Comparative Perspective* (Albany: State University of New York Press,
      1998); Mike Desch, "Why Latin America May Miss the Cold War: The United
      States and the Future of Inter-American Security Relations" in Jorge I. Domín-
      guez, ed., *International Security and Democracy* (Pittsburgh: University of Pitts-
      burgh Press, 1998), pp. 245–65.
2.   Kenneth Waltz, *Theory of International Politics* (New York: Random House,
      1979), pp. 185–189; John J. Mearsheimer, "Back to the Future: Instability in
      Europe After the Cold War" *International Security* 15 (Summer 1990): 5–56.
3.   Michael Doyle, "Liberalism and World Politics" *American Political Science
      Review* 80(4) (December 1986): 1151–69; Bruce Russett, Grasping the Dem-
      ocratic Peace (Princeton: Princeton University Press, 1993); John M. Owen,
      "How Liberalism Produces Democratic Peace" *International Security* 19(2)
      (Fall 1994): 87–125.
4.   Robert O. Keohane and Joseph Nye, *Power and Interdependence* (Boston: Little,
      Brown, 1977); Etel Solingen, "Economic Liberalization, Political Coalitions,
      and Emerging Regional Orders" in David Lake and Patrick J. Morgan, eds.
      Regional Orders (Pennsylvania State University Press, 1997), pp. 68–100.
5.   Huntington, "The Clash of Civilizations?" *Foreign Affairs* 72(3) (Summer
      1993): 22–49.
6.   John E. Mueller, *Retreat from Doomsday: The Obsolescence of Major War* (New
      York: Basic Books, 1989).
7.   Cf. Robert Paarlberg, "Domesticating Global Management" *Foreign Affairs*
      54(3) (1976): 563–576; Peter Evans, Harold K. Jacobson, and Robert D. Put-
      nam, eds., *Double-Edged Diplomacy: International Bargaining and Domestic
      Politics* (Berkeley: University of California Press, 1993).
8.   Definitions of democracy vary dramatically, even among democratic peace ad-
      vocates. See my discussion in chapter 4.
9.   Analysts who extrapolate international behavior from citizens' willingness in a
      democracy to resolve even fundamental disagreements via the ballot box cannot

be comfortable with the empirical reality of democracies threatening and shooting at each other, even when they produce fewer than 1,000 battlefield deaths. Consequently, a number of democratic peace advocates have turned to the issue of violence below war levels. Cf. Michael A. Doyle, "To the Editors " *International Security* 19(4) (Spring 1995): 180–94; Zeev Maoz and Bruce Russett, "Normative and Structural Causes of Democratic Peace" *American Political Science Review* 87(3) (September 1993): 624–38. Russet has even felt it necessary to try to explain why a democracy would use covert action against another democracy, *Grasping the Democratic Peace*, pp. 120–24. For my critique, see chapter 4.

10. The Japanese attack on Pearl Harbor was preceded by years of diplomatic bargaining and economic sanctioning by the U.S. James B. Crowley, *Japan's Quest for Autonomy: National Security and Foreign Policy, 1930–1938* (Princeton: Princeton University Press, 1966). Iraq's invasion of Kuwait came not only after months of tense negotiations, but after a meeting with the U.S. Ambassador as well. "Kuwait: How the West Blundered" *The Economist* September 29, 1990, reprinted in Micah L. Sifry and Christopher Cerf, eds., *The Gulf War Reader: History, Documents, Opinions* (New York: Times Books, 1991), pp. 99–106.

11. The U.S. is the only democratic country in which a minor can be given a death sentence. Amnesty International, *United States of America: "A Macabre Assembly Line of Death" Death Penalty Developments in 1997*. April 1998 AMR 51/20/98, p. 14.

12. Victor Davis Hanson, *The Western Way of War* (New York: Oxford University Press, 1990).

13. Hanson, *Western Way of War*, pp. 219–27; for a general treatment, see Raphael Sealey, *A History of the Greek City States, 700–338 B.C.* (Berkeley: University of California Press, 1976).

14. David E. Spiro, "The Insignificance of the Liberal Peace" *International Security* 19(2) (Fall 1994): 50–86.

15. John Lewis Gaddis, "The Long Peace: Elements of Stability in the Postwar International System" *International Security* 10(4) (Spring 1986).

16. Thomas C. Schelling, *The Strategy of Conflict* (Cambridge: Harvard University Press, 1980), pp. 43–46; James Fearon, "Domestic Political Audiences and the Escalation of International Disputes" *American Political Science Review* 88(3) (September 1994): 577–92.

17. I. William Zartmann, "Prenegotiations: Phases and Functions" in Janet Gross Stein, ed., *Getting to the Table: The Process of International Prenegotiation* (Baltimore: Johns Hopkins University Press, 1989), pp. 1–17, focuses on costs, but Stein (p. x) suggests that increasing benefits falls into the realm of prenegotiations as well.

18. Roger Fisher, William Ury, and Bruce Patton, *Getting to Yes: Negotiating Agreement without Giving In* (New York: Penguin, 1991), 2nd edition, p. 141.

19. Schelling, *The Strategy of Conflict*, pp. 35–43.

20. These distinctions are categorized in great detail in the Militarized Interstate Disputes data base. Charles S. Gochman and Zeev Maoz, "Militarized Interstate Disputes, 1816–1976: Procedures, Patterns and Insights" *Journal of Conflict Resolution* 28(4) (December 1984): 585–615; an updated version is discussed in Daniel M. Jones, Stuart A. Bremer, and J. David Singer, "Militarized Interstate Disputes, 1816–1992: Rationale, Coding Rules and Empirical Patterns" *Conflict Management and Peace Science* 15(2) (Fall 1996): 163–213.

21. On the issue of binding commitments, see Schelling, *Strategy of Conflict*, pp. 21–52 and Fearon, "Domestic Political Audiences."

22. On bargaining over the characteristics of the bargain once both parties see an agreement is in their interest, see Stephen D. Krasner, "Global Communications and National Power: Life on the Pareto Frontier" *World Politics* (April 1991): 336–66; P. Terrance Hopmann, *The Negotiation Process and the Resolution of International Conflicts* (Columbia, SC: University of South Carolina Press, 1996), pp. 87–96.

23. Schelling, *The Strategy of Conflict*, pp. 21–52.

24. See the discussion in Hopmann, *The Negotiation Process*, pp. 53–75.

25. Waltz notes that explaining national foreign policies, as compared to systemic outcomes, requires unit level factors. The idea of "two level games" tries to incorporate domestic and international factors. Cf., Evans, et. al., *Double-Edged Diplomacy*. For review articles concerning the state of the literature in successfully incorporating such factors, see Ethan B. Kapstein, "Is Realism Dead? The Domestic Sources of International Politics" *International Organization* 49(4) (Autumn 1995): 751–74 and Fareed Zakaria, "Realism and Domestic Politics: A Review Essay" *International Security* 17(1) (Summer 1992).

26. Alexander George and Richard Smoke, *Deterrence in American Foreign Policy: Theory and Practice* (New York: Columbia University Press, 1974); Alexander L. George, David K. Hall, and William E. Simons, *The Limits to Coercive Diplomacy* (Boston: Little, Brown, 1971).

27. John D. Montgomery, *The Politics of Foreign Aid: American Experience in Southeast Asia* (New York: Published for the Council on Foreign Relations by Praeger, c. 1962); Robert O. Keohane, "The Big Influence of Small Allies" *Foreign Policy* (Spring 1969): 161–82; and T.V. Paul, *Asymmetric Conflicts* (Cambridge: Cambridge University Press, 1994).

28. W. Robert Reed, "A Retrospective Voting Model with Heterogeneous Politicians" *Economics and Politics* 6(1) (March 1994): 39–57; Bruce Bueno de Mesquita, *The War Trap* (New Haven: Yale University Press, 1981); Bruce Bueno de Mesquita, Randolph M. Siverson, and Gary Woller, "War and the

Fate of Regimes" *American Political Science Review* 86(3) (September 1992): 638–46; Bruce Bueno de Mesquita and David Lalman, *Reason and War* (New Haven: Yale University Press, 1992); and Bruce Bueno de Mesquita, James Morrow and Ethan R. Zorick, "Capabilities, Perceptions and Escalation" *American Political Science Review* March 1997 91(1) 15–27. See also Fearon, "Domestic Political Audiences.

29. In the international arena, this logic underlies the dynamics of the security dilemma, offense-defense explanations of war, and even the stability of the bipolar Cold War. Cf., Robert Jervis, "Cooperation Under the Security Dilemma" and James Fearon, "Rationalist Explanations of War" *International Organization* 49(3) (Summer 1995): 379–414. Waltz himself has argued that nuclear weapons, a unit level attribute, is a fundamental determinant of the absence of war between the U.S. and Soviet Union, even taking into account the expected stability of a bipolar world. "The Origins of War in NeoRealist Theory" *Journal of Interdisciplinary History* 28(4) (Spring 1988): 615–28. In the domestic arena, see the literature on retrospective voting, including Reed, "A Retrospective Voting Model with Heterogeneous Politicians."

30. A wide range of international relations analysts agrees on this approach to studying international politics. Cf. Waltz, *Theory of International Politics*, pp. 95–96 and one of his archnemises, Bruce Bueno de Mesquita in *War and Reason*, pp. 16–19.

31. This is the traditional realist approach, which began with Thucydides' *The Peloponnesian War*, translated by Rex Warner (London: Penguin, 1972 revised edition), passed through Hans Morgenthau, *Politics Among Nations: The Struggle for Power and Peace* 5th ed. (New York: Knopf; distributed by Random House, 1973) and is present in John J. Mearsheimer, "The False Promise of International Institutions" *International Security* 19(3) (Winter 1994): 5–49.

32. Krasner, "Global Communications and National Power" *passim*; Bueno de Mesquita and Lalman, *War and Reason*, p. 19.

33. Cf. The discussion in Holsti, *Peace and War*. This approach is similar to the argument that the stakes in question matter for the use of military force. On this point see Paul F. Diehl, "What Are They Fighting For? The Importance of Issues in International Conflict Research" *Journal of Peace Research* 29(3) (August 1992): 333–44; Gary Goertz and Paul F. Diehl, *Territorial Changes and International Conflict* (London: Routledge, 1992); For an analysis distinguishing territorial from nonterritorial issues in Latin American MIDs, see Paul R. Hensel, "One Thing Leads to Another: Recurrent Militarized Disputes in Latin America, 1816–1986" *Journal of Peace Research* 31(3) 1994): 281–97.

34. Stephen D. Krasner, *Defending the National Interest* (Princeton: Princeton University Press, 1978).

35. Here I follow Peter A. Gourevitch's definition of the ruling coalition, *Politics in Hard Times: Comparative Responses to International Economic Crises* (Ithaca: Cornell University Press, 1986); see also Peter J. Katzenstein, *Small States in World Markets: Industrial Policy in Europe* (Ithaca: Cornell University Press, 1985).

36. Cf., Russett, *Grasping the Democratic Peace*, pp. 31–37; Bueno de Mesquita and Lalman, *War and Reason*, pp. 45–52; Doyle limits this preference ordering to relations among liberal states and worries that liberal states have a tendency to provoke violence with non-liberal states. See Michael W. Doyle, "Kant, Liberal Legacies and Foreign Affairs, Part I" pp. 230–32 and "Part 2" pp. 323–53, in *Philosophy and World Affairs*, Summer 1983 12(3) and Fall 1983, 12(4), respectively ; Kapstein, "Is realism dead?" also objects to this assumption, pp. 761–62.

37. On Fashoda, see Christopher Layne, "Kant or Cant: the Myth of the Democratic Peace" *International Security* 19(2) (Fall 1994): 28–33; on Venezuela, see Leandro Area, Elke Nieschulz de Stockhausen, *El Golfo de Venezuela: Documentación y cronología. Vol. II (1981–1989)* (Caracas: Universidad Central de Venezuela, 1991).

38. There is a large body of work demonstrating that the military requires support from key sectors in civil society in order to govern, and by extension, to threaten to govern if their policy preferences are not met. Cf., Alfred Stepan, *The Military in Politics* (Princeton: Princeton University Press, 1971); Alain Rouquie, *The Military and the State in Latin America*, trans., Paul E. Sigmund (Berkeley: University of California Press, 1987).

39. It had long been assumed that foreign policy had little impact on U.S. Presidential elections, but recent work is calling this into question. John H. Aldrich, John L. Sullivan, and Eugene Brogida "Foreign Affairs and Issue Voting: Do Presidential Candidates 'Waltz Before a Blind Audience'?" *American Political Science Review* 83(1) (March 1989): 123–42. A historical case is made in Charles P. Korr, *Cromwell and the New Model Foreign Policy: England's Policy Toward France, 1649–1658* (Berkeley: University of California Press, 1975).

40. Bueno de Mesquita, Siverson and Woller, "War and the Fate of Regimes."

41. Arno J. Mayer, "Internal Causes and Purposes of War in Europe, 1870–1956: A Research Assignment" *Journal of Modern History* (September 1969): 291–303 ; Jack Levy, "The Diversionary Theory of War: A Critique" in Manus I. Midlarsky, ed., *Handbook of War Studies* (Ann Arbor: University of Michigan Press, 1993, reprint of 1989 Unwin Hyman edition), pp. 259–88.

42. Caesar D. Sereseres, "The Interplay of Internal War and Democratization in Guatemala since 1982" in David R. Mares, ed., *Civil-Military Relations: Building Democracy and Regional Security in Latin America, Southern Asia and Central Europe* (Boulder: Westview, 1998), pp. 206–22. Serrano shortly there-

after overstepped his bounds, however. When he attempted to suspend the constitution and rule by emergency degree, the military opted to support the constitution instead and Serrano fell from office.

43. Bueno de Mesquita, Morrow, and Zorick, "Capabilities, Perception and Escalation"; Fearon, "Rationalist Explanations for War," p. 381.

44. Keisuke Iida attempts to model this possibility formally, but makes too many simplifying assumptions and imposes too many restrictions on players' moves (e.g., voting is sincere, rather than strategic), for the model to be empirically useful. "When and How do Domestic Constraints Matter? Two-Level Games with Uncertainty" *Journal of Conflict Resolution* 37(3) (September 1993): 403–26. One could use bureaucratic politics, legislative-executive bargaining, or principal-agent arguments to explain how these incomplete costs arise in domestic politics.

45. Examples include the U.S. mobilization of the Navy and ultimatum to Chile in 1891 after police arrested U.S. sailors involved in a barroom brawl. Peru also mobilized in 1977 after Chile began discussing Bolivian sovereign access to the sea via territory that Chile seized from Peru in the War of the Pacific 1879–1884. Joyce S. Goldberg *The Baltimore Affair* (Lincoln: University of Nebraska Press, 1986) and José de la Puente Radbill, "La mediterraneidad de Bolivia" in Eduardo Ferrero Costa, ed., *Relaciones del Perú con Chile y Bolivia*. (Lima: Centro Peruano de Estudios Internacionales, 1989), pp. 399–58, Daniel M. Masterson, *Militarism and Politics in Latin America: Peru from Sánchez Cerro to Sendero Luminoso* (Westport, CT: Greenwood, 1991), p. 265 respectively.

46. Paul, *Asymmetric Conflicts*; Paul K. Huth, *Extended Deterrence and the Prevention of War* (New Haven: Yale University Press, 1988).

47. George and Smoke, *Deterrence in American Foreign Policy*; John J. Mearsheimer, *Conventional Deterrence* (Ithaca: Cornell University Press, 1983); Alan Alexandroff and Richard Rosecrance "Deterrence in 1939" *World Politics* (April 1977): 404–24; Paul, *Asymmetric Conflicts*.

48. David A. Baldwin, *Economic Statecraft* (Princeton: Princeton University Press, 1985); I.M. Destler and John Odell, assisted by Kimberly Ann Elliott, *Anti-Protection: Changing Forces in United States Trade Politics* (Washington D.C.: Institute for International Economics, 1987); Lisa L. Martin, *Coercive Cooperation: Exploring Multilateral Economic Sanctions* (Princeton: Princeton University Press, 1992).

49. Thomas P. Anderson, *The War of the Dispossessed: Honduras and El Salvador, 1969* (Lincoln: University of Nebraska Press, 1981); Mark Rosenberg, et. al., *Honduras : Pieza clave de la política de Estados Unidos en Centro América.* (Tegucigalpa: Centro de Documentacion de Honduras (CEDOH), 1990).

50. Elliot A. Cohen, *Citizens and Soldiers: the Dilemmas of Military Service* (Ithaca: Cornell University Press, 1985); Jack Snyder, *The Ideology of the Offensive:*

Military Decision-Making and the Disasters of 1914 (Ithaca: Cornell University Press, 1984).

51. Cf. studies on mobilization in World War I, especially Marc Trachtenberg, "The Meaning of Mobilization in 1914" in Steven E. Miller, Sean M. Lynn-Jones, and Stephen Van Evera, eds. *Military Strategy and the Origins of the First World War* (Princeton: Princeton University Press, 1991) revised and expanded edition; and analyses of nonoffensive defense, including Robert Jervis, "Cooperation Under the Security Dilemma" *World Politics* 30 (January 1978): 167–214.

52. For a similar focus on partisan votes, see T. Clifton Morgan and Kenneth Bickers, "Domestic Discontent and the External Use of Force" *Journal of Conflict Resolution* (1992) 36: 25–52. Since the median voter theorem has specific requirements that clearly do not exist in all countries, I don't use this approach. On the median voter and its requirements, see Dennis C. Mueller, *Public Choice* (Cambridge: Cambridge University Press, 1979), pp. 97–124.

53. For corroborating evidence, see Bruce Bueno de Mesquita and Randolph M. Siverson, "Nasty or Nice? Political Systems, Endogenous Norms, and the Treatment of Adversaries" *Journal of Conflict Resolution* 41(1) (February 1997): 175–99.

54. Robert A. Dahl, *Polyarchy: Participation and Opposition* (New Haven: Yale University Press, 1972); Arendt Lipjhart, *Democracies* (New Haven: Yale University Press, 1984); Gary Cox, *Making Votes Count* (Cambridge: Cambridge University Press, 1997); David Scott Palmer, "Peru's 1995 Elections: A Second Look" *LASA Forum* 26(2) (Summer 1995): 17–20. The literature on international political economy has long recognized that variations in the characteristics of democratic states have important implications for their international behavior; cf. Peter J. Katzenstein, ed., *Between Power and Plenty: Foreign Economic Policies of Advanced Industrial States* (Madison: University of Wisconsin Press 1978) and Peter F. Cowhey, "Domestic Institutions and the Credibility of International Commitments: Japan and the United States" *International Organization* 47(2) (Spring 1993): 299–326.

55. D. Roderick Kiewiet and Mathew D. McCubbins, *The Logic of Delegation: Congressional Parties and the Appropriations Process* (Chicago: University of Chicago Press, 1991), pp. 22–38.

56. Cf. the debate over the War Powers Act in Thomas M. Franck and Edward Weisband, *Foreign Policy by Congress* (New York: Oxford University Press, 1979). See also Patrick James and John R. Oneal, "The Influence of Domestic and International Politics on the President's Use of Force" *Journal of Conflict Resolution* 35(2) (June 1991): 307–32.

57. Zeev Maoz and Nasrin Abdolali, "Regime Types and International Conflict, 1816–1976" *Journal of Conflict Resolution* 33(1) (March 1989): 23. For argu-

ments that governments led by professional militaries should be peaceful, see Stanislav Andreski, "On the Peaceful Disposition of Military Dictatorships" *Journal of Strategic Studies* 3 (December 1980) and David C. Rapoport, "A Comparative Theory of Military Political Types" in Samuel P. Huntington, ed., *Changing Patterns of Military Politics* (New York: Free Press, 1962), pp. 71–101.

58. Analysts of the international political economy recognize the importance of this factor in explaining the success of leaders who initially impose severe economic adjustment costs on voters and are reelected (e.g., U.S. president Ronald Reagan in 1980–84; Argentine president Carlos Saul Menem 1990–1994). Stephan Haggard and Robert R. Kaufman, "Economic Adjustment and the Prospects for Democracy" in Stephan Haggard and Robert R. Kaufman, eds., *The Politics of Economic Adjustment* (Princeton: Princeton University Press, 1992), pp. 319–50 and Barbara Geddes, "Challenging the Conventional Wisdom" in Larry Diamond and Marc F. Plattner, eds., *Economic Reform and Democracy* (Baltimore: Johns Hopkins University Press, 1995), pp. 66–72. But security analysts have ignored this aspect of domestic constraints.

59. Alexander L. George and Timothy J. McKowen, "Case Studies and Theories of Organizational Decision Making" in Lee S. Sproul and Patrick D. Larkey, eds., *Advances in Information Processing in Organizations* (Greenwich, CT: Jai Press, 1985), pp. 221–58.

60. Zeev Maoz and Ben D. Mor, "The Strategic Structure of Enduring International Rivalries," Paper presented at the Workshop on Processes of Enduring Rivalries (Indiana University, Bloomington, May 1993), pp. 3–4. I want to thank Elli Lieberman for providing me with this information.

61. Not all democratic peace advocates would accept this claim. Since Huntington ("Clash of Civilizations?") does not believe that any Latin American democracies are members of Western Civilization (in contrast to Doyle ["Liberalism and World Politics"] who classifies many as Liberal Republics), their experience is irrelevant to his claims about the democratic peace.

2. *Latin America's Violent Peace*

1. Cf. Robert Rothstein, *Alliances and Small Powers* (New York: Columbia University Press, 1968), p. 5; Kacowicz, *Zones of Peace*; Desch, "Why Latin America May Miss the Cold War"; one exception is Paul R. Hensel, "One Thing Leads to Another: Recurrent Militarized Disputes in Latin America, 1816–1986" *Journal of Peace Research* 31(3) (1994): 281–97.

2. Cf., Dirk Kruijt and Edelberto Torres Rivas, eds., *América Latina: Militares y Sociedad I* (San José, Costa Rica: FLACSO, 1991), pp. 8–9.

3.   Large sections of Guyana are claimed by Venezuela; Guatemala, which only recognized Belize in 1992, continues to dispute the territorial and maritime borders; Guyana and Brazil contest Suriname's borders.

4.   On the Monroe Doctrine see Dexter Perkins, *The Monroe Doctrine, 1823– 26* (Cambridge: Harvard University Press, 1927) and on the Venezuela dispute see Owen, "How Liberalism Produces the Democratic Peace," pp. 114– 19.

5.   Arthur P. Whitaker, *The Western Hemisphere Idea* (Ithaca: Cornell University Press, 1954); J. Lloyd Mecham, *The United States and Inter-American Security, 1889–1960* (Austin: University of Texas Press, 1962).

6.   See the response by the U.S. to the Colombian Minister in Washington in Perkins, *The Monroe Doctrine, 1823–26*, p. 192. Britain intervened actively in the region: in the 1828 Argentine-Brazilian war, Britain forced the combatants to create Uruguay as a buffer state; in 1833 it seized the Malvinas Islands and in 1843 a Honduran island; in 1841 it occupied a Nicaraguan port. The French were also active, occupying a Mexican port and an Argentine island in 1838 and participating with the British in a blockage of the Rio Plata in 1845. In none of these cases was the U.S. willing to aid the Latin Americans. Aid would come only when the U.S. itself perceived a threat, and not when a Latin American country defined the threat. Gordon Connell-Smith, *The United States and Latin America* (New York: Wiley 1974), p. 69; Mecham *The United States and Inter-American Security*, pp. 37–38.

7.   Mecham, *The United States and Inter-American Security*, p. 40; Guido DiTella and D. Cameron Watt, eds., *Argentina Between the Great Powers, 1939–46* (Pittsburgh: University of Pittsburgh Press, 1990); Amado Luiz Cervo and Clo- doaldo Bueno, *Historia da Política Exterior do Brasil* (Sao Paulo: Editora Atica, 1992); Cole Blasier, *The Hovering Giant* (Pittsburgh: University of Pittsburgh Press, 1976).

8.   *Diario* (August 7, 1993):32; *Hoy* April 4, 1995; see also United States, Depart- ment of Defense, *United States Security Strategy for the Americas* (Washington, D.C.: The Pentagon, Office of International Security Affairs 1995), pp. 12–14; Victor Millan and Michael A. Morris, *Conflicts in Latin America: Democratic Alternatives in the 1990s* (London: Research Institute for the Study of Conflict and Terrorism, 1990), pp. 8–16; David R. Mares, "Deterrence Bargaining in the Ecuador-Peru Enduring Rivalry: Designing Strategies Around Military Weakness" *Security Studies* 6(2) (Winter 1996/97): 91–123.

9.   For the ideas of a security complex and security externalities, see Lake, "Re- gional Security Complexes."

10.   Dana G.Munro, *Intervention and Dollar Diplomacy in the Caribbean, 1900– 1921* (Princeton: Princeton University Press, 1964); Foster Rhea Dulles, *Prelude to World Power* (New York: Macmillan, 1971, 2nd edition).

11. Even Brazil, an extremely large country located at the southern end of the hemisphere, worried about the implications of U.S. intervention in the Caribbean for its own security. McCann, Jr. "The Brazilian General Staff and Brazil's Military Situation, 1900–1945."

12. Cf., the State Department White Paper on El Salvador. "Flaws in El Salvador White Paper Raise Questions About Its Analysis" *The Washington Post* (June 9, 1991): A1, A114.

13. U.S. government officials and security analysts often point to such participation as evidence of "external" security threats. But they conveniently forget that the U.S. War of Independence itself attracted idealists from outside its territorial boundaries, as well as money and troops from a pre-Revolutionary France that could hardly have held the same ideals as those of the "Founding Fathers."

14. Stanley E. Hilton, *Brazil and the Soviet Challenge 1917–1947* (Austin: University of Texas Press, 1991); Mecham, *The United States and Inter-American Security*; Jorge I. Domínguez, *To Make a World Safe for Revolution: Cuba's Foreign Policy* (Cambridge: Harvard University Press, 1989); Charles D. Ameringer, *The Caribbean Legion: Patriots, Politicians, Soldiers of Fortune, 1946–1950* (University Park: Pennsylvania State University Press, 1996).

15. Mohammed Ayoob, *The Third World Security Predicament: State Making, Regional Conflict, and the International System* (Boulder: Lynne Rienner 1995); Buzan, *People, States and Fear*.

16. I want to thank Leon Zamosc for pointing this out, and Jennifer Collins for providing me with supporting materials. Cf. the package distributed for a march on the Ecuadorian national capital by the Organización de Pueblos Indígenas de Pastaza, March 10, 1992 #0129-OPIP-92; also the pamphlet produced in support of a continent-wide campaign "Campaña Nacional: 500 anos de resistencia indígena y popular" Folleto 1, Secretaría Operativa, Guatemala November 1, 1990.

17. David R. Mares, "Middle Powers Under Regional Hegemony: To Challenge or Acquiesce in Hegemonic Enforcement," *International Studies Quarterly*, December 1988) 32: 453–71.

18. Michael J. Francis, *The Limits of Hegemony: United States Relations with Argentina and Chile During World War II* (Notre Dame: University of Notre Dame Press, 1977); Stanley E. Hilton, *Hitler's Secret War in South America, 1939–1945: German Military Espionage and Allied Counterespionage in Brazil* (Baton Rouge: Louisiana State University Press, 1981). Argentina paid a high price for betting that the U.S. would be unwilling to pressure the British to help rein in Argentina's independent foreign policy. See the discussion in Guido DiTella and Cameron Watt, eds., *Argentina Between the Great Powers, 1939–46* (Pittsburgh: University of Pittsburgh Press, 1990).

19. Ecuador was abandoned to the Peruvians in the 1939–41 war and Chile felt isolated in 1977–78 as it confronted war scares with first Peru, then Argentina (see chapters 6 and 7 below). The landed oligarchy throughout Latin America believed that the U.S. push for land reform after the Cuban Revolution meant that they were being abandoned by the U.S., while anti-Communist military regimes in the 1970s also perceived U.S. human rights policies in a similar light. Federico G. Gil, "The Kennedy-Johnson Years" in John D. Martz, ed., *United States Policy in Latin America: A Quarter Century of Crisis and Challenge, 1961–1986* (Lincoln: University of Nebraska Press, 1988), pp. 3–25; Frederick M. Nunn, *The Time of the Generals: Latin American Professional Militarism in World Perspective* (Lincoln: University of Nebraska Press, 1992), esp. pp. 240–61.

20. E.g., the Acre War (1906) between Bolivia and Brazil, and the Cenepa War of 1981 between Ecuador and Peru.

21. Peruvian losses in Adrian J. English, *Armed Forces of Latin America: Their Histories, Development, Present Strength, and Military Potential* (London; New York: Jane's, 1984), p. 169; population estimates from James L. Wilkie and Enrique Ochoal, *Statistical Abstract of Latin America* v. 27 (Los Angeles: UCLA Latin American Center Publication, University of California, 1989), pp. 112–13.

22. Bryce Wood, *The United States and Latin American Wars, 1932–1942* (New York: Columbia University Press, 1966).

23. *Keesings Contemporary Archives*, various issues.

24. This threshold is akin to those used in the general analysis of international politics, such as "post 1816" (Napoleonic Wars settlement), "post WWII" and now "post Cold War."

25. Joseph Grunwald, Miguel S. Wionczek, and Martin Carnoy, *Latin American Economic Integration and U.S. Policy* (Washington: Brookings, 1972).

26. MIDS defined in chapter 1.

27. Jones, Bremer, and Singer, "Militarized Interstate Disputes, 1816–1992," pp. 183–85.

28. Charles S. Gochman and Zeev Maoz, "Militarized Interstate Disputes, 1816–1976" *Journal of Conflict Resolution* 28(4) (December 1984): 606–9.

29. Stuart Bremer, "Dangerous Dyads: Conditions Affecting the Likelihood of Interstate War, 1816–1965" *Journal of Conflict Resolution* 36 (1992): 309–41; D. Scott Bennett, "Measuring Rivalry Termination, 1816–1992" *Journal of Conflict Resolution* 41(2) (April 1997): 236.

30. Gochman and Maoz, "Militarized Interstate Disputes," pp. 585–615.

31. For purposes of tractability, the relatively few MIDs with non-Western hemisphere states (mainly Great Britain, France, Germany, and Japan) are omitted

from the analysis, except for the Falklands War between Argentina and Great Britain.

32. Gochman and Maoz, "Militarized Interstate Disputes," pp. 600–02; see also Jorge I. Domínguez, "Los conflictos internacionales en América Latina y la amenaza de guerra" *Foro Internacional* 97 25 (1) (July–September 1984): 1–13.

33. Data obtained by Steven A. Bernstein from Keith Jaggers' update of Polity II, compiled by Ted Robert Gurr, Keith Jaggers, and Will H. Moore. *Polity II: Political Structures and Regime Change, 1800–1986* (Ann Arbor: Inter-university Consortium for Political and Social Research, 1990).

34. William Dixon, "Democracy and the Peaceful Settlement of International Conflict" *American Political Science Review* 88(1) (March 1994): 22 also uses 6 as the determinant for his dichotomous democracy variable in a study of 264 interstate conflicts after WWII.

35. "País no ampliará la Amnistía" *La Nación* (San José, Costa Rica) July 17, 1999, p. 5A.

36. Gabriel Marcella, "Epilogue: The Peace of October 1998" in Gabriel Marcella and Richard Downes, eds., *Security Cooperation in the Western Hemisphere: Resolving the Ecuador-Peru Conflict* (Coral Gables, FL: University of Miami, North-South Center Press, 1999), pp. 231–35.

37. Edgar Camacho Omiste, "El Enclaustramiento Marítimo de Bolivia" (La Paz: FLACSO-Bolivia, July 1988) Documento de Trabajo #22; Juan Ignacio Siles, ed., *La Política Exterior de Bolivia, 1989–1993* (La Paz: Ministerio de Relaciones Exteriores y Culto, Government of Bolivia, 1993); Despite a 1997 agreement to remove them, as of 1999 Chile had not de-mined the area. "Border Mines Not Being Removed" *Santiago Times* June 30, 1999.

38. For a discussion of early plans see Whitaker, *The Western Hemisphere Idea*; Native American political units had already been incorporated *de jure* into Latin American states during colonial days but many still resisted *de facto* integration. Latin American states advanced their internal security interests by militarily defeating independence minded indigenous populations.

39. Ronald Bruce St. John, *The Foreign Policy of Peru* (Boulder: Lynne Rienner, 1992), pp. 34–38.

40. English, *Armed Forces of Latin America*; Ralph Lee Woodward, Jr., *Central America: A Nation Divided* (New York: Oxford University Press, 1976).

41. For example, Brazil (largely because it saw itself as a Latin American great power that would soon be recognized as such by the Europeans—see discussion in Chapter 5), opposed these efforts in the early twentieth century.

42. David Sheinin, *Argentina and the United States at the Sixth Pan American Conference (Havana 1928)* (London: Institute of Latin American Studies, University of London, 1991) Research Papers 25. As late as 1945 the U.S. was still

using this policy against Argentina for its neutrality in the war, even though Argentine beef and grains contributed to the British war effort. For a discussion of the differences between the manner in which Britain and the U.S. dealt with Argentine neutrality, see Di Tella and Watt, eds., *Argentina Between the Great Powers*.

43. Mecham *The United States and Inter-American Security*, p. 46.

44. Hector Gros Espiell, *Conflictos Territoriales en Iberoamérica y Solución Pacífica de Controversias* (Madrid: Ediciones Cultura Hispánica, 1986), p. 16; Binding arbitration of inter-American disputes met with the disapproval of the U.S., Chile, and others at the 1902 Pan American Meetings. Mecham, *The United States and Inter-American Security*, pp. 59–61; *Segunda Conferencia Internacional Americana* (Mexico: Tipografía de la Oficina Impresora de Estampillas, 1901), pp. 310–84.

45. Latin America Data Base, "El Salvador & Honduras Sign Treaties to End Border Conflicts" *EcoCentral: Central American Economy & Sustainable Development* ISSN 1089–1560 3(4) (January 29, 1998).

46. Latin America Data Base, "Chile and Argentina Resolve Last Border Dispute" *NotiSur—Latin American Affairs* Latin American Institute, University of New Mexico, ISSN 1060–41889 9(1) (January 8, 1999).

47. Carlos Portales, "Seguridad regional en Sudamérica: escenarios prospectivos" in Augusto Varas, ed., *Paz, Desarme y Desarrollo en América Latina* (Buenos Aires: Grupo Editor Latinoamericano 1987); Augusto Varas, "Zonas de Paz en América Latina: Una propuesta factible?" in *Seguridad, paz y desarme: Propuestas de concertación pacífica en América Latina y el Caribe* (Santiago: FLACSO-CLADDE 1992). On Contadora, see Alicia Frohmann, "De contadora al grupo de los ocho: El reaprendizaje de la concertación política regional" *Estudios Internacionales* 22(87) (July–September 1989): 365–427.

48. Both undertook this step in 1994. Paz V. Milet, "La desmilitarización en Haití" and Ebrahim Asvat, "La desmilitarización Panameña y sus desafíos futuros," both in *Paz y Seguridad en las Américas* No. 12, July 1997, pp. 14–15 and 15–18, respectively.

49. John R. Redick, "The Tlatelolco Regime and Nonproliferation in Latin America" *International Organization* 35(1) (Winter 1981): 103–34.

50. St. John, *The Foreign Policy of Peru*, pp. 204, 210.

51. E.g., the OAS organized the Seminario Regional Sobre la Aplicación Nacional de la Convención Sobre Armas Químicas in Lima in September 1994; during the XXIV Assembly the member countries also approved a resolution against arms proliferation; and at the IX Plenary Session the Commission for Hemispheric Security approved a resolution calling on members to redouble their efforts on disarmament and arms control. Since 1987 the Latin American Center for Defense and Disarmament (CLADDE) and the Joint Study Program of

Latin American International Relations (RIAL) have edited an annual study of progress in the area of arms control and disarmament, *Estudio Estratégico de América Latina* (Santiago, Chile).

52. Timothy J. Dunn, *The Militarization of the U.S.-Mexican Border, 1978–1992: Low Intensity Conflict Doctrine Comes Home* (Austin: The Center for Mexican American Studies, The University of Texas Press, 1997, 2nd ed.).

3. *The Myth of Hegemonic Management*

1. The list of scholars who casually assert that the U.S. has been able to control interstate conflicts in Latin America is long; cf. Phillipe C. Schmitter, "Introduction" in Phillipe C. Schmitter, ed., *Military Rule in Latin America: Function, Consequences, and Perspectives* (Beverly Hills: Sage Publications, 1973), p.xi; Carlos Portales, "Seguridad regional en Sudamérica"; Heraldo Munoz, "Beyond the Malvinas Crisis" *Latin American Research Review* 19(1) (1984); Richard Millett "The Limits of Influence: The United States and the Military in Central America and the Caribbean" in Louis W. Goodman, Johanna S. R. Mendelson, and Juan Rial, eds. , *The Military and Democracy: the Future of Civil-Military Relations in Latin America* (Lexington, MA: Lexington Books, 1990), pp. 123–40. More developed discussions of the positive impact of the U.S. for Latin American security are found in Wood, *The United States and Latin American Wars, 1932–1942*; Domínguez, "Los conflictos internacionales en América Latina y la amenaza de guerra"; and Clifford E. Griffin, "Power Relations and Conflict Neutralization in Latin America" International Studies Working Paper, Hoover Institute, March 1992.

2. Inis L. Claude, Jr., *Power and International Relations* (New York: Random House, 1962).

3. Steven Lukes, *Power: A Radical View* (New York: Macmillan, 1974); Scott C. James and David A. Lake, "The Second Face of Hegemony: Britain's repeal of the Corn Laws and the American Walker Tariff of 1846" *International Organization* 43(1) (Winter 1989): 3–9.

4. This description holds even if one would claim that the rules of the international market, rather than those of a particular state, structure international incentives. My point is that the market is emphatically not "free," but rather that the leading states in a system allow certain markets to function more or less freely while others are not. This argument is developed at length in my book *Penetrating the International Market* (New York: Columbia University Press, 1987), pp. 3–38 and examined in the case of the illegal drug trade in the Americas in my "The Logic of Inter-American Cooperation on Drugs: Insights from Models of Strategic Interaction" in Peter S. Smith, ed., *Drug Policy in the Americas* (Boulder: Westview, 1992), pp. 329–42.

.

5. An excellent analysis of this struggle in Mexico is Charles Hale, *Mexican Liberalism in the Age of Mora: 1821–1853* (New Haven, Yale University Press, 1968); see also Woodward, *Central America*; the Liberal-Conservative struggle also reflected the battle between the forces of national centralization and decentralization. A fascinating account of this complex situation can be found in Domingo F. Sarmiento, *Facundo, or Civilization and Barbarism* trans. Mary Mann, introduction by Ilan Stevens (New York: Penguin Books, 1998).

6. Whitaker, *The Western Hemisphere Idea.*

7. The list of Latin American Liberal dictators is long and includes Porfirio Díaz (1885–1911) in Mexico, the Liberal Oligarchy of the Monagas brothers (1847–1857) in Venezuela, Tomás Guardia (1870–1882) in Costa Rica, José Santos Zelaya (1894–1909) in Nicaragua, Justo Rufino Barrios (1873–1885) and Manuel Estrada Cabrera (1989–1920) in Guatemala. See also, Frederick B. Pike, *The United States and the Andean Republics: Peru, Bolivia, and Ecuador* (Cambridge: Harvard University Press, 1977), pp. 143–53.

8. Thomas F. McGann, *Argentina, The United States, and the Inter-American System 1880–1914* (Cambridge: Harvard University Press, 1957), pp. 130–64.

9. Ernest R. May, *The Making of the Monroe Doctrine* (Cambridge: Belknap Press of Harvard University Press, 1975). Most analysts, especially those who perceive the Doctrine as legitimate and in effect up through the Cold War, ignore the U.S. promise to stay out of European security affairs. The issue came up at the time because Greece was seeking its independence from the Ottoman Empire. European great powers were concerned about the impact of a weakening of the Ottoman Empire upon the balance of power.

10. In a dispute between Venezuela and Great Britain over the boundary with British Guiana in 1895 the U.S. took a forceful position favoring Venezuelan suggestions to arbitrate the controversy, with Secretary of State Richard Olney's claiming that the U.S. was "practically sovereign in the continent and its fiat is law upon the subjects to which it confines its interposition . . ." The British initially rejected this position, noting that the Monroe Doctrine had no standing in international law. But when President Grover Cleveland told Congress that he was willing to go to war to defend the U.S. position, the British realized the seriousness of the situation and negotiated a compromise. Dulles, *Prelude to World Power*, pp. 134–48; Lester D. Langley, *Struggle for the American Mediterranean: United States - European Rivalry in the Gulf-Caribbean 1776–1904* (Athens GA: University of Georgia Press, 1976), pp. 152–60. After this episode the British paid deference to U.S. security interests in the Caribbean region. Warren G. Kneer, *Great Britain and the Caribbean 1901–1913: A Study in Anglo-American Relations* (East Lansing, MI: Michigan State University Press, 1975).

11. Langley, *Struggle for the American Mediterranean*, p. 160; U.S. naval forces at the time were still no match for the British. David Healy, *Drive to Hegemony* (Madison: University of Wisconsin Press, 1988), pp. 32–35. Britain steadily gave way to the U.S. on control of a trans-isthmusian canal, according it equal responsibility in the Clayton Bulwer treaty of 1850 and ultimately ceding co-defense in the Hay-Pauncefote treaty of 1901.

12. Compare Kneer's discussion of German Foreign Office preoccupation with U.S. positions on joint German and British military coercion of Guatemala and Venezuela in 1901 with the naval arms competition discussed in Holger H. Herwig, *Politics of Frustration: The United States in German Naval Planning, 1889–1941* (Boston: Little, Brown, 1976), pp. 67–109. Herwig also notes that U.S. naval planners did not adequately update their perceptions of German intentions in the region.

13. An extensive discussion and analysis of U.S.-Cuban relations is found in Jorge I. Domínguez, *Cuba: Order and Revolution* (Cambridge: Belknap Press of Harvard University Press, 1978).

14. General discussions of U.S.-Caribbean/Central American relations in this period can be found in two books by Munro, *Intervention and Dollar Diplomacy in the Caribbean 1900–1921* and *The United States and the Caribbean Area* (Boston: World Peace Foundation, 1934).

15. Daniel Cosío Villegas, *Historia Moderna de México* (México: Editorial Hermes, 1955) Vol. 7: 23, 174–83; and passim.

16. Ibid., pp. 424–26.

17. Ibid.

18. Ibid., p. 565.

19. Ibid., pp. 473–81.

20. Whitaker, *The Western Hemisphere Idea*, pp. 74–81; Gordon Connell-Smith, *The Inter-American System*. (London: Oxford University Press, 1966), pp. 39–42.

21. Robert John Deger, Jr., "Porfirian Foreign Policy and Mexican Nationalism: A Study of Cooperation and Conflict in Mexican-American Relations, 1884–1904," unpublished Ph.D. dissertation, Indiana University, 1979, p. 220–21.

22. For U.S. interests, see Munro, *Intervention and Dollar Diplomacy*, p. 147.

23. Woodward, *Central America*, p. 187; for U.S. interests in this episode, see Walter LaFaber, *The New Empire: An Interpretation of American Expansion 1860–1898* (Ithaca: Cornell University Press, 1969, 7th Printing), pp. 218–29.

24. Munro, *Intervention and Dollar Diplomacy*, p. 41.

25. Munro, *Intervention and Dollar Diplomacy*.

26. Cosío Villegas, *Historia Moderna de México*, pp. 648–79; Munro, *Intervention and Dollar Diplomacy*, p. 151.

27. Munro, *Intervention and Dollar Diplomacy.*, pp. 152–55; Munro, *The United States and the Caribbean Area*, pp. 195–202; Perkins, *Constraint of Empire*, p. 23.

28. Cosío Villegas, *Historia Moderna de México*, pp. 687–97.

29. Munro, *Intervention and Dollar Diplomacy*, pp. 165–66.

30. Cosío Villegas, *Historia Moderna de México*, pp. 699–703.

31. The consul was most likely acting on his own, and not under orders from the State Department, see Perkins, *Constraint of Empire*, pp. 25–26; Munro, *Intervention and Dollar Diplomacy*, pp. 174–75. Nevertheless, the incentives from Washington encouraged this type of behavior. If independent action failed to produce benefits for the U.S., the consul rarely seems to have paid a price, while if such actions brought benefits Washington was very happy to accept them.

32. Cosío Villegas, *Historia Moderna de México*, pp. 705–7; Munro, *Intervention and Dollar Diplomacy*, pp. 175–77; Perkins, *Constraint of Empire*, p. 26.

33. Cosío Villegas, *Historia Moderna de México*, pp. 699–723; Munro, *Intervention and Dollar Diplomacy*, p. 179.

34. Cosío Villegas, *Historia Moderna de México*, pp. 708–23; Munro, *Intervention and Dollar Diplomacy*, pp. 182–83.

35. Munro, *Intervention and Dollar Diplomacy*, p. 181.

36. Joyce S. Goldberg, *The Baltimore Affair* (Lincoln: University of Nebraska Press, 1986). Chile's Navy had new British-built ironclads which were superior to U.S. ships in 1879. See p. 116 and *passim*.

37. Joseph Tulchin, *The Aftermath of War: World War I and U.S. Policy toward Latin America* (New York: New York University Press, 1971), p. 35.

38. Frederick M. Nunn, *Yesterday's Soldiers: European Military Professionalism in South America, 1890–1940* (Lincoln: University of Nebraska Press, 1983).

39. William F. Sater, *Chile and the United States* (Athens: University of Georgia Press, 1990), p. 91.

40. Michael L. Krenn, *U.S. Policy toward Economic Nationalism in Latin America, 1917–1929* (Wilmington, DE: Scholarly Resources, 1990), chapter 1.

41. Tulchin focuses on these aspects in his analysis, *The Aftermath of War*.

42. Krenn, *U.S. Policy toward Economic Nationalism*, p. 8.

43. Michael Grow, *The Good Neighbor Policy and Authoritarianism in Paraguay: United States Economic Expansion and Great-Power Rivalry in Latin America during World War II* (Lawrence: The Regents Press of Kansas, 1981), pp. 25–42.

44. For U.S.-Brazilian relations at the time, see E. Bradford Burns, *The Unwritten Alliance: Rio-Branco and Brazilian-American Relations* (New York: Columbia University Press, 1966); Amado Luiz Cervo and Clodomiro Bueno, *Historia da Política Exterior do Brasil* (Sao Paulo: Ed. Atica, 1992).

45. Tulchin, *The Aftermath of War*, pp. 63–64; Richard V. Salisbury, *Anti-Imperialism and International Competition in Central America* (Wilmington, DE: Scholarly Resources, 1989) and Chapter 3 below.

46. At the San Francisco conference to set up the United Nations in 1945, the Soviet Union had insulted the Latin American governments by referring to them as "client states." Mecham, *The United States and Inter-American Security*, p. 269.

47. Wood does not use the 1,000 battlefield deaths cutoff, therefore he includes the Leticia Dispute between Peru and Colombia. On the other hand, he does not include the attack by the Dominican Republic's army against Haitians, in which estimates run up to 12,000 dead. Mecham, *The United States and Inter-American Security*, pp. 175–76.

48. Wood, *The United States and Latin American Wars, 1932–1942*, pp. 8–15.

49. For Wood the Good Neighbor Policy weakened in 1943–44 when the U.S. pressured Argentina to break relations with the Axis powers and ended with the U.S. covert intervention against Guatemala in 1954. He also does not see either the OAS or the Rio Treaty as providing effective mechanisms for conflict resolution. *The Unmaking of the Good Neighbor Policy*.

50. Wood, *The United States and Latin America Wars*, p. 8 gives the U.S. the major credit, but see the detailed discussions in Lawrence A. Clayton, *Peru and the United States: The Condor and the Eagle* (Athens, GA: University of Georgia Press, 1999), pp. 137–41 and St. John, *The Foreign Policy of Peru*, pp. 160–64.

51. Joseph S. Tulchin, *Argentina and the United States: A Conflicted Relationship* (Boston: Twayne, 1990), pp. 46–47; Arthur P. Whitaker, *The United States and the Southern Cone: Argentina, Chile, and Uruguay* (Cambridge: Harvard University Press, 1976), pp. 368–72; Sater, *Chile and the United States*, pp. 94–104.

52. Sater, Ibid., p. 88–91.

53. Sater, Ibid., p. 95; Pike *The United States and the Andean Republics*, p. 237.

54. Sater, *Chile and the United States*, pp. 94–97; St. John, *The Foreign Policy of Peru*, pp. 160–64; Frederick B. Pike, *The Modern History of Peru* (New York: Praeger, 1967), pp. 232; Daniel M. Masterson, *Militarism and Politics in Latin America: Peru from Sanchez Cerro to Sendero Luminoso* (Westhaven, CT: Greenwood Press, 1991), p. 33.

55. Oscar Espinosa Mora, *Bolivia y el mar, 1810–1964* (Santiago: Editorial Nascimiento, 1964), pp. 350–57; Pike, *The United States and the Andean Republics*, p. 202. In 1977–78 Peru and Chile were on the brink of war as a result of Chile's discussions with Bolivia concerning an exchange of territory in the area. José de la Puente Radbill, "La mediterraneidad de Bolivia" in Eduardo Ferrero Costa, ed., *Las Relaciones del Perú con Chile y Bolivia* (Lima: Centro

Peruano de Estudios Internacionales, 1989), pp. 39–58 Chile has kept the border zone mined for years.

56. Sater, *Chile and the United States*, p. 100. Sater notes that Britain did not make the trade when it discovered that doing so would violate the Washington Naval Armament Limitation Treaty of 1922, but is silent on Japanese reasoning.

57. Pike, *The United States and the Andean Republics*, p. 203.

58. Wood, *The United States and Latin American Wars*, pp. 169–72; St. John, *Foreign Policy of Peru*, pp. 165–66; Pike *Modern History of Peru*, p. 230; and *The United States and the Andean Republics*, pp. 203–4.

59. In 1932 the U.S. Ambassador in Peru, upon reviewing Embassy records, asked the State Department why it had pressured Leguia and his Foreign Minister into accepting a treaty "against their will." Wood, *The United States and Latin American Wars*, p. 172.

60. Wood, Ibid., p. 171. Citation from Francisco Andrade S., "Límites entre Colombia y Ecuador" *Boletín de Historia y Antiguedades* (Bogotá) 47 (March–April, 1961): 201–29 at p. 217.

61. Masterson, *Militarism and Politics in Latin America*, p. 33.

62. Wood, *The United States and Latin American Wars*, p. 21.

63. Leslie B. Rout, Jr., *The Politics of the Chaco Peace Conference, 1935–39* (Austin: University of Texas Press, 1970), pp. 8–27.

64. Ibid.; Mecham, *The United States and Inter-American Security*, pp. 154–59; Wood, *The United States and Latin American Wars*, pp. 19–166.

65. Wood, Ibid., pp. 169–251; St. John, *Foreign Policy of Peru*, pp. 173–77.

66. Wood, *The United States and Latin American Wars*, pp. 255–344.

67. In Chapter 2 I extended the democratic rankings and MID occurrences to 1998. I am not, however, extending the quantitative studies past the Polity III and MID II periods. This decision avoids introducing problems of disagreements among coders into the analyses.

68. According to Waltz' structural realism theory, under conditions of bipolarity a great power should not be concerned with external balancing, but instead focus on internal resources. *Theory of International Relations*, p. 163. But the argument about regional hegemonic management by definition does not accept this claim and so we need to ask how systemic polarity might affect the hegemon's management, *assuming the hegemon wanted to manage regional conflict*. Note that this situation is not necessarily opposed to Waltz. If the management of regional conflict can be accomplished without impinging upon the great power's ability to internally balance against the other great power, Waltz has nothing to say concerning hegemonic management. For him, this lies more in the realm of foreign policy, rather than systemic outcome. Kenneth Waltz, "The Stability of a Bipolar World" *Daedalus* 93 (Summer 1964): 881–909.

69. Cf., Schmitter, "Introduction"; Rothstein, *Alliances and Small Powers*.

70. Eg., Kacowicz, *Zones of Peace*, pp. 67–81 sees the impact of hegemony as greater in Central America, while Wood, *The United States and Latin American Wars*, pp. 1–15, makes no such distinction.

71. Cf., Salisbury, *Anti-Imperialism and International Competition*; Krenn, *U.S. Policy toward Economic Nationalism in Latin America, 1917–1929*; Richard E. Feinberg, *The Intemperate Zone: the Third World Challenge to U.S. Foreign Policy* (New York: Norton, 1983) makes this argument for all of U.S. foreign policy during the Cold War.

72. Mexican workers in 1915 were organized into Red Brigades to fight in the Mexican Revolution. In 1925 the U.S. President warned Congress that war might have to be declared against the Mexican "Bolshevik" government which was spreading revolution in Central America.

73. The military government carried out a "Dirty War" internally in which tens of thousands of people were killed and "disappeared," and the generals believed that they were in the good graces of the Reagan administration because they were helping the U.S.-supported Contras in Nicaragua. See my discussion of the regime in Chapter 6.

4. Democracy, Restrained Leadership

1. Department of Defense, *United States Security Strategy for the Americas*, pp. 1–5.

2. Levy had proclaimed it to be perhaps the only lawlike statement in the study of international relations. Jack S. Levy, "Democratic Politics and War" *Journal of Interdisciplinary History* 18(4) (Spring 1988): 653–73. The claim for absolute peace among democracies is clearly incorrect: The clearest cases include the U.S. against Spain in 1898, Great Britain against Finland during World War II, and Ecuador-Peru in 1995. If we want to go back in history, ancient Athens attacked Syracuse, among other democratic city-states.

3. My reading of the literature turns up five different versions of the dependent variable, two variations on normative and four on institutional constraints, four different claims concerning how long a state needed to be democratic and finally, three different ways of measuring whether a state was democratic or not (without including differences on what to measure in determining democrat-icness, where the variations are too numerous to mention). Among the better critiques are Joanne Gowa, "Democratic states and international disputes" *International Organization* 49(3) (Summer 1995): 511–22 and William R. Thompson and Richard Tucker, "A tale of two democratic peace critiques" *Journal of Conflict Resolution* 41(3) (June 1997): 428–54.

4. David A. Lake, "Powerful pacifists: democratic states and war" *American Political Science Review* 86(1) (March 1992): 24–37 focuses on institutional con-

straints. Doyle, "Liberalism and World Politics" and Maoz and Russett "Normative and Structural Causes of the Democratic Peace, 1946–1986," pp. 624–38 emphasize norms and institutional constraints. Mearsheimer, "Back to the Future" credits international power relations and alliance structure. David E. Spiro, "The Insignificance of the Liberal Peace" *International Security* argues that the findings are statistically insignificant.

5. Maoz and Abdolali, "Regime Types and International Conflict, 1816–1976," pp. 3–35, argue that the findings vary by level of analysis, time period and measures used. Maoz and Russett, "Normative and Structural Causes of the Democratic Peace, 1946–86," claim that post-1945 democratic states also use force short of war against other democracies and nondemocracies less often than would be expected. Steve Chan, "Mirror, Mirror on the Wall . . . Are the Freer Countries More Pacific?" *Journal of Conflict Resolution* 28(4) (1984): 617–48 found that democratic states were most likely to be involved in extra-systemic wars and implies that if one included violence against anti-colonial movements, democracies would also score high in this category. Morgan, and Bickers, "Domestic Discontent and the External Use of Force," while not a comparative analysis, present data demonstrating that the U.S. engages in the overt use of force internationally quite often. Henry S. Farber and Joanne Gowa, "Polities and Peace" *International Security* 20(2) (Fall 1995): 123–46 found that, before 1914, democracies were more likely to engage in low-level military violence against each other than any other pairing of states. Russett and Antholis' analysis of the data demonstrates that democratic city states in ancient Greece were more likely to fight each other than were any other type of dyad, although the authors misinterpret their evidence in discussing their own table. Bruce Russett with William Antholis, "The Imperfect Democratic Peace of Ancient Greece" in Bruce Russett, *Grasping the Democratic Peace* (Princeton: Princeton University Press, 1993), p. 53.

6. An introduction to the historical sociological strain is found in Sven Steinmo, Kathleen Thelen, and Frank Longstreth, eds., *Structuring Politics: Historical Institutionalism in Comparative Analysis* (New York: Cambridge University Press, 1992); for the public choice view, see Douglass C. North, *Institutions, Institutional Change and Economic Performance* (New York: Cambridge University Press, 1992).

7. Although Kant and Doyle make the argument that the liberal peace requires both normative and institutional constraints, most of the analyses have focused on the latter.

8. Brian Barry, *Sociologists, Economists & Democracy* (Chicago: University of Chicago Press, 1978), pp. 99–100.

9. For discussions of how the cost of a political act influences its use, see Charles S. Tilly, *From Mobilization to Revolution* (Reading MA: Addison-Wesley, 1978)

and Albert O. Hirschman, *Exit, Voice and Loyalty* (Cambridge: Harvard University Press, 1970).

10. If one assumes these other interests, the people may push leaders into war or willingly respond to the call to arms whenever and against whomever it is made. Thus Machiavelli, who assumed the people wanted glory, saw republics as the most efficient fighting institution and expected them to fight each other for greater glory. Doyle, "Liberalism and World Politics," pp. 1154–55. Thucydides reports similiar advantages and aspirations for democracies. *Peloponnesian War* Book I.

11. Maoz and Russett, "Normative and Structural Causes," p. 625; Lake "Powerful Pacifists" discusses the conditions under which democratic states will themselves be the aggressors: "when the initial cost of conquest and the ongoing costs of rule are less than the discounted present value of future economic profits," p. 29.

12. Lake's article is unfortunately mistitled ("Powerful Pacifists") In the text he makes it clear that democracies will *not* turn the other cheek.

13. Russet and Maoz, "Normative and Structural Causes," p. 625.

14. Huntington "The Clash of Civilizations?" and Doyle "Liberalism and World Politics" have similar arguments on this point, except that they ignore the subjective elements in the evaluations of other polities, even by Western or Liberal nations. For further discussion, see below.

15. Owen, "How Liberalism Produces the Democratic Peace," pp. 93–94; but for an interesting argument that post World War II liberals have overemphasized the distinction between nationalism and liberal individualism, see Yael Tamir, *Liberal Nationalism* (Princeton: Princeton University Press, 1993). In addition, John Stuart Mill believed that Liberals could treat "savages" in authoritarian ways. *Considerations On Representative Government* (Indianapolis: Bobbs Merrill, 1958), pp. 59, 256; *On Liberty* reprinted in Mary Warnock, ed., *John Stuart Mill* (New York: The New American Library, Meridian Books, 1962), p. 136 and *Civilization*, p. 60; see also, Gerald Sirkin and Natalie Robinson Sirkin, "John Stuart Mill and Disutilitarianism in Indian Education" *Journal of General Education* 34(4) (January 1973).

16. Howard J. Wiarda, ed., *Politics and Social Change in Latin America: Still a Distinct Tradition?* 3rd ed. (Boulder: Westview, 1992); Brian Loveman, *The Constitution of Tyranny: Regimes of Exception in Spanish America* (Pittsburgh: University of Pittsburgh Press, 1993).

17. V. R. Berghahn, *Militarism: the History of an International Debate, 1861–1979* (Cambridge: Cambridge University Press, 1981).

18. Note that not all militaries are more willing to utilize military force than civilians. In a study of the U.S. behavior during Cold War crises, Richard Betts found that, in all but one of the cases (Cuban Missile Crisis), military officers

were generally no more likely than civilians to advocate the use of military force. *Soldiers, Statesmen and Cold War Crises* (Cambridge: Harvard University Press, 1977), pp. 4, 215–16.

19. Doyle, "Liberalism and World Politics"; Owen, "How Liberalism," pp. 108–15; Douglass C. North and Barry R. Weingast, "Constitutions and Commitment: The Evolution of Institutions Governing Public Choice in 17th Century England" in *Working Papers Series, Domestic Studies Program* Hoover Institute, Stanford University, pp. 8–11, November 1988; quote is on p. 33.

20. Ida Oren, "The Subjectivity of the 'Democratic' Peace: Changing U.S. Perceptions of Imperial Germany" *International Security* 20(2) (Fall 1995): 147–84.

21. Leandro Area and Elke Nieschulz de Stockhausen, *El Golfo de Venezuela: Documentación y Cronologia* Vol. 2 (1981–1989) (Caracas: Universidad Central de Venezuela, 1991), pp. 64–87; for Ecuador, see the discussion in chapter 7 below.

22. These are analyses which claim that both normative and institutional constraints matter, and then procede to classify "democracy" by a certain time threshold on the institutional side. Doyle "Liberalism and World Politics" uses three years, Edward D. Mansfield and Jack Snyder, "Democratization and the Danger of War" *International Security* 20(1) (Summer 1995): 5–38 go up to ten years and Russet and Maoz, "Normative and Structural Causes," pp. 625 and 636 claim "new" democracies must develop the norms but do not provide any time period in which those norms can be expected to develop.

23. Thucydides, *The Peloponnesian War*; Russett (with a chapter co-author William Antholis), *Grasping the Democratic Peace* (pp. 55–56, 61) argues that perhaps Athens did not know that Syracuse was democratic or perceived it as less democratic because of the great distance between them and difficulty of communications at the time. Yet the Athenian leader Nicias himself was the official representative of Syracuse's interests in Athens and told the Assembly that Syracuseans had freedom and power so the war would be difficult and expensive. The people believed him enough to vote to increase their forces for the war. Thucydides, *Peloponnesian War* Book VI: 20–26; Adcock, *Diplomacy in Ancient Greece* (New York: St. Martin's Press, 1975), p. 60.

24. Doyle, "Liberalism and World Politics"and Huntington, "The Clash of Civilizations?," respectively. Despite their agreement on this point, Doyle believes most Latin America republics have been Liberal (see his appendix in "Liberalism and World Politics," whereas Huntington does not, and thus classifies the region as a non-Western civilization. See also, Fareed Zakaria, "The Rise of Illiberal Democracy" *Foreign Affairs* 76(6) (November/December 1997): 36–38 who also seems to exclude Latin America from the group of Liberal republics.

25. Oren, "The Subjectivity of the 'Democratic' Peace"; Owen, "How Liberalism Produces the Democratic Peace."

26. The U.S. and Great Britain are liberal societies, and the rational choice analyses of voting behavior mainly draw on these two electorates for their empirical referents.

27. Owen recognizes that liberal societies may elect illiberal leaders, but expects the other constraints to keep the country from using force against another liberal state. "How Liberalism," p. 120. For a critique, see below.

28. Dennis C. Mueller, *Public Choice* (Cambridge: Cambridge University Press, 1979), pp. 41–42 discusses the dimensionality of issues. An excellent discussion of this phenomenon applied to the use of force is Kurt Taylor Gaubatz, "Intervention and Intransitivity: Public Opinion, Social Choice, and the Use of Military Force Abroad," *World Politics* 47 (July 1995): 534–54.

29. Mueller, *Public Choice*, pp. 43–49.

30. Ronald Hinckley, "Public Attitudes toward Key Foreign Policy Events," *Journal of Conflict Resolution* 32 (June 1988). Hinckley labels the variations within each group differently, but for our purposes "hard" and "soft" suffice.

31. In 1996 eight countries of Latin America were participating in UN peacekeeping missions. Antonio L. Pala, "Peacekeeping and Its Effects on Civil-Military Relations: The Argentine Experience" in Domínguez, ed., *International Security and Democracy*, p. 135. While most of these missions were outside the hemisphere, during the 1990s Venezuelan troops participated in the Central American missions and Argentine ships helped patrol Haiti. The U.S., Brazil, Argentina, and Chile also contributed troops to the peacekeeping force on the Ecuador-Peruvian border after the 1995 war.

32. On the Andean Pact, see Lynn Krieger Mytelka, *Regional Development in a Global Economy: The Multinational Corporation, Technology, and Andean Integration* (New Haven: Yale University Press, 1979). For a discussion of regionally competitive and collaborative geopolitics see Phillip Kelly and Jack Child, "An Overview: Geopolitics, Integration, and Conflict in the Southern Cone and Antartica," pp. 1–12 in Kelly and Child, eds., *Geopolitics of the Southern Cone and Antartica* (Boulder: Lynne Rienner, 1988).

33. This section is guided by the analysis of U.S. public opinion on participation in the 1990 Gulf War in Gaubatz, "Intervention and Intransitivity," pp. 542–49.

34. Juan Rial and Daniel Zovatto G., "La Política, los Partidos y las Elecciones en América Latina," pp. xxxvii-xlvi and Juan E. Mendez and Luis Alberto Cordero, "Presentación," p. xi, both in Juan Rial and Daniel Zovatto G., eds., *Elecciones y democracia en* América Latina, *1992–1996: Urnas y Desencanto Político* (San José, Costa Rica: Instituto Interamericano de Derechos Humanos, 1998).

35. Mueller, *Public Choice* p. 102, including fn. 3.

36. Donald E. Schulz and Gabriel Marcella, *Reconciling the Irreconcilable: The Troubled Outlook for U.S. Policy Toward Haiti* (Carlisle Barracks, PA: U.S. Army War College, Strategic Studies Institute, March 10, 1994), pp. 1–2.

37. Latin America Data Base, "Honduran, Salvadoran, & Nicaraguan Naval Forces Agree to Reduce Tensions in Gulf of Fonseca" *EcoCentral: Central American Economy & Sustainable Development* ISSN 1089–1560 2(32) (September 4, 1997).

38. Interview, Luis Alberto Huerta Guerrero, Comisión Andina de Juristas, Lima, Peru March 25, 1999.

39. Cf., the discussion in Part I of Peter F. Cowhey and Matthew D. McCubbins, eds., *Structure and Policy in Japan and the United States* (Cambridge: Cambridge University Press, 1995).

40. Winner take all elections discourage the formation of third parties and a two party system pushes the electorate toward the center. Thus it is theoretically erroneous to argue that U.S. citizens are represented by the median voter. Instead one needs to clarify that the median voter represents the citizens who actually vote, which in turn is affected by the institutional structure of elections.

41. Arendt Lipjhart "Presidential address" Western Political Science Association, Annual Meetings, March 1995, published in *American Political Science Review* 91(1) (March 1997): 1–14.

42. Palmer, Peru's 1995 Elections," p. 18.

43. Mathew Soberg Shugart and John M. Carey, *Presidents and Assemblies* (Cambridge: Cambridge University Press, 1992), pp. 31–32; Oscar Godoy Arcaya, ed., *Hacia Una Democracia Moderna: La Opción Parlamentaria* (Santiago: Universidad Católica de Chile, 1990).

44. Shugart and Carey, *Presidents and Assemblies*, pp. 87–91.

45. Scott Mainwaring and Timothy R. Scully, eds., *Building Democratic Institutions: Party Systems in Latin America* (Stanford: Stanford University Press, 1995), p. 1. The fourth category is implicit, although they explicitly discuss only the three categories in which party systems exist. Currently, Venezuela may be moving toward an inchoate and Mexico towards an institutionalized competitive party system.

46. Cf., Arthur M. Schlesinger, Jr., *The Imperial Presidency* (Boston, Houghton Mifflin, 1973); Holly Sklar, *Washington's War on Nicaragua* (Boston: South End Press, 1988).

47. Bueno de Mesquita and Lalman, *War and Reason*; Lake, "Powerful Pacifists."

48. An excellent comparative analysis of this relationship as it concerns domestic issues is Shugart and Carey, *Presidents and Assemblies*, pp. 106–66.

49. Framers of presidentialist constitutions recognize that legislatures may not be able to act quickly or may not be in session when a crisis occurs, therefore they provide the chief executive with the tools to act quickly. In addition, some

aspects of foreign policy may be the exclusive domain of the executive, including the use of force. The U.S. Constitution gives Congress control over budgets (including that of the military and the intelligence services) and the sole right to declare war. It also gives the executive the right to make foreign policy and defend the national interests of the U.S. See Franck and Weisband, *Foreign Policy by Congress*; on Latin America, Loveman, *Constitution of Tyranny*.

50. Shugart and Carey, *Presidents and Assemblies*, p. 141.

51. Franck and Weisband, *Foreign Policy by Congress*, pp. 14–19.

52. William H. Freivogel, "Gulf Debate May Decide War Powers, President could Gain Authority" *St. Louis Post-Dispatch*, January 10, 1991, p. 1C.

53. Franck and Weisband, *Foreign Policy by Congress*, pp. 61–82; Sklar, *Washington's War on Nicaragua*, pp. 321–49; for Venezuela, Latin American Data Base, *NotiSur* ISSN 1060–4189 6(23) (June 7, 1996); "Venezuela: Former President Carlos Andres Pérez Sentenced to 28 Months for Misappropriation of Funds"; the exact Chilean share has changed over time, Francisco Rojas Aravena, "Chile y el gasto militar: un criterio histórico y jurídico de asignación" in Francisco Rojas Aravena, ed., *Gasto Militar en América Latina* (Santiago: CINDE & FLACSO, 1994), pp. 255–56; Brenes, Arnoldo and Kevin Casas, *Soldados como empresarios* (San José: Fundación Arias Para la Paz y el Progreso Humano, 1998).

54. Brian Loveman, *The Constitution of Tyranny* examines the colonial and 19th century origins of these provisions, which continue in today's democratic constitutions.

55. Shugart and Carey, *Presidents and Assemblies*, pp. 141–42; Loveman, *The Constitution of Tyranny*, for Colombia, pp. 179–80; Peru, 232–33; Venezuela, p. 159.

56. Shugart and Carey, *Presidents and Assemblies* chapter 6.

57. Ibid., pp. 126–29.

58. Rhoda Rabkin, "The Aylwin Government and Tutelary Democracy: A Concept in Search of a Case?" *Journal of InterAmerican Economic and World Affairs* 34(4) (Winter 1992/93): 119–94; Francisco Rojas and Claudio Fuentes, " Civil-Military Relations in Chile's Geopolitical Transition" in Mares, ed., *Civil-Military Relations*, pp. 165–86.

59. Charles Sellers, "Hard War Averted—Easy War Gained" in Archie P. McDonald, ed., *The Mexican War: Crisis for American Diplomacy* (Lexington, MA: D.C. Heath, 1969), pp. 13–22; COW also codes the U.S. as initiator.

60. Mares, "Deterrence Bargaining."

61. Morgan and Bickers, "Domestic Discontent and the External Use of Force."

62. The authors did not test for this relationship.

63. *Grasping the Democratic Peace*, pp. 36–38, 120–24. In Maoz and Russett, "Normative and Structural Sources," however, the theoretical framework for the normative argument did not contemplate such a possibility; cf., p. 625.

64. From 1891 to 1973 Chile was governed by elected governments except for the brief period 1924–31 and the Socialists had participated in National Front governments from 1938–41 without provoking domestic disorder. For a discussion, see Paul Drake, *Socialism and Populism in Chile 1932–52* (Urbana: University of Illinois Press, 1978).

65. Paul E. Sigmund, *The United States and Democracy in Chile* (Baltimore: Johns Hopkins University Press, 1993).

66. I want to thank Steven Bernstein for running the statistical analyses.

67. Analysts familiar with Latin American politics might find another type of constraint on leaders particularly useful given the historical role of the military in Latin American politics; cf., Stepan, *The Military in Politics*. Categorizing civil-military relations would enable us to test whether the degree of military domination of government affects a state's militarized dispute behavior. Although Posen, *The Sources of Military Doctrine France, Britain, and Germany Between the World Wars* (Ithaca: Cornell University Press, 1984), and Snyder, *The Ideology of the Offensive* argue that militaries prefer offensive doctrines, in *Soldiers, Statesmen and Cold War Crises* Betts finds that military leaders are not quicker than civilians to advocate the use of force in a crisis. Rapoport, "A Comparative Theory of Military and Political Types" and Andreski, "On the Peaceful Disposition of Military Dictatorships," claim that militaries involved in combating domestic civilian disturbances and paramilitary threats will be unable to successfully fight another army, consequently, military governments are peaceful internationally. (Of course, this claim of reticence based on a weak military would only hold if the potential targeted country did not use its military force in the same way, otherwise both militaries are weak and the determinants of the use of force have to be found elsewhere.) Banks' index of military domination of a polity looked promising for these purposes. Unfortunately, the large number of missing values precludes its use in this analysis. (For South America's 130 MIDs in this time period, 24 disputes cannot be coded because of missing values; for Central America 50 of 124 MIDs are missing.) He also develops a *constraint on the executive* variable. These constraints can be imposed by any political groups (legislatures, nobles, parties, the military); all that is required is that they be a recognized part of the decisionmaking process. But again, the time period covered by this variable does extend into the recent redemocratization wave in the region.

68. Gurr, *Polity II*, pp. 38–39. Bruce Bueno de Mesquita and Randolph M. Siverson, "War and the Survival of Political Leaders: A Comparative Study of Regime Types and Political Accountability" *American Political Science Review* 98(4) (December 1995): 841–55 also use this indicator for regime type, labeling it a "relatively rigorous measure."

69. *Polity III* was constructed by one of the authors of *Polity II* and is less complete. Some of the revisions of the prior data seem problematic. Mexico is reclassified as a 0 on the 0–10 scale up through 1978, giving it the same score as Castro's Cuba and the first 14 years of Pinochet's Chile! Since 1978 Mexico is a 2, which is the same score merited by the last two years of Pinochet's military dictatorship. Chile from 1955 to 1962, a period in which the Socialist candidate narrowly lost the 1958 Presidential election, is given the same score that the Imperial Japan of World War II earned in *Polity II*! The downgrading of El Salvador from a 8 to a 3 in 1969 (despite the fact that the President's party had a bare majority in the Legislature and that he had to negotiate with the non-Communist opposition groups before engaging in the Soccer War [Anderson, *War of the Dispossessed*, pp. 107–08]), puts it at the same level as Peru in 1992–93 when President Fujimori dissolved Congress and ruled by decree and military force. In the face of these problems, two points are worth emphasizing. First, the bias seems to be to lower democracy scores, which should strengthen the support for an argument that democracies are inherently peaceful by eliminating many of the cases in which countries otherwise thought to be democracies engaged in MIDs. Secondly, if we utilize just *Polity II* the analysis must end in 1982, just when redemocratization begins in Latin America. Consequently, I use *Polity III* and note its limitations.

70. Doyle's "Pacific Union" listing also includes many of these Latin American countries as pacific liberal republics. "Liberalism and World Politics" Appendix.

71. R.J. Rummel, "Libertarianism and International Violence" *Journal of Conflict Resolution* 27(1) 1983 and "Libertarian Propositions on Violence Within and Between Nations: A Test Against Published Research Results" *Journal of Conflict Resolution* 29(3) 1985; Maoz and Russett, "Normative and Structural Causes," p. 635; Chan, "Mirror, Mirror on the Wall . . ." p. 621; but see Erich Weede, "Democracy and War Involvement" *Journal of Conflict Resolution* 28(4) (December 1984): 660; Maoz and Abdolali, "Regime Types and International Conflict, 1816–1976," pp. 18, 20; T. Clifton Morgan and Sally Howard Campbell, "Domestic Structure, Decisional Constraints, and War: So Why Kant Democracies Fight?" *Journal of Conflict Resolution* 35(2) (1991): 195.

72. Except for Rummel, "Libertarianism and International Violence" and "Libertarian Propositions" and Maoz and Russett, "Normative and Structural Sources."

5. The Distribution of Power and Military Conflict

1. Cf. the diplomatic correspondence from the British Ministers in Buenos Aires and Rio de Janeiro in the Foreign Office files, Public Records Office, London, 1906–14.

2.   John Child, *The Unequal Alliance: The Inter-American Military System, 1938–1978* (Boulder: Westview Press, 1980).

3.   For example, the Colombian legislature approved a large arms buildup after the 1987 war scare with Venezuela. Area and Nieschulz de Stockhausen, *El Golfo de Venezuela*, pp. 64–87. In 1958 Chile's Congress adopted legislation guaranteeing its military a percentage of copper export revenue for weapons purchases; there have been subsequent modifications in both the percentages and the manner in which they are calculated. Rojas Aravena, "Chile y el gasto militar," pp. 254–59. See also, Miguel Navarro, Equilibrios estratégicos en el Cono Sur: una aproximación chilena" in Francisco Rojas Aravena, ed., *Balance Estratégico y Medidas de Confianza Mutua* (Santiago: FLACSO, 1996), pp. 271–302.

4.   Thomaz Guedes da Costa critiques recent U.S. policymakers' suggestions for the future role of the Latin American military in "Post-Cold War Military Relations between the United States and Latin America," in Lars Schoultz, William C. Smith, and Augusto Varas, eds., *Security, Democracy, and Development in U.S.-Latin American Relations* (Miami: North-South Center, University of Miami, 1994), esp. pp. 143–44.

5.   Thucydides, *The Peloponnesian War*; Niccolo Machiavelli, *The Prince*, edited and translated by David Wootton (Indianapolis: Hackett Pub. Co., c. 1995); Morgenthau, *Politics Among Nations*; Mearsheimer, "The False Promise of Institutions."

6.   Waltz, *The Theory of International Politics*; Jervis, "Cooperation Under the Security Dilemma"; Charles L. Glaser, "Realists as Optimists: Cooperation as Self-Help," *International Security* Winter 1994/95 19(3): 50–90.

7.   Some analysts wish to make the heroic assumption that anarchy does not necessarily imply a concern for security. Cf. Wendt "Anarchy Is What States Make of It: The Social Construction of State Politics," *International Organization* 46(2) (Spring 1992): 391–425. But this argument requires two difficult and related situations in order to succeed. States must be able to confide completely in the signals they are sending each other, and they must be perfectly pacific. The argument that states fear for their security, on the other hand, simply requires that communication not be perfect and that some states, even a minority of one whose identity is unknown, be willing to act first and ask questions later.

8.   Cf. Mearsheimer, "False Promise."

9.   Jervis, "Cooperation Under the Security Dilemma;" Mearsheimer, *Conventional Deterrence*, pp. 24–27; Jack Levy, "The Offensive/Defensive Balance of Military Technology: A Theoretical and Historical Analysis" *International Studies Quarterly* 28(2) (June 1984): 219–38.

10.   Barry R. Posen, "Measuring the European Conventional Balance" *International Security* 9(3) (Winter 1984–85): 47–88. Even when Realists look to eco-

nomic and political variables, it is because they affect how many resources and for how long a country can commit to the battlefield.

11. Lebow argues that the existence of nonmilitary proximate causes refutes Realism. *Between Peace and War: The Nature of International Crisis* (Baltimore: Johns Hopkins University Press, 1981), pp. 334–37.

12. See the discussion in Bremer, "Dangerous Dyads," pp. 313–14; A.F.K. Organski and Jacek Kugler go so far as to argue that no distribution of power model can explain war in the "periphery." *The War Ledger* (Chicago: University of Chicago Press, 1980), pp. 29, 32, 45, and 51–53.

13. Organski and Kugler, *War Ledger*, p. 49 favor 80% while Bremer, "Dangerous Dyads" uses 3/1 and 10/1.

14. Organski and Kugler, *The War Ledger*; Jacek Kugler and A.F.K. Organski, "The Power Transition: A Retrospective and Prospective Evaluation" in Manus I. Midlarsky, ed., *Handbook of War Studies* (Ann Arbor: University of Michigan Press, 1993 reprint of Unwin Hyman 1989), pp. 173–74.

15. Organski and Kugler, *War Ledger*, pp. 19–22; 206.

16. A.F.K. Organski, *World Politics* (New York: Knopf, 1968, 2nd ed), p. 373.

17. Organski and Kugler, *The War Ledger*, p. 45.

18. Joseph E. Loftus, *Latin American Defense Expenditures, 1938–1965* (Santa Monica: RAND, 1968) RM-5310-PR/ISA.

19. Martin C. Needler, "United States Government Figures on Latin American Military Expenditures" *Latin American Research Review* 1973 8(2): 101–3.

20. See the dispatches from the British Ministers in South America during the arms buildup in South America at the beginning of the twentieth century. Foreign Office, Public Records Office, London.

21. Discussed in J. David Singer, ed., *The Correlates of War* (New York: Free Press, 1979).

22. I want to thank Steven A. Bernstein for undertaking this statistical analysis. An earlier version was published in David R. Mares and Steven A. Bernstein, "Explaining the Use of Force in Latin America" in Jorge I. Domínguez, ed., *International Security and Democracy*, pp. 29–47. Although in chapter 2 I updated MID and Democracy data to 1998, I did not have the opportunity to confirm or calibrate my calculations across the relevant categories and components of the data bases with those done by the other research teams. In particular, I refrained from distinguishing between democracy levels 6–10. Consequently, I have not incorporated these extra years into the statistical analysis.

23. David Spiro, "On the statistical insignificance of the Democratic Peace."

24. U.S. Department of Defense figures. *Keesings* 36(1) (January 1990) #37181.

25. Max G. Manwaring, "Monitoring Latin American Arms Control Agreements" in Morris and Millan, *Controlling Latin American Conflicts* Table 9.3, p. 182.

26. For a discussion of the National Period see chapter 2.

27. The impression for the first four and last wars is based on total population, GNP and my reading of the secondary literature on the status of the military in each country at the time. See especially Rout, *Politics of the Chaco Peace Conference*, pp. 41–45 and Wood, *The United States and Latin American Wars*. I use Manwaring's analysis of Relative Military Capability for the 1969 and 1982 wars,.

28. Gary W. Wynia, *Argentina Illusions and Realities* (New York: Holmes & Meier, 1986), p. 21. Michael Brzoska and Frederic S. Pearson, *Arms and Warfare: Escalation, De-escalation and Negotiation* (Columbia: University of South Carolina, 1994), p. 80.

29. Augusto Varas, *Militarization and the International Arms Race in Latin America* (Boulder: Westview, 1985), p. 55.

30. See the annual volumes edited by the Centro Latinoamericano de Defensa y Desarme *Estudio Estratégico de América Latina* Santiago, Chile and the monthly newsletter of the UN Centro Regional Para la Paz, El Desarme y el Desarrollo en América Latina y el Caribe, based in Lima, Peru. The case for unilateral arms reduction is made in Bennett Ramberg, ed., *Arms Control Without Negotiation: From the Cold War to the New World Order* (Boulder: Lynne Rienner, 1993). Costa Rica (1949), Haiti (1994) and Panama (1994) disbanded their militaries.

31. Graham T. Allison. "Questions About the Arms Race: Who's Racing Whom? A Bureaucratic Perspective" in Robert L. Pfaltzgraff Jr., ed. *Contrasting Approaches to Strategic Arms Control* (Lexington: Lexington Books, 1974); Robert E. Looney, *The Political Economy of Latin American Defense Expenditures* (Lexington, MA: D.C. Heath, 1986) examines the impact of macroeconomic conditions on defense expenditures. Jose O. Maldifassi and Pier A. Abetti, *Defense Industries in Latin American Countries: Argentina, Brazil, Chile* (Westport CT: Praeger 1984) argue that an inability to procure arms in the quantity and quality desired stimulated the development of defense industries in these South American countries.

32. Luiz Cervo and Bueno, *Historia da Política Exterior do Brasil*, pp. 98–104.

33. By some estimates up to 80% of Paraguayan males perished in the six year war. For a discussion of the aftermath, see Harris Gaylord Warren, *Paraguay and the Triple Alliance: The Postwar Decade, 1869–1978* (Austin: University of Texas Press, 1974).

34. Luiz Cervo and Bueno, *Historia da Política Exterior do Brasil*, pp. 107–14.

35. Nunn, *Yesterday's Soldiers*.

36. Bello, *A History of Modern Brazil*, p. 189; D.R. O'Sullivan to Sir Earl Grey, November 10, 1906, Haggard to Grey, 30 September 1906, and Barclay to Grey, October 5, 1906, all Public Records Office, Foreign Office, London; Nunn,

Yesterday's Soldiers, pp. 56–61; Joseph Smith, *Unequal Giants: Diplomatic Relations Between the United States and Brazil, 1889–1930* (Pittsburgh: University of Pittsburgh Press, 1991), pp. 62–67.

37. Burns, *By Reason or Force*, pp. 183–84.

38. Hanford to Grey, July 30, 1906, Public Records Office, Foreign Office, London 1906, Folio 371.5 f28811, p. 157.

39. Burns, *By Reason or Force*, p. 182.

40. Nunn, *Yesterday's Soldiers*, p. 124; Public Records Office, Foreign Office, London for years 1906–1910. Cable traffic between the British Minister in Buenos Aires and London at this time contains many Argentine admonitions for Her Majesty's Government to pressure Brazil to moderate its naval program.

41. Burns, *The Unwritten Alliance*, pp. 185–191; Haggard to Grey, November 28, 1910, Public Record Office, Foreign Office FO 371/833. XC16815.

42. Javier Villanueva, "Economic Development" in Mark Falcoff and Ronald H. Dolkart, eds., *Prologue to Peron: Argentina in Depression and War, 1930–1943* (Berkeley: University of California Press, 1975), pp. 65–78; Wynia, *Argentina*, pp. 37–38.

43. Robert A. Potash, *The Army and Politics in Argentina, 1928–1945* (Stanford: Stanford University Press, 1969), pp. 5–17; Glen Barclay, *Struggle for a Continent* (New York: SUNY Press, 1972), pp. 34, 36, 44–45; 68–76.

44. McCann, Jr. "The Brazilian General Staff and Brazil's Military Situation, 1900–1945," p. 307.

45. Hilton, *Brazil and the Soviet Challenge, 1917–1947*, pp. 34, 47–48, 61, 99–101, 163, and 180.

46. Barclay, *Struggle for a Continent*, p. 96.

47. U.S. State Department Press Releases, August 21, 1937, p. 162, as cited in Graham H. Stuart, *Latin America and the United States* (New York: Appleton-Century-Crofts, 1955, 5th edition).

48. David R. Mares, "Middle Powers under Regional Hegemony: To Challenge or Acquiesce in Hegemonic Enforcement" *International Studies Quarterly* 32 (1988): pp. 453–71; McCann, Jr., "The Brazilian General Staff and Brazil's Military Situation, 1900–1945," p. 314.

49. The U.S. claimed that the Argentine military was pro-fascist. But their fascist tendencies were not very different from those of Getulio Vargas' Estado Novo in Brazil. For an examination of the U.S.-Argentine relationship see Francis, *The Limits of Hegemony* and Di Tella and Watt, eds., *Argentina Between the Great Powers, 1939–46*.

50. Potash, *Army and Politics in Argentina, 1928–1945*, pp. 168–74. The quote is from German documents cited on p. 172, fn. 103.

51. Brazilian combat experience in Italy is detailed in Frank D. McCann, Jr., *The Brazilian-American Alliance 1937–1945* (Princeton: Princeton University Press, 1973), pp. 403–42.

52. Loftus, *Latin American Defense Expenditures, 1938–1965*. The author cautions that the figures are not entirely reliable, but they are the best we have and confirm impressionistic conclusions. McCann also sees a shift in the trend after World War II "The Brazilian General Staff and Brazil's Military Situation, 1900–1945," p. 317; Nunn says manpower decreased between 1955 and 1965 *The Military in Chilean History: Essays on Civil-Military Relations, 1810–1973* (Albuquerque: University of New Mexico Press, 1976), p. 251.

53. In an analysis of military expenditures from 1950–1970 Schmitter claims that Brazilian expenditures were not stimulated by Argentine expenditures, but that Argentina's did react to Brazil's. Philippe C. Schmitter, "Foreign Military Assistance, National Military Spending and Military Rule in Latin America" in Schmitter, ed., *Military Rule in Latin America* (Beverly Hills: SAGE, 1973), p. 169.

54. Wayne A. Selcher, "Brasilian-Argentine Relations in the 1980s: From Wary Rivalry to Friendly Competition" *Journal of InterAmerican and World Affairs* 27(2) (Summer 1985): 25–54.

55. Manwaring, "Monitoring Latin American Arms Control," pp. 172–73; 182–83. Indicative of the problems of estimating the military balance in Latin America at this time, the sources cited in footnote 49 would have a difficult time believing that Argentina had a 4 to 1 advantage in 1970.

56. McCann, Jr., "The Brazilian General Staff and Brazil's Military Situation, 1900–1945," p. 299.

57. Thomaz Guedes da Costa, "La percepción de amenazas desde el punto de vista de los militares brasileros en las décadas del 70 y 80" in VA Rigoberto Cruz Johnson and Augusto Varas Fernández, eds., *Percepciones de Amenaza y Políticas de Defensa en América Latina* (Santiago: FLACSO, 1993), pp. 193–210; Selcher, "Brasilian-Argentine Relations," p. 30.

58. Wayne A. Selcher, *Brazil's Multilateral Relations: Between First and Third Worlds* (Boulder: Westview, 1978), pp. 264–66; Paul L. Leventhal and Sharon Tanzer, eds., *Averting a Latin American Nuclear Arms Race: New Prospects and Challenges for Argentine-Brazilian Nuclear Cooperation* (New York: St. Martin's, 1992); Riordan Roett, ed., *Mercosur: Regional Integration, World Markets* (Boulder, CO: Lynne Rienner, 1999).

59. Camilión at the Argentine-American Forum, October 31–November 2, 1993 and Domínguez in "Chile comprará más mísiles: equilibrio militar en el Cono Sur" *Clarín* (Buenos Aires) January 23, 1998. Argentina has significantly increased its radar capabilities in the recent purchases of 53 U.S. Skyhawk A4s equipped with the same radar found in the F-16. Luis Garasino, "Aviones para la Fuerza Aerea" *Clarín* December 15, 1997. Though old, the Skyhawks had been responsible for destroying some of the British ships during the Malvinas

War. Adrian J. English, *Battle for the Falklands (2) Naval Forces* (London: Osprey, 1982), pp. 27–29.

60. "La OTAN rechazó el pedido de incorporación de la Argentina," *Clarín* July 29, 1999.

61. "Chile comprará más mísiles" *Clarín*. "Old Latin American Rivalries Re-emerge, Generating Concerns About U.S. Diplomacy in the Region" *Eco-Central* ISSN 1060–4189 7(31) (August 29, 1997). The Brazilians worried about the political and military effects on the South American security environment of having Argentina join a military alliance outside the region. "OTAN: ya se quejó Brasil" *Clarín* July 10, 1999.

62. Tomaz Guedes da Costa, "Democratization and International Integration: The Role of the Armed Forces in Brazil's Grand Strategy" in Mares, ed., *Civil-Military Relations*, pp. 223–37.

63. For a review of actions and the accusations traded by important politicians and policymakers in both countries during the crisis, see Area and Nieschulz de Stockhausen, *El Golfo de Venezuela*, pp. 64–87 and Liliana Obregón T. and Carlo Nasi L., *Colombia Venezuela: Conflicto o Integracíon* (Bogotá: FESCOL, 1990).

64. "Uslar Pietri: puede estallar un gran conflicto" *El Nacional* (Caracas) March 17, 1995, pp. Al, 8.

65. "Chile Acquires Mirage Jets" CHIPnews March 20, 1995; for a discussion of the Chilean Mirages see *América Vuela* (No. 25, 1995): 22–27. On Peruvian threat perceptions, see St. John, *Foreign Policy of Peru*, pp. 203–5; Masterson, *Militarism and Politics in Latin America*, p. 265. Citing Pentagon sources, CLADDE-RIAL reports that the Soviet Union provided Peru with 115 military advisers in the Army and Air Force, and trained 200 commissioned and non-commissioned officers, *Limitación de Armamentos y Confianza Mutua en América Latina* Santiago: Ediciones ChileAmerica, 1988, p. 348. Military expenditures can be found in ACDA, *World Military Expenditures and Arms Transfers* various issues.

6. Military Leadership and the Use of Force

1. Andreski; "On the Peaceful Disposition"; Kurt Dassel, "Civilians, Soldiers, and Strife: Domestic Sources of International Aggression" *International Security* 23(1) (Summer 1998): 107–40, focuses on the trade-offs for militaries whose institutions are "contested."

2. Cf. Arturo Valenzuela, "The Military in Power: The Consolidation of One-Man Rule" in Paul Drake and Ivan Jaskic, eds., *The Struggle for Democracy in Chile* (Lincoln: University of Nebraska Press, 1995), revised edition. But Gen-

aro Arriagada Herrera, "The Legal and Institutional Framework of the Armed Forces in Chile" in J. Samuel Valenzuela and Arturo Valenzuela, eds., *Military Rule in Chile: Dictatorship and Oppositions* (Baltimore: Johns Hopkins University Press, 1986), pp. 117–43, sees some negative impact on Chilean professionalism.

3.   Antonio Cavalla, *El conflicto del Beagle* (Mexico: Casa del Chile, 1979), pp. 19–23; Burr, *By Reason or Force*, pp. 247–56.

4.   Stephen M. Gorman, "Geopolitics and Peruvian Foreign Policy" *Journal of Inter-American Economic Affairs* 36(2) (Autumn 1982): 81 and "The High Stakes of Geopolitics in Tierra del Fuego" *Parameters* 8(2) (1978): 45–46.

5.   Juan Archibaldo Lanús, *De Chapultepec al Beagle* (Buenos Aires: Emece, 1984), pp. 510–12; James L. Garrett, "The Beagle Dispute: Confrontation and Negotiation in the Southern Cone" *Journal of Inter-American Studies and World Affairs* 27(3) (Fall 1985): 90.

6.   Thomas Princen, *Beagle Channel Negotiations*. Pew Case Studies in International Affairs, Case 401. Institute for the Study of Diplomacy, Georgetown University, 1988, p. 2. Thomas Princen, *Intermediaries in International Conflict* (Princeton: Princeton University Press, 1992), p. 134.

7.   Lanús, *De Chapultepec al Beagle*, p. 517.

8.   Ibid. On the 1976 coup, see David G. Erro, *Resolving the Argentine Paradox: Politics and Development, 1966–1992* (Boulder: Lynne Rienner, 1993), pp. 73–98.

9.   Princen, *Beagle Channel Negotiations*, p. 3; Lanús, *De Chapultepec al Beagle*, p. 517.

10.   Garrett, "The Beagle Dispute," p. 93; Roberto Russell, "El Proceso de toma de decisiones en la política exterior argentina" in Roberto Russell, ed., *Política Exterior y El Proceso de Toma de Decisiones en América Latina* (Buenos Aires: Grupo Editorial Latinoamericano, 1990), p. 36.

11.   Cf. The proposal by the Argentine Junta to Chile that it not use the Award to extend its sovereign claims to new Antarctic territories. Roberto Russell, "El Proceso de toma de decisiones," p. 38.

12.   Italics are those of the author. Russell, "El Proceso de toma de decisiones," p. 36 citing *La Opinión* of May 4 , 1977.

13.   Garrett, "Beagle Channel," p. 93.

14.   Russell, "El proceso de toma de decisiones," pp. 38–39.

15.   Lanús, *De Chapultepec al Beagle*, p. 519.

16.   If Argentina had merely rejected the Arbitral Award Chile would have had legal standing to appeal to the ICJ. Russell, "El proceso de toma de decisiones," pp. 41–42.

17.   Andreas Keller Sarmiento, "The Dynamics of Decision-Making in the Argentine Military Government, 1976–82: The Beagle Crisis" BA Thesis, Depart-

ment of Government, Harvard College March 1984, p. 89, citing his interview with Admiral Allara on January 4, 1984.

18. There is some speculation that Argentina planned to seize the still disputed Beagle Channel islands in 1982 if the seizure of the Malvinas/Falklands Islands had been successful. Cf. Martin Middlebrook, *Task Force: The Falklands War, 1982* (London: Penguin, 1987, revised edition), p. 36.

19. Princen, *Intermediaries in International Conflict*, pp. 144–50.

20. Russell, "El Proceso de Toma," pp. 54–58.

21. General Pinochet, now Senator-for-life, was arrested in 1998 in London for possible extradition to Spain on charges of genocide stemming from his military government. During his defense, both his attorneys and former British Prime Minister Margaret Thatcher highlighted Pinochet's aid to Britain during the 1982 Malvinas/Falklands War. *ChipNews* "Foreign Office Ends Immunity Dispute: Thatcher Calls for Immediate Release" October 22, 1998. In retaliation for Pinochet's arrest Chile suspended its transportation links to the islands and joined Mercosur in calling for recognition of Argentine sovereignty over the islands. Foreign Minister Jose Miguel Insulza even said that Chile "should never have supported Great Britain" in the 1982 war! *Noti-Sur* "Chile & Argentina Resolve Last Border Dispute" ISSN 1060–4189 9(1) (January 8, 1999).

22. Note that the General and his military cohorts were willing to violate international laws and treaties that would constrain them in violating the human and political rights of anyone they believed posed a threat to their ability to restructure Chilean society, economy and politics. Thus this was not a stance on the legitimacy of international law *per se*.

23. Masterson, *Militarism and Politics in Latin America*, p. 265.

24. Burr, *By Reason or Force*, pp. 245–63; Emilio Meneses, *Ayuda Económica, Política Exterior y Política de Defensa en Chile, 1943–1973* (Santiago: Centro de Estudios Políticos, 1989) Documento de Trabajo 117.

25. See discussion in chapter 5.

26. Lanús, *De Chapultepec al Beagle*, p. 528; Princen, *Intermediaries in International Conflict*, pp. 142–43.

27. Kurt Dassel, "Domestic Instability, the Military, and War," PhD Dissertation, Columbia University, Department of Political Science, 1996.

28. English, *Armed Forces of Latin America*; figures are based on 1980 and 1981.

29. Gorman, "The High Stakes," pp. 9–10.

30. English, *Armed Forces of Latin America*, p. 134; In August 1999 there were unconfirmed rumors that Chile might agree to de-mine the border area. Atilio Bleta, "Tras los incidentes en Jujuy, Ménem se despidió de Frei" *Clarín* August 20, 1999.

31. Peru did provide fighter aircraft to Argentina during the Malvinas/Falklands War in 1982. But that aid was largely symbolic and there was little reason for Peru to fear retaliation by the British.

32. Lanús, *De Chapultepec al Beagle*, p. 518–23; Russell, "El proceso de toma de decisiones," p. 46. Chile did not accept the possibility of joint sovereignty over the islands. Pinochet also rejected the idea of continuing with direct negotiations after November 2, 1978.

33. See the declaration by Alfonsín's Minister of the Interior, Antonio Troccoli, in Russell, "El Proceso de Toma de Decisiones," p. 55.

34. Andres Miguel Fontana, "Political Decision-Making By a Military Corporation: Argentina, 1976–1983" (PhD Dissertation, University of Texas at Austin, 1987), pp. 57–59.

35. Russell, "El Proceso de Toma de Decisiones," p. 18; Keller Sarmiento, "The Dynamics of Decision-Making in the Argentine Military Government," p. 53, citing *La Prensa* April 15, 1978.

36. Lanús, *De Chapultepec al Beagle*, p. 521.

37. Fontana, "Political Decision-Making By a Military Corporation," p. 74. Videla requested the resignations of numerous military cabinet ministers and governors and reassigned ministerial responsibilities. The navy perceived all of this to the detriment of their influence. Russell, "El Proceso de Toma de Decisiones," p. 19.

38. Russell, "El Proceso de Toma de Decisiones," p. 50; fn. 111, 112, citing investigative report in the newspaper *Somos* (February 17, 1984): 31–32.

39. Russell, "El Proceso de Toma de Decisiones," pp. 50–51.

40. Russell, Ibid., p. 52; Princen, *Intermediaries in International Conflict*, does not refer to the meeting of the 22nd in his discussion. P. 144, nor does Lanús, *De Chapultepec al Beagle*, p. 529.

41. Princen, *Intermediaries in International Conflict*, p. 148–49.

42. Keller Sarmiento, "The Dynamics of Decision-Making in the Argentine Military Government," p. 110.

43. Russell, "El Proceso de Toma de Decisiones," p. 53.

44. A Chilean reserve officer told me in confidence that Argentine troops had indeed crossed the border in the north on the day that the islands were to be seized but retreated quickly once the order to occupy the islands had been postponed. I could not, however, corroborate this claim and it seems unlikely that Chilean troops would have been caught unawares of an Argentine crossing.

45. *La Nación* (Buenos Aires), October 4, 1977 as cited in Russell, "El Proceso de Toma de Decisiones," p. 42.

46. Russell "El Proceso de toma de decisiones," p. 47 fn. 100 and p. 49, fn. 107, respectively.

47. *Tiempo Argentino* June 8, 1994 and *Clarín*, July 22, 1984, respectively, and as cited in Russell, "El Proceso de Toma," pp. 54–55.

48. Russell, "El Proceso de Toma," pp. 54–58.

49. Cf., Cavalla, *El conflicto del Beagle*.

50. On Videla's efforts to liberalize politically, see Fontana, "Political Decision-Making by a Military Corporation," pp. 72–90; Keller Sarmiento, "The Dynamics of Decision-Making in the Argentine Military Government," pp. 56–60.

51. Russell, "El Proceso de Toma de Decisiones," p. 46.

52. Lanús, *De Chapultepec al Beagle*, pp. 523–25; Princen, *International Intermediaries* reports on the collapse of negotiations but focuses only on whether the Pope would be the mediator, not on the disagreement over the grounds for mediation, pp. 138–43.

53. Lanús, *De Chapultepec al Beagle*, pp. 526–28; Princen, *International Intermediaries*, pp. 142–43.

54. Fontana, "Political Decision-Making By a Military Corporation," pp. 66–72.

55. Mónica Peralta Ramos, "Toward an Analysis of the Structural Basis of Coercion in Argentina: The Behavior of the Major Factions of the Bourgeoisie, 1976–1983" in Mónica Peralta Ramos and Carlos H. Waisman, eds., *From Military Rule to Liberal Democracy in Argentina* (Boulder: Westview, 1987), pp. 55–56; Erro, *Resolving the Argentine Paradox*, pp. 124–25.

56. Fontana, "Political Decision-Making By a Military Corporation," pp. 121–22.

57. Erro, *Resolving the Argentine Paradox*, pp. 123–26.

58. Fontana, "Political Decision-Making By a Military Corporation," pp. 126–31.

59. Middlebrook, *Task Force*, p. 36; Fontana, "Political Decision-Making By a Military Corporation," pp. 140–41, but Lawrence Freedman and Virginia Gamba-Stonehouse, *Signals of War: The Falklands Conflict of 1982* (Princeton: Princeton University Press, 1991) see the Malvinas issue as secondary to those concerning economic policies, pp. 3–4.

60. Latin American Bureau, *Falklands/Malvinas: Whose Crisis?* (London: Latin American Bureau Ltd, 1982), p. 80.

61. Carlos J. Moneta, "The Malvinas Conflict: Some Elements for an Analysis of the Argentine Military Regime's Decision-Making Process" in Heraldo Munoz and Joseph S. Tulchin, eds., *Latin American Nations in World Politics* (Boulder: Westview, 1984), pp. 128–29, also reprinted in *Millenium* 13(3): 198ff.

62. The plebiscite was in response to United Nations condemnation of the Chilean government for massive human rights violations. Under the repressive conditions of the times, the vote was hardly "free and unfettered" but it did allow Pinochet to claim a popular basis for his government. To a military who saw themselves acting in the name of the nation, it would be difficult to discard the results entirely. Valenzuela, "The Military in Power," p. 38.

63. Valenzuela, "The Military in Power," p. 61; Eduardo Silva, "The Political Economy of Chile's Regime Transition: From Radical to 'Pragmatic' Neo-Liberal Policies" in Drake and Jaskic, *The Struggle for Democracy in Chile*, pp.

98–127 discusses the economic concessions Pinochet made to his constituencies between 1983–1985.

64. In 1988 Pinochet lost his bid for re-election, garnering "only" 43 percent of the vote against a combined opposition. Probably to his detriment, Pinochet had structured the vote to be either "yes or no" on whether he should continue in office. As it became clear that Pinochet was losing the 1988 plebiscite on whether he should remain in power for another ten years, he looked for a way to continue his regime but the other members of the Junta refused to support such a move. Chile held democratic elections the following year. Sigmund, *The United States and Democracy in Chile*, pp. 167–78.

65. Nora Femenia, *National Identity in Times of Crises: The Scripts of the Falklands-Malvinas War* (Commack, New York: Nova Science Publishers, Inc. 1996), *passim*.

66. See the analysis of decisionmaking in the Malvinas case undertaken by the military government that assumed office after the defeat: Rattenbach Commission, *Informe Rattenbach: El Drama de Malvinas* (Buenos Aires: Ediciones Espártaco, 1988), pp. 25–42; also, Freedman and Gamba-Stonehouse, *Signals of War*, pp. 7–11; Guillermo A. Makin, "Argentine approaches to the Falklands/Malvinas: Was the Resort to Violence Foreseeable?" *International Affairs* (1983): 403.

67. Freedman and Gamba-Stonehouse, *Signals of War*, pp. 10–11, 78–81.

68. Rattenbach Commission, *Informe Rattenbach* is highly critical of the Junta's military planning, pp. 45–61.

69. Freedman and Gamba-Stonehouse, *Signals of War*, pp. 4–13; Femenia, *National Identity in Times of Crises*, pp. 84–102.

70. *Informe Rattenbach*, pp. 63–87.

71. Prime Minister Margaret Thatcher's decision to respond with military force cannot be analyzed in the limited space available here. But the five factors determining costs and cost acceptability for the use of force in the militarized bargaining model also explain her decision. The costs produced by (S) recover islands before negotiating + (SB) overwhelming in favor of Britain in the diplomatic, economic and military arenas + (F) large naval task force, aided by U.S. material and intelligence support were less than those willing to be paid by her constituency (CC) and she was very constrained by her constituency, given the British parliamentary system (A). Cf., Walter Little, "Public Opinion in Britain" in Wayne S. Smith, ed., *Toward Resolution? The Falklands/Malvinas Dispute* (Boulder: Lynne Rienner, 1991), pp. 63–80; Latin American Bureau, *Falklands/Malvinas*, pp. 101–26; Femenia, *National Identity in Time of Crisis*, pp. 121–204; Freedman and Gamba-Stonehouse, *Signals of War*, *passim*.

72. Rettenbach Commission, *Informe Rettenbach*, p. 56.

7. Democracies and the Use of Force

1.   According to the MID data base all the Ecuador-Peru disputes in this period included displays or actual use of force by one of the participants, and not merely verbal threats. Other sources include Loftus, *Latin American Defense Expenditures*, pp. 27–29; *Hoy* December 29, 1995 and "Peru and Ecuador Hold Fresh Talks" *Financial Times* September 8, 1998, p. 9; 1998; Carlos E. Scheggia Flores, *Orígen del Pueblo Ecuatoriano y Sus Infundadas Pretensiones Amazónicas* (Lima: Talleres de Linea, 1992), p. 61; Ministry of Foreign Affairs, *Hacia la Solución del Problema Territorial con el Perú: Libro Blanco* (Quito: Ministry of Foreign Affairs, 1992), pp. 194–95.

2.   This brief historical summary is based largely upon Julio Tóbar Donoso and Alfredo Luna Tóbar, *Derecho Territorial Ecuatoriano* (Quito: Ministry of Foreign Affairs, 1994, 4th edition); Gustavo Pons Muzzo, *Estudio Histórico sobre el Protocolo de Rio de Janeiro* (Lima: n.p., 1994); Scheggia Flores, *Orígen del Pueblo Ecuatoriano*; Ministry of Foreign Affairs, *Hacia la Solución*; Wood, *The United States and Latin American Wars, 1932–42.*

3.   Burr, *By Reason or Force*, pp. 44–45; 80–88; 146–47.

4.   Peru was fearful of renewed Chilean attacks, since they remained in possession of Peruvian territory in Tacna and Arica. For a discussion, see chapter 3.

5.   *Foreign Relations of the United States* (hereafter FRUS) (1910): 439.

6.   Chile had also made explicit offers of alliance to Ecuador in the nineteenth century: St. John, *Foreign Policy of Peru*, pp. 153–54, 34, and 111. U.S. and Argentine diplomats also believed that Chile had significant influence in Quito. FRUS 1910, pp. 492–93.

7.   Ironically, the contemplated settlement in 1910, while depriving Ecuador of vast territory, provided for Ecuadorian access to the Maranon River and the treaty following the 1941 war would not.

8.   FRUS (1910): 171–83.

9.   See the discussion in chapter 3.

10.   Perkins, *Constraint of Empire.*

11.   The payoff to Colombia was settled borders with Ecuador and Peru (although they had to fight a war in 1932 to ensure it), leaving the country with only disputes with Nicaragua and Venezuela (both of which continue to flare up). Wood, *The United States and Latin American Wars*, pp. 169–72; Bruce St. John, *The Boundary Between Ecuador and Peru*, Vol 1. No. 4 of *Boundary & Territory Briefing* (Durham, UK: International Boundaries Research Unit, University of Durham, 1994), p. 12; Pike *The United States and the Andean Republics*, pp. 203–4.

12.   Wood, *The United States and Latin American Wars*, pp. 69–251; Pike, *The Modern History of Peru*, pp. 266–69.

13. Anita Isaacs, *Military Rule and Transition in Ecuador, 1972–92* (Pittsburgh: University of Pittsburgh Press, 1993), pp. 1–3; Victor Villanueva, *100 años del ejército peruano: frustraciones y cambios* (Lima: Editorial Juan Mejía Baca, 1971), pp. 100–107; The U.S. military attaché in Lima rated Peru's combat efficiency as significantly better than Ecuador's. Masterson, *Militarism and Politics*, pp. 65–70; Wood, *The United States and Latin American Wars*, pp. 268–69.

14. Although Peruvian President Manuel Prado was opposed to a war with Ecuador, the commander of the northern army insisted upon attacking the Ecuadorian forces. Geoffrey Bertram, "Peru 1930–60" in Leslie Bethel, ed., *The Cambridge History of Latin America*, vol. 8 (Cambridge: Cambridge University Press, 1991), p. 423; Wood, *The United States and Latin American Wars*, pp. 255–331.

15. See the comments by the Ecuadorian negotiator in Tóbar Donoso and Luna Tóbar, *Derecho Territorial Ecuatoriano*, pp. 212–22 and by General José W. Gallardo R., Commander-in-Chief of the Army, "Comentario Militar" in Hernán Alonso Altamirano Escobar, *EL POR QUE del ávido expansionismo del PERU [Peru's Avid Expansionism Explained]* (Quito: Instituto Geográfico Militar, 1991), pp. 34–35 (Gallardo was Defense Minister during the 1995 war). Captain Altamirano Escobar's book begins with a discussion of Incan expansionism. Also, Lt. General Frank Vargas Pazzos (ret.), *Tiwintza: Toda La Verdad* (Quito: Color Gráfica, 1995) [Vargas Pazzos was leader of one of the political parties in Congress upon which President Bucaram depended.] and Wood, *The United States and Latin American Wars*, pp. 326–30.

16. Tóbar Donoso and Luna Tóbar, *Derecho Territorial Ecuatoriano*, pp. 212–26; 234–35. With hindsight the authors claim that Ecuador expected the guarantors to find some way to compensate Ecuador, but since the Protocol did not foresee anything at issue other than border demarcation this appears to be post hoc justification for the position taken by Ecuador after the Zamora-Santiago problem arose.

17. *Análisis Semanal* (Quito) 25(6) (February 10, 1995): 11–12 noted that Ecuadorian leaders never specified where access to the Amazon would occur, but that access via the Maranon River in the Zamora-Santiago region would provide the country with only the appearance of an Amazonian country since the Maranon is not navigable to the Amazon in that sector.

18. Pons Muzzo, *Estudio Histórico*, pp. 277–78.

19. Ministry of Foreign Affairs, *Hacia la Solución*, pp. 78–79; Fernando Bustamante, "Ecuador: Putting an End to Ghosts of the Past?" *Journal of Interamerican Studies and World Affairs* 34 (4) (Winter) 1992/93): 205–13.

20. William P. Avery, "Origins and Consequences of the Border Dispute between Ecuador and Peru" *Journal of Inter-American Economic Affairs* 38 (1) (Summer 1984): 74.

21. Avery, "Origins and Consequences," p. 69.
22. Gorman, "Geopolitics and Peruvian Foreign Policy," pp. 83–84.
23. Ministry of Foreign Affairs, *Hacia la Solución*, p. 182.
24. Stockholm International Peace Research Institute, *1982 World Armaments and Disarmament*, p. 412; Pons Muzzo, *Estudio Histórico*, pp. 310–54; *Análisis Semanal*, p. 46 reports the payment, but Ecuadorian political leaders denied it. *Hoy*, March 2, 1995 "No se Pagó Indemnización a Perú."
25. *El Universo* (Quito) special supplement "Ni Un Paso Atrás" c. March 22, 1995, p. 2.
26. Scheggia Flores, *Orígen del Pueblo Ecuatoriano*, pp. 71–73.
27. Gabriel Marcella, "War and Peace in the Amazon: Strategic Implications for the United States and Latin America of the Ecuador-Peru War of 1995" (MS US Army War College, Department of National Security and Strategy. September 1, 1995), pp. 2–3.
28. At the time there was speculation that by appealing to the guarantors Ecuador had retreated from its nullification thesis and accepted the Protocol. But the President's wording on the appeal was ambiguous and never clarified. The majority of people polled in Ecuador's two major cities believed that he did not accept the Protocol. Among respondents with graduate school level of education, the figure is even higher. Poll of January 6, 1996 in Quito and Quayaquil by Informe Confidencial, archives in Quito offices.
29. *Hoy* (Quito) December 29, 1995, February 12, 13 14, 23, and 26, 1996; the planes have U.S. built engines and therefore their sale to third parties requires U.S. approval.
30. Latin American Data Base, "Peru: Foreign Minister Resigns in Midst of Negotiations with Ecuador" *NotiSur—Latin American Affairs*, ISSN 1060–4189 8(37) (October 9, 1998) and a confidential interview with a former high ranking Peruvian diplomat. Lima, March 26 1999.
31. St. John, *The Boundary*, p. 16.
32. Pons Muzzo, *Estudio Histórico*, p. 362.
33. Confidential interviews August 1995; in addition, Dr. Luis Proaño, Political Advisor, Ministry of Defense, Quito, August 14, 1995; Col. Hernández, Personal Secretary to the Minister of Defense (and commander of the Tiwintza defense during the war), August 14, 1995.
34. Ministry of Foreign Affairs, *Hacia La Solución*, p. 145.
35. Luis Carrera de la Torre, *El proyecto binacional Puyango Tumbes* Quito: AFESE, 1990; Scheggia Flores, *Orígen del Pueblo Ecuatoriano*, pp. 71–73.
36. Between 1983–1993 Ecuador increased its number of soldiers dramatically (by 50%), while Peru decreased its own (by almost 1/3). Yet Peru's armed forces still outnumbered their rival by 2–1. U.S. Arms Control and Disarmament Agency, *World Military Expenditures and Arms Transfers, 1993–1994*, pp. 61 and 78.

37. J. Samuel Fitch, *The Military Coup d'Etat as a Poltical Process: Ecuador 1948–1966* (Baltimore: Johns Hopkins University Press, 1977); Isaacs, *Military Rule and Transition*, pp. 2–3 also does not reference the question of border in her summary of why the military grew disenchanted with democracy in the 1960s.

38. St. John, *The Boundary*, p. 16.

39. Confidential interviews August 1995; in addition, interviews with Proaño and Hernández; see also, Gen. Vargas Pazzos, *Tiwintza*, 45–62.

40. ACDA does not record China having delivered or made any agreements to deliver arms to Ecuador from 1979 to 1993. U.S. Arms Control and Disarmament Agency, *World Military Expenditures and Arms Transfers, 1993–94* Vols. 1985 and 1993–94 (Washington: U.S. Government Printing Office, 1995), pp. 133 and 140, respectively.

41. Confidential interviews with Ecuadorian, Peruvian and U.S. military and civilian analysts August and September 1995. The Navy had been bottled up in port in 1981.

42. Gorman, "Geopolitics and Peruvian Foreign Policy," p. 80; Masterson, *Militarism and Politics in Latin America*, p. 265. During the 1995 conflict Peruvian President Fujimori maintained that Peru could escalate the conflict despite initial loses because the military government of the 1970s had stockpiled weapons in preparation for a war with Chile. *CHIP News* "Peru was preparing for War with Chile, Reveals President Fujimori" March 3, 1995.

43. The poll is discussed in Ministry of Foreign Affairs, *Hacia la Solución*, pp. 192–93; diplomatic sentiment is discussed in *Latin American Regional Reports* November 14, 1991, p. 6 and confirmed in my confidential interviews of 1995.

44. Pons Muzzo, *Estudio Histórico*, p. 358.

45. Jaime Durán Barga, "Actitud de los Ecuatorianos Frente al Perú: Estudio de Opinión Pública" in *Ecuador y Perú: vecinos distantes* (Quito: Corporación de Estudios para el Desarrollo, 1993), 171–202.

46. *Informe Confidencial* February 25, 1995 and January 6, 1996. Archives.

47. *Informe Confidencial* January 6, 1995. Archives.

48. Pedro Saad Herrería, *La Caída de Abdalá* (Quito: El Conejo, 1997), pp. 137–38.

49. ACDA's estimates of Ecuadorian military expenditures as a percent of GNP indicate that they were never large. A slight increase developed after the military government had been in power for a few years (from 2.1 percent to 2.4 percent, except for 1978 when it reached 2.9 percent), followed by a slight decline with the return of democracy to the level of the early years of military government, an important increase after the 1981 mini-war (reaching 3.3 percent in 1983), and declining dramatically after 1987, reaching 1.1 percent in 1993. *World Military Expenditures* Vols. 1985 and 1993–94, pp. 60 and 61, respectively.

50. For a detailed analysis, see Mares, "Deterrence Bargaining."

51. Based on responses by Army and Air Force officers to my presentation "La Disuasión y el Conflicto Ecuador-Perú" at the Air Force War College, Quito, August 1995; interviews with Army Chief General Paco Moncayo and Adrian Bonilla and public opinion data analyzed in this chapter.

52. Fernando Tuesta Soldevilla, *Perú Político en Cifras* (Lima: Fundación Friedrich Ebert, 1994, 2nd edition), p. 71; Raul P. Saba, *Political Development and Democracy in Peru: Continuity in Change and Crisis* (Boulder: Westview, 1987), pp. 72–76; Philip Mauceri, *State Under Siege: Development and Policy-Making in Peru* (Boulder: Westview Press, 1966), pp. 46–58; Julio Cotler, "Political Parties and the Problems of Democratic Consolidation in Peru" in Mainwaring and Scully, eds., *Building Democratic Institutions*, pp. 337–43.

53. Saba, *Political Development and Democracy in Peru*, p. 137; none of the other authors in the previous footnote even mentions the 1981 mini-war in their discussions of political protests against Belaunde. Edward Schumacher, "Behind Ecuador War, Long-Smoldering Resentment" *New York Times*, February 10, 1981, p. A2.

54. Tuesta Soldevilla, *Perú Político en Cifras*, p. 68.

55. Mauceri, *State Under Siege*, pp. 59–77; John Crabtree, *Peru Under Garcia: An Opportunity Lost* (Pittsburgh: University of Pittsburgh Press, 1992), pp. 69–93,121–83.

56. Tuesta Soldevilla, *Perú Político en Cifras*, p. 64 for 1990 and Palmer, "Peru's 1995 Elections," pp. 17–20 for 1995.

57. Tuesta Soldevilla, *Perú Político en Cifras*, pp. 23, Table 2 and 149.

58. In March 1999, nine years after assuming office, which include two years of authoritarian government, Fujimori's approval ratings were still 64.5%. "En popularidad, Fujimori cede terreno a Andrade" *El Comercio* March 21, 1999, p. a5.

59. Polling data from Apoyo, S.A. (Lima) via Roper Center for Public Opinion Research, University of Connecticut, Storrs, CT. January 1994 #62001 questions 9.1 and 9.2 and April 94 #62004 questions 6.1 and 6.2.

60. Apoyo, S.A. (Lima) via Roper Center for Public Opinion Research, February 1995 "Elections" #63004 question 2, 3, 4, 6 and 7; February 1995 "Political and Economic Situation" #62002, question 2.1, 2.2, and 2.5; and March 1995 #62003 questions 4.1a, 4.1c, and 4.1e, 4.1f,.

61. Apoyo, S.A. (Lima) via Roper Center for Public Opinion Research, February 1995 "Elections" #63004 question 5; February 1995 "Political and Economic Situation" #62002, question 2.4; and March 1995 #62003 questions 4.2 and 4.3.

62. Shugart and Carey, *Presidents and Assemblies*, pp. 149–55.

63. Catherine M. Conaghan, "Politicians Against Parties: Discord and Disconnection in Ecuador's Party System" in Mainwaring and Scully, eds., *Building Democratic Institutions*, pp. 434–58.

64. Shugart and Carey, *Presidents and Assemblies*, pp. 114–15.
65. *Hoy* (Quito) February 19, 1997 "Reforma contra Bucaram;" *Hoy* February 24, 1977 Francisco Rosales Ramos "Dilema." *NotiSur* April 11, 1997 "Ecaudor: Interim Government Calls Referendum as Supreme Court Orders Arrest of Former President."
66. *Hoy* "Jueces Unen a Políticos" October 4, 1996 and "Como despolitizar la justicia?" April 18, 1997.
67. Latin American Data Base, *NotiSur* "Ecuador: Compromise Between President Jamil Mahuad & Congress on Economic Measures Ends Crisis" ISSN 1060–4189 9(11) (March 19, 1999).
68. *NotiSur* "Ecuador: Institutional Crisis Continues with Investigation of President Sixto Durán Ballen" November 10, 1995; Adrian Bonilla, "Las Imágenes nacionales y la guerra: Una lectura crítica del conflicto entre Ecuador y Perú," paper presented at the XXI Annual Meeting of the Latin American Studies Association, April 17–19, 1997 Guadalajara, Mexico.
69. For a discussion of the varieties of civil-military relations, see Mares, "Civil-Military Relations, Democracy and the Regional Neighborhood."
70. Ministry of Foreign Affairs, *Misión en Washington*, p. 61.
71. Two confidential Ecuadorian interviews, Quito, August 1995.
72. Confidential interview with a former high ranking diplomat. My 1995 interviews, Gen. Vargas Pazzos (*Tiwintza*) and Minister of Defense General Gallardo ("Comentario Militar"), suggest that some military officers have reinterpreted the events of 1981 to suggest that they were holding their own and civilians capitulated. On the other hand, Army Chief General Moncayo claimed that, as a result of having focused on governing the country between 1973 and 1979, the armed forces were not ready to defend themselves against a broad Peruvian attack in 1981. Interview, August 16, 1995.
73. Isaacs, *Military Rule and Transition*, pp. 137–40.
74. Confidential Ecuadorian interview, Quito, August 1995.
75. For example, in the controversy over Bucaram's demise, Congress and the Vice President disputed who would succeed him. Thus for a few days Ecuador had three Presidents, since Bucaram rejected his ouster. The military initially remained aloof despite the President's efforts to garner their political support. When they finally decided to publicly withdraw support from Bucaram they refused to name his successor, insisting that Congress and the Vice President resolve the issue themselves. Although they, along with the U.S. Embassy, favored naming the Vice President, everyone accepted the maneuvering by Congress which placed its leader in the presidency. *Hoy* January 29–February 13, 1997 for discussions of the crisis, in particular "Los militares tras Rosalía" and "EEUU no ha intervenido en la crisis," both in *Hoy* February 11, 1997; *Notisur* "Ecuador: Congress Votes to Oust President Abdala Bucaram" February 7, 1997; interview with Adrian Bonilla, April 1997 Guadalajara, Mexico.

76. Cf. The discussion in NotiSur.

77. In May 1990 52% of respondents believed the legislature had performed either "badly" or "very badly" during the García presidency of 1985–90 and 54% wanted the Senate and House to fuse into one chamber. APOYO S.A., Lima, as cited in Enrique Bernales Ballesteros, *Parlamento y democracia* (Lima: Constitución y Sociedad, 1990), pp. 239, 260.

78. Carol Graham, "Government and Politics" in Rex A. Hudson, ed., *Peru: A Country Study* (Washington, DC: Federal Research Division, Library of Congress, 1993, 4th edition), pp. 212–17; an excellent overview is Cynthia McClintock, "Presidents, Messiahs, and Constitutional Breakdowns in Peru" in Juan J. Linz and Arturo Valenzuela, eds., *The Failure of Presidential Democracy: The Case of Latin America* (Baltimore: Johns Hopkins University Press, 1994), pp. 286–321.

79. 1979 Constitution, Articles 227–30.

80. 1993 Constitution, Articles 134–36.

81. 1979 Constitution, a majority of both houses Article 193; 1993 Constitution Article 108.

82. McClintock, "Presidents, Messiahs, and Constitutional Breakdowns," p. 309; the number of decrees is from Samuel B. Abad Yupanqui and Carolina Garces Peralta, "El gobierno de Fujimori: antes y después del golpe" in Comisión Andina de Juristas, ed., *Del Golpe de Estado a la Nueva Constitución*. Series: *Lecturas sobre Temas Constitucionales* 9(Lima: Comision Andina de Juristas, 1993), p. 103.

83. 1993 Constitution Article 118, XIX.

84. 1979 Constitution, Article 188, 211 and 1993 Constitution, Articles 104 and 137.

85. Polls by Apoyo and CPI as cited in Federico Prieto Celi, *El golpe* (Lima: B&C Editores, 1992), p. 41; see also, Carlos Ivan Degregori and Carlos Rivera, "Perú 1980–1993: Fuerzas Armadas, Subversión y Democracia" *Documento de Trabajo No. 53* (Lima: Instituto de Estudios Peruanos, 1994), pp. 8–14.

86. *Hoy*, March 22, April 3, 1995; Abraham Lamas, "Ecuador–Perú: Quién Ganó y Quién Perdió en la Guerra Empatada" *InterPress Service*, March 10, 1995.

87. Latin America Data Base, *NotiSur—Latin American Political Affairs*, March 10, 1995.

88. See footnote 68.

89. Crabtree, *Peru Under Garcia*, pp. 108–12; Interview, César Azabache, Defensoria del Pueblo, Lima, April 5, 1999.

90. Interview, Azabache.

91. Susan Stokes, "Peru: The Rupture of Democratic Rule" in Jorge I. Domínguez and Abraham F. Lowenthal, eds., *Constructing Democratic Governance: South America in the 1990s* (Baltimore: Johns Hopkins University Press, 1996), pp. 66–71.

92. David Pion-Berlin, "From Confrontation to Cooperation: Democratic Gover-
    nance and Argentine Foreign Relations" in Mares, ed., *Civil-Military Relations*,
    pp. 79–100; Carlos Escudé, *Foreign Policy Theory in Menem's Argentina*
    (Gainesville: University Press of Florida, 1997).
93. He failed because the military juntas were accused in 1998 of kidnapping and
    selling the babies of political prisoners, a crime which had not been considered
    under the 1990 amnesty. The Junta leaders are currently back in jail, awaiting
    new trials.
94. Teodoro Hidalgo Morey, *Las Ganancias de Ecuador* (Lima: Producciones Gráf-
    icas "Borjas," 1997).
95. Interview with Luis Huerta, Comisión Andina de Juristas, Lima, March 25,
    1999.
96. see the discussion in chapter 5, footnote 100.
97. Pons Muzzo, *Estudio Histórico*, p. 364.
98. In a little over a year, a Constituent Assembly was elected, a new constitution
    increasing executive powers adopted, and the country returned to democracy.

8. *Militarized Bargaining*

1. Cf., the declarations by opposition politicians as the war began to wind down.
   Femenia, *National Identity in Times of Crises*, pp. 108–19.
2. Latin American Bureau, *Falklands/Malvinas*, pp. 101–26.
3. For example, the Organization of American States created a committee to examine the relationship between the social-political-economic components of
   the organization and their military counterpart. Academic institutions in the
   U.S., Canada and Latin America (e.g., The North-South Center at the University of Miami; the Latin American Program of the Woodrow Wilson Center
   of the Smithsonian Institution; The Queens University, University of Montreal,
   and FLACSO-Chile) have organized conferences and research on this topic.
4. In 1991 the OAS adopted the Santiago Resolution, which stipulates that the
   defense of democracy is vital to the security of the region. The United States
   Southern Command now has among its priorities to aid the countries of the
   region in sustaining democracy. See also the newsletter edited jointly by
   FLACSO-Chile and the Latin America Program of the Woodrow Wilson Center, *Paz y Seguridad en las Américas* and the various committee reports for the
   Organization of American States: Working Group on Hemispheric Security,
   Working Group on Cooperation for Hemispheric Security and the Special
   Committee on Hemispheric Security.
5. Riordan Roett, "Introduction" in Roett, *Mercosur*, pp. 1–5; Escudé, *Foreign
   Policy Theory in Menem's Argentina*; Pion-Berlin, "From Confrontation to Co-
   operation."

6. Cf., Carlos Escudé and Andrés Fontana, "Argentina's Security Policies: Their Rationale and Regional Context" in Jorge I. Domínguez, ed., *International Security and Democracy* (Pittsburgh: University of Pittsburgh Press, 1998), pp. 51–79.

7. Roett, ed., *Mercosur*; Martin Bywater, *Andean Integration: A New Lease on Life?* London: The Economist Intelligence Unit, Special Report No. 2018, March 1990; Francisco Rojas Aravena, "Centroamérica: Nueva Agenda de Seguridad" in *Paz y Seguridad en las Américas* No. 9 (December 1996): 3–7.

8. David R. Mares, "Latin American Economic Integration and Democratic Control of the Military: Is There a Symbiotic Relationship?" Forthcoming in David Pion-Berlin, ed., *Civil-Military Relations in Latin America: New Analytical Perspectives* (Chapel Hill: University of North Carolina Press).

9. Even in Central America, which has the example of Costa Rica and in which many U.S. and Central American analysts had hoped that the end of the Central American civil wars would demilitarize the region, the hope now seems lost. LADB (Latin America Data Base, Latin American Institute, University of New Mexico) June 9, 1995.

10. Israel's strategy that the "best defense is a strong offense" is a prime example. Many Chilean military analysts find important parallels between Israel and Chile's strategic predicament. On the general subject of the relationship between capability and doctrine, see Mearsheimer, *Conventional Deterrence* .

11. Venezuela had already been reinforcing border defenses after Colombian guerrillas crossed. But the appearance of a Colombian navy vessel in Venezuelan claimed waters provoked a major interstate dispute. For a review of actions and the accusations traded by important politicians and policymakers in both countries during the crisis, see Area and Nieschulz de Stockhausen, *El Golfo de Venezuela*, pp. 64–87.

12. E.g., the comments by Argentine Defense Minister Jorge Domínguez in "Chile comprará más mísiles."

13. See the discussions concerning the recent purchases of Skyhawk A4s with top-down radar from the U.S. Though old, the Skyhawks had been responsible for destroying some of the British ships during the Malvinas War. Adrian J. English, *Battle for the Falklands (2) Naval Forces* (London: Osprey), 1982, pp. 27–29.

14. "Chile Acquires Mirage Jets" CHIPnews March 20, 1995; for a discussion of the Chilean Mirages see *América Vuela* (No. 25, 1995): 22–27.

15. For Ecuador, data from an interview with the Director of *Informe Confidencial*. Polls were taken in Quito and Guayaquil, January 1996; for Chile, Rojas Aravena, "Chile y el gasto militar," p. 244, citing a survey by FLACSO, "Percepciones y Opiniones sobre las Fuerzas Armadas en Chile" June 1992 in Santiago.

Bibliography

Abad Yupanqui, Samuel B. and Carolina Garces Peralta. "El gobierno de Fujimori: antes y después del golpe." In Comisión Andina de Juristas, ed. *Del Golpe de Estado a la Nueva Constitución.* Series: *Lecturas sobre Temas Constitucionales* 9. Lima: Comisión Andina de Juristas, 1993, pp. 85–190.

Adcock, Sir Frank and D. J. Mosley. *Diplomacy in Ancient Greece.* New York: St. Martin's Press, 1975.

Aldrich, John H., John L. Sullivan, and Eugene Brogida. "Foreign Affairs and Issue Voting: Do Presidential Candidates 'Waltz Before a Blind Audience'?" *American Political Science Review* 83(1) (March 1989): 123–42.

Alexandroff, Alan and Richard Rosecrance. "Deterrence in 1939" *World Politics* (April 1977): 404–24.

Allison, Graham T. "Questions About the Arms Race: Who's Racing Whom? A Bureaucratic Perspective." In Robert L. Pfaltzgraff Jr., ed. *Contrasting Approaches to Strategic Arms Control.* Lexington: Lexington Books, 1974.

Ameringer, Charles D. *The Caribbean Legion: Patriots, Politicians, Soldiers of Fortune, 1946–1950.* University Park: The Pennsylvania State University Press, 1996.

Anderson, Thomas P. *The War of the Dispossessed: Honduras and El Salvador, 1969.* Lincoln: University of Nebraska Press, 1981.

Andreski, Stanislav. "On the Peaceful Disposition of Military Dictatorships" *Journal of Strategic Studies* 3 (December 1980): 3–10.

Area, Leandro and Elke Nieschulz de Stockhausen. *El Golfo de Venezuela: Documentación y cronología. Vol. II (1981–1989).* Caracas: Universidad Central de Venezuela, 1991.

Arriagada Herrera, Genaro. "The Legal and Institutional Framework of the Armed Forces in Chile." In J. Samuel Valenzuela and Arturo Valenzuela, eds. *Military Rule in Chile: Dictatorship and Oppositions*. Baltimore: Johns Hopkins University Press, pp. 117–43.

Asvat, Ebrahim. "La desmilitarización Panameña y sus desafíos futuros," *Paz y Seguridad en las Américas* No. 12, July 1997, pp 15–18.

Avery, William P. "Origins and Consequences of the Border Dispute between Ecuador and Peru" *Journal of Inter-American Economic Affairs*, 38, no. 1 (Summer 1984).

Ayoob, Mohammed. *The Third World Security Predicament: State Making, Regional Conflict, and the International System*. Boulder: Lynne Rienner, 1995.

Baldwin, David A. *Economic Statecraft*. Princeton: Princeton University Press, 1985.

Barclay, Glen. *Struggle for a Continent*. New York: SUNY Press, 1972.

Barry, Brian. *Sociologists, Economists & Democracy*. Chicago: University of Chicago Press, 1978.

Bennett, D. Scott. "Measuring Rivalry Termination, 1816–1992" *Journal of Conflict Resolution* 41(2) (April 1997): 227–54.

Berghahn, V. R. *Militarism: the History of an International Debate, 1861–1979*. Cambridge: Cambridge University Press, 1981.

Bernales Ballesteros, Enrique. *Parlamento y democracia*. Lima: Constitución y Sociedad, 1990.

Bertram, Geoffrey. "Peru 1930–60." In Leslie Bethel, ed. *The Cambridge History of Latin America* vol. 8. Cambridge: Cambridge University Press, 1991.

Betts, Richard. *Soldiers, Statesmen and Cold War Crises*. Cambridge: Harvard University Press, 1977.

Blainey, Geoffery. *The Causes of War*. New York: Free Press, 1973.

Blasier, Cole. *The Hovering Giant*. Pittsburgh: University of Pittsburgh Press, 1976.

Bonilla, Adrian. "Las imágenes nacionales y la guerra: Una lectura crítica del conflicto entre Ecuador y Perú." Paper presented at the XXI Annual Meeting of the Latin American Studies Association, April 17–19, 1997 Guadalajara, Mexico.

Bremer, Stuart. "Dangerous Dyads: Conditions Affecting the Likelihood of Interstate War, 1816–1965." *Journal of Conflict Resolution* 36: (1992): 309–41.

Brenes, Arnoldo and Kevin Casas. *Soldados como empresarios*. San José: Fundación Arias Para la Paz y el Progreso Humano, 1998.

Brzoska, Michael and Frederic S. Pearson. *Arms and Warfare: Escalation, De-escalation, and Negotiation*. Columbia: University of South Carolina, 1994.

Bueno de Mesquita, Bruce and David Lalman. *Reason and War*. New Haven: Yale University Press, 1992.

Bueno de Mesquita, Bruce and Randolph M. Siverson. "Nasty or Nice? Political Systems, Endogenous Norms, and the Treatment of Adversaries." *Journal of Conflict Resolution* 41(1) (February 1997): 175–99.

Bueno de Mesquita, Bruce and Randolph M. Siverson. "War and the Survival of Political Leaders: A Comparative Study of Regime Types and Political Accountability." *American Political Science Review* 98(4) (December 1995): 841–55.

Bueno de Mesquita, Bruce, James Morrow and Ethan R. Zorick. "Capabilities, Perceptions and Escalation." *American Political Science Review* 91(1) (March 1997): 15–27.

Bueno de Mesquita, Bruce, Randolph M. Siverson, and Gary Woller. "War and the Fate of Regimes." *American Political Science Review* 86(3) (September 1992): 638–46.

Bueno de Mesquita, Bruce. *The War Trap*. New Haven: Yale University Press, 1981.

Burns, E. Bradford. *The Unwritten Alliance: Rio-Branco and Brazilian-American Relations*. New York: Columbia University Press, 1966.

Bustamante, Fernando. "Ecuador: Putting an End to Ghosts of the Past?" *Journal of Interamerican Studies and World Affairs* 34(4) (Winter 1992/93): 195–224.

Buzan, Barry. *People, States and Fear*. Boulder: Lynne Rienner, 1991, 2nd ed.

Bywater, Martin. *Andean Integration: A New Lease on Life?* London: The Economist Intelligence Unit, Special Report No. 2018, March 1990.

Camacho Omiste, Edgar. "El Enclaustramiento Marítimo de Bolivia." La Paz: FLACSO-Bolivia, July 1988. Documento de Trabajo #22.

Carrera de la Torre, Luís. *El proyecto binacional Puyango Tumbes*. Quito: AFESE, 1990.

Cavalla, Antonio. *El conflicto del Beagle*. México: Casa del Chile, 1979.

Centro Latinoamericano de Defensa y Desarme and Relaciones Internacionales de América Latina. *Estudio Estratégico de América Latina*. Various annual issues Santiago: Ediciones ChileAmerica.

Cervo, Amado Luiz & Clodoaldo Bueno. *Historia da Política Exterior do Brasil*. Sao Paulo: Editora Atica, 1992.

Chan, Steve. "Mirror, Mirror on the Wall . . . Are the Freer Countries More Pacific?" *Journal of Conflict Resolution* 28(4) (1984): 617–48.

Child, John. *The Unequal Alliance: The Inter-American Military System, 1938–1978*. Boulder: Westview Press, 1980.

Chile Information Press (CHIPnews), subsequently *Santiago Times*.

Claude, Jr., Inis L. *Power and International Relations*. New York: Random House, 1962.

Clayton, Lawrence A. *Peru and the United States: The Condor and the Eagle*. Athens, GA: University of Georgia Press, 1999.

Cohen, Elliot A. *Citizens and Soldiers: The Dilemmas of Military Service*. Ithaca: Cornell University Press, 1985.

Conaghan, Catherine M. "Politicians Against Parties: Discord and Disconnection in Ecuador's Party System." In Mainwaring and Scully, eds. *Building Democratic Institutions*, pp. 434–58.

Connell-Smith, Gordon. *The Inter-American System*. London: Oxford University Press, 1966.

Connell-Smith, Gordon. *The United States and Latin America*. New York: Wiley, 1974.

Cosío Villegas, Daniel. *Historia Moderna de México*. México: Editorial Hermes, 1955 Vol. 7.

Cotler, Julio. "Political Parties and the Problems of Democratic Consolidation in Peru." In Mainwaring and Scully, eds. *Building Democratic Institutions*, pp. 323–53.

Cowhey, Peter F. and Matthew D. McCubbins, eds. *Structure and Policy in Japan and the United States*. Cambridge: Cambridge University Press, 1995.

Cowhey, Peter F. "Domestic Institutions and the Credibility of International Commitments: Japan and the United States." *International Organization* 47(2) (Spring 1993): 299–326.

Cox, Gary. *Making Votes Count*. Cambridge: Cambridge University Press, 1997.

Crabtree, John. *Peru Under Garcia: An Opportunity Lost*. Pittsburgh: University of Pittsburgh Press, 1992.

Crowley, James B. *Japan's Quest for Autonomy: national security and foreign policy, 1930–1938*. Princeton: Princeton University Press, 1966.

Dahl, Robert A. *Polyarchy: Participation and Opposition*. New Haven: Yale University Press, 1972.

Dassel, Kurt. "Civilians, Soldiers, and Strife: Domestic Sources of International Aggression." *International Security* 23(1) (Summer 1998): 107–40.

Dassel, Kurt. "Domestic Instability, the Military, and War." PhD Dissertation, Columbia University, Department of Political Science, 1996.

de la Puente Radbill, José. "La mediterraneidad de Bolivia." In Eduardo Ferrero Costa, ed. *Relaciones del Perú con Chile y Bolivia*. Lima: Centro Peruano de Estudios Internacionales, 1989, pp. 399–58.

Deger, Jr., Robert John. "Porfirian Foreign Policy and Mexican Nationalism: A Study of Cooperation and Conflict in Mexican-American Relations, 1884–1904." Unpublished Ph.D. dissertation, Indiana University, 1979.

Degregori,Carlos Ivan and Carlos Rivera. "Perú 1980–1993: Fuerzas Armadas, Subversión y Democracia." *Documento de Trabajo No. 53*. Lima: Instituto de Estudios Peruanos, 1994.

Desch, Mike. "Why Latin America May Miss the Cold War: The United States and the Future of Inter-American Security Relations." In Jorge I. Dominguez, ed. *International Security and Democracy*. Pittsburgh: University of Pittsburgh Press, 1998, pp. 245–65.

Destler, I.M. and John Odell, assisted by Kimberly Ann Elliott. *Anti-Protection: Changing Forces in United States Trade Politics*. Washington D.C.: Institute for International Economics, 1987.

Diehl, Paul F. "What Are They Fighting For? The Importance of Issues in International Conflict Research." *Journal of Peace Research* 29(3) (August 1992): 333–44.

DiTella, Guido and D. Cameron Watt, eds. *Argentina Between the Great Powers, 1939–46*. Pittsburgh: University of Pittsburgh Press, 1990.

Dixon, William. "Democracy and the Peaceful Settlement of International Conflict." *American Political Science Review* 88(1) (March 1994): 14–32.

Domínguez, Jorge I. *Cuba: Order and Revolution*. Cambridge: Belknap Press of Harvard University Press, 1978.

Dominguez, Jorge I. ed. *International Security and Democracy: Latin America and the Caribbean in the post-Cold War Era*. Pittsburgh: University of Pittsburgh Press, 1998.

Domínguez, Jorge I. *To Make a World Safe for Revolution: Cuba's Foreign Policy*. Cambridge: Harvard University Press, 1989.

Domínguez, Jorge I. "Los conflictos internacionales en América Latina y la amenaza de guerra." *Foro Internacional* 97 25(1) (July-September 1984): 1–13.

Doyle, Michael A. "To the Editors." *International Security* 19(4) (Spring 1995): 180–94.

Doyle, Michael W. "Kant, Liberal Legacies and Foreign Affairs," parts 1 and 2. In *Philosophy and World Affairs* 12(3) (Summer 1983): 205-35; and 12(4) (Fall 1983): 323–53.

Doyle, Michael. "Liberalism and World Politics." *American Political Science Review* 80(4) (December 1986): 1151–69.

Drake, Paul. *Socialism and Populism in Chile 1932–52*. Urbana: University of Illinois Press, 1978.

Dunn, Timothy J. *The Militarization of the U.S.-Mexican Border 1978–1992. Low Intensity Conflict Doctrine Comes Home*. Austin: The Center for Mexican American Studies, The University of Texas Press, 1997, 2nd ed.

Duran Barga, Jaime. "Actitud de los Ecuatorianos Frente al Perú: Estudio de Opinión Pública." In *Ecuador y Perú: vecinos distantes*. Quito: Corporación de Estudios para el Desarrollo, 1993, pp. 171–202.

English, Adrian J. *Armed Forces of Latin America: Their Histories, Development, Present Strength, and Military Potential*. London, New York: Jane's, 1984.

English, Adrian J. *Battle for the Falklands (2) Naval Forces*. London: Osprey, 1982, pp. 27–29.

Erro, David G. *Resolving the Argentine Paradox: Politics and Development, 1966–1992*. Boulder: Lynne Rienner, 1993, pp. 73–98.

Escudé, Carlos and Andrés Fontana. "Argentina's Security Policies: Their Rationale and Regional Context." In Jorge I. Dominguez, ed. *International Security and Democracy*. Pittsburgh: University of Pittsburgh Press, 1998, pp. 51–79.

Escudé, Carlos. *Foreign Policy Theory in Menem's Argentina*. Gainesville: University Press of Florida, 1997.

Espinosa Mora, Oscar. *Bolivia y el mar, 1810–1964*. Santiago: Editorial Nascimento, 1964.

Estudio Estratégico de América Latina. Santiago, Chile.

Evans, Peter, Harold K. Jacobson, and Robert D. Putnam, eds. *Double-Edged Diplomacy: International Bargaining and Domestic Politics*. Berkeley: University of California Press, 1993.

Farber, Henry S. and Joanne Gowa. "Polities and Peace." *International Security* 20(2) (Fall 1995): 123–46.

Fearon, James D. "Domestic Political Audiences and the Escalation of International Disputes." *American Political Science Review* 88(3) (September 1994): 577–92.

Fearon, James D. "Rationalist Explanations of War." *International Organization* 49(3) (Summer 1995): 379–414.

Feinberg, Richard E. *The Intemperate Zone: The Third World Challenge to U.S. Foreign Policy*. New York: Norton, 1983.

Femenia, Nora. *National Identity in Times of Crises: The Scripts of the Falklands-Malvinas War*. Commack, New York: Nova Science Publishers, Inc. 1996.

Fisher, Roger William Ury and Bruce Patton. *Getting to Yes: Negotiating Agreement Without Giving In*. New York: Penguin, 1991, 2nd edition.

Fitch, J. Samuel. *The Military Coup d'Etat as a Poltical Process: Ecuador 1948–1966*. Baltimore: Johns Hopkins University Press, 1977.

FLACSO-Chile and the Latin America Program of the Woodrow Wilson Center. *Paz y Seguridad en las Américas* .

Fontana, Andres Miguel. "Political Decision-Making By a Military Corporation: Argentina, 1976–1983." PhD Dissertation, University of Texas at Austin, 1987.

Francis, Michael J. *The Limits of Hegemony: United States Relations with Argentina and Chile During World War II*. Notre Dame: University of Notre Dame Press, 1977.

Franck, Thomas M. and Edward Weisband. *Foreign Policy by Congress*. New York: Oxford University Press, 1979.

Freedman, Lawrence and Virginia Gamba-Stonehouse. *Signals of War: The Falklands Conflict of 1982*. Princeton: Princeton University Press, 1991.

Freivogel, William H. "Gulf Debate May Decide War Powers, President could Gain Authority." *St. Louis Post-Dispatch* January 10, 1991, p. 1C.

Frohmann, Alicia. "De contadora al grupo de los ocho: El reaprendizaje de la concertación política regional." *Estudios Internacionales* 22(87) (July–September 1989): 365–427.

Gaddis, John Lewis. "The Long Peace: Elements of Stability in the Postwar International System." *International Security* 10(4) (Spring 1986): 99–142.

Gallardo R., General José W. "Comentario Militar." In Hernán Alonso Altamirano Escobar. *EL POR QUE del ávido expansionismo del PERU [Peru's Avid Expansionism Explained]*. Quito: Instituto Geográfico Militar, 1991, pp. 34–35.

Garrett, James L. "The Beagle Dispute: Confrontation and Negotiation in the Southern Cone." *Journal of Inter-American Studies and World Affairs* 27(3) (Fall 1985): 81–110.

Gaubatz, Kurt Taylor. "Intervention and Intransitivity: Public Opinion, Social Choice, and the Use of Military Force Abroad." *World Politics* 47 July 1995 534–54.

Geddes, Barbara. "Challenging the Conventional Wisdom." In Larry Diamond and Marc F. Plattner, eds. *Economic Reform and Democracy*. Baltimore: Johns Hopkins University Press, 1995, pp. 66–72.

George, Alexander L. and Richard Smoke. *Deterrence in American Foreign Policy: Theory and Practice*. New York, Columbia University Press, 1974.

George, Alexander L. and Timothy J. McKowen. "Case Studies and Theories of Organizational Decision Making." In Lee S. Sproul and Patrick D. Larkey, eds. *Advances in Information Processing in Organizations*. Greenwich, CT: Jai Press, 1985, pp. 21–58.

George, Alexander L. David K. Hall, and William E. Simons. *The Limits to Coercive Diplomacy*. Boston: Little, Brown, 1971.

Gil, Federico G. "The Kennedy-Johnson Years." In John D. Martz, ed. *United States Policy in Latin America: A Quarter Century of Crisis and Challenge, 1961–1986*. Lincoln: University of Nebraska Press, 1988, pp. 3–25.

Glaser, Charles L. "Realists as Optimists: Cooperation as Self-Help." *International Security* Winter 1994/95 19(3): 50–90.

Gochman Charles S., and Zeev Maoz. "Militarized Interstate Disputes, 1816–1976." *Journal of Conflict Resolution* 28(4) (December 1984): 606–9.

Gochman, Charles S. and Zeev Maoz. "Militarized Interstate Disputes, 1816–1976: Procedures, Patterns and Insights." *Journal of Conflict Resolution* 28(4) (December 1984): 585–615.

Godoy Arcaya, Oscar ed. *Hacia Una Democracia Moderna: La Opción Parlamentaria*. Santiago: Universidad Católica de Chile, 1990.

Goertz,Gary and Paul F. Diehl. *Territorial Changes and International Conflict*. London: Routledge, 1992.

Goldberg Joyce S. *The Baltimore Affair*. Lincoln: University of Nebraska Press, 1986.

Gorman, Stephen M. "Geopolitics and Peruvian Foreign Policy." *Journal of Inter-American Economic Affairs* 36(2) (Autumn 1982): 65–88.

Gorman, Stephen M. "The High Stakes of Geopolitics in Tierra del Fuego." *Parameters* 8(2) (1978).

Gourevitch, Peter A. *Politics in Hard Times: Comparative Responses to International Economic Crises*. Ithaca: Cornell University Press, 1986.

Gowa, Joanne. "Democratic States and International Disputes." *International Organization* 49(3) (Summer, 1995): 511–22.

Graham, Carol. "Government and Politics." In Rex A. Hudson, ed. *Peru: A Country Study*. Washington, DC: Federal Research Division, Library of Congress, 1993, 4th ed., pp. 205–63.

Griffin, Clifford E. "Power Relations and Conflict Neutralization in Latin America." International Studies Working Paper, Hoover Institute, March 1992.

Gros Espiell, Hector. *Conflictos Territoriales en Iberoamérica y Solución Pacífica de Controversias*. Madrid: Ediciones Cultura Hispánica, 1986.

Grow, Michael. *The Good Neighbor Policy and Authoritarianism in Paraguay: United States Economic Expansion and Great-Power Rivalry in Latin America During World War II*. Lawrence: The Regents Press of Kansas, 1981.

Grunwald, Joseph, Miguel S. Wionczek and Martin Carnoy. *Latin American Economic Integration and U.S. Policy*. Washington: Brookings, 1972.

Guedes da Costa, Thomaz. "Democratization and International Integration: The Role of the Armed Forces in Brazil's Grand Strategy." In Mares, ed. *Civil-Military Relations*, pp. 223–37.

Guedes da Costa, Thomaz. "La percepción de amenazas desde el punto de vista de los militares brasileros en las décadas del 70 y 80." In VA Rigoberto Cruz Johnson and Augusto Varas Fernández, eds. *Percepciones de Amenaza y Políticas de Defensa en América Latina*. Santiago: FLACSO, 1993, pp. 193–210.

Guedes da Costa, Thomaz. "Post-Cold War Military Relations between the United States and Latin America." In Lars Schoultz, William C. Smith and Augusto Varas, eds. *Security, Democracy and Development in U.S.-Latin American Relations*. Miami: North-South Center, University of Miami, 1994, pp. 137–50.

Gurr, Ted Robert, Keith Jaggers and Will H. Moore. *Polity II: Political Structures and Regime Change, 1800–1986*. Ann Arbor: Inter-university Consortium for Political and Social Research, 1990.

Haggard, Stephan and Robert R. Kaufman. "Economic Adjustment and the Prospects for Democracy." In Stephan Haggard and Robert R. Kaufman, eds. *The Politics of Economic Adjustment*. Princeton: Princeton University Press, 1992, pp. 319–50.

Hale, Charles. *Mexican Liberalism in the Age of Mora 1821–1853*. New Haven, Yale University Press, 1968.

Hanson, Victor Davis. *The Western Way of War*. New York: Oxford University Press, 1990.

Healy, David. *Drive to Hegemony*. Madison: University of Wisconsin Press, 1988.

Hensel, Paul R. "One Thing Leads to Another: Recurrent Militarized Disputes in Latin America, 1816–1986." *Journal of Peace Research* 31(3) (1994): 281–97.

Herwig. Holger H. *Politics of Frustration: The United States in German Naval Planning, 1889–1941*. Boston: Little, Brown, 1976.

Hidalgo Morey, Teodoro. *Las Ganancias de Ecuador*. Lima: Producciones Gráficas "Borjas," 1997.

Hilton, Stanley E. *Brazil and the Soviet Challenge 1917–1947*. Austin: University of
Texas Press, 1991.

Hilton, Stanley E. *Hitler's Secret War in South America, 1939–1945: German Military
Espionage and Allied Counterespionage in Brazil*. Baton Rouge: Louisiana State
University Press, 1981.

Hinckley, Ronald. "Public Attitudes Toward Key Foreign Policy Events." *Journal of
Conflict Resolution* 32 (June 1988): 295–316.

Hirschman, Albert O. *Exit, Voice and Loyalty*. Cambridge: Harvard University Press,
1970.

Holsti, Kalevi J. *Peace and War: Armed Conflicts and International Order 1648–1989*.
Cambridge: Cambridge University Press, 1991.

Hopmann, P. Terrance. *The Negotiation Process and the Resolution of International
Conflicts*. Columbia, SC: University of South Carolina Press, 1996.

Huntington, Samuel P. "The Clash of Civilizations?" *Foreign Affairs* 72(3) (Summer
1993): 22–49.

Huth, Paul K. *Extended Deterrence and the Prevention of War*. New Haven: Yale
University Press, 1988.

Iida, Keisuke. "When and How do Domestic Constraints Matter? Two-Level Games
with Uncertainty." *Journal of Conflict Resolution* 37(3) (September 1993): 403–
26.

Isaacs, Anita. *Military Rule and Transition in Ecuador, 1972–92*. Pittsburgh: University of Pittsburgh Press, 1993.

James, Patrick and John R. Oneal. "The Influence of Domestic and International
Politics on the President's Use of Force." *Journal of Conflict Resolution* 35(2)
(June 1991): 307–32.

James, Scott C. and David A. Lake. "The Second Face of Hegemony: Britain's Repeal
of the Corn Laws and the American Walker Tariff of 1846." *International Organization* 43(1) (Winter 1989): 1–29.

Jervis, Robert. "Cooperation Under the Security Dilemma." *World Politics* 30 (January 1978): 167–214.

Jones, Daniel M., Stuart A. Bremer, and J. David Singer. "Militarized Interstate
Disputes, 1816–1992: Rationale, Coding Rules and Empirical Patterns." *Conflict Management and Peace Science* 15(2) (Fall, 1996): 163–213.

Kacowicz, Arie. *Zones of Peace in the Third World: South America and West Africa
in Comparative Perspective*. Albany: State University of New York Press, 1998.

Kapstein, Ethan B. "Is Realism Dead? The Domestic Sources of International Politics." *International Organization* 49(4) (Autumn 1995): 751–74.

Katzenstein, Peter J. ed. *Between Power and Plenty: Foreign Economic Policies of
Advanced Industrial States*. Madison: University of Wisconsin Press 1978.

Katzenstein, Peter J. *Small States in World Markets: Industrial Policy in Europe*.
Ithaca: Cornell University Press, 1985.

Keller Sarmiento, Andreas. "The Dynamics of Decision-Making in the Argentine Military Government, 1976–82: The Beagle Crisis." BA Thesis, Department of Government, Harvard College March.

Kelly, Phillip and Jack Child. "An Overview: Geopolitics, Integration, and Conflict in the Southern Cone and Antartica." In Kelly and Child, eds. *Geopolitics of the Southern Cone and Antartica.* Boulder: Lynne Rienner, 1988, pp. 1–12.

Keohane, Robert O. and Joseph Nye. *Power and Interdependence.* Boston: Little, Brown, 1977.

Keohane, Robert O. "The Big Influence of Small Allies." *Foreign Policy* No. 2 (Spring 1969): 161–82.

Kiewiet, D. Roderick and Mathew D. McCubbins. *The Logic of Delegation: Congressional Parties and the Appropriations Process.* Chicago: University of Chicago Press, 1991.

Kneer, Warren G. *Great Britain and the Caribbean 1901–1913: A Study in Anglo-American Relations.* East Lansing, MI: Michigan State University Press, 1975.

Kolodziej, Edward J. and Roger E. Kanet, eds. *Coping with Conflict After the Cold War.* Baltimore: Johns Hopkins University Press, 1996.

Korr, Charles P. *Cromwell and the New Model Foreign Policy: England's Policy Toward France, 1649–1658.* Berkeley: University of California Press, 1975.

Krasner, Stephen D. *Defending the National Interest.* Princeton: Princeton University Press, 1978.

Krasner, Stephen D. "Global Communications and National Power: Life on the Pareto Frontier." *World Politics* (April 1991): 336–66.

Krenn, Michael L. *U.S. Policy Toward Economic Nationalism in Latin America, 1917–1929.* Wilmington, DE: Scholarly Resources, 1990.

Kruijt, Dirk and Edelberto Torres Rivas, eds. *América Latina: Militares y Sociedad I.* San José, Costa Rica: FLACSO, 1991.

Kugler, Jacek and A.F.K. Organski. "The Power Transition: A Retrospective and Propsective Evaluation." In Manus I. Midlarsky, ed. *Handbook of War Studies.* Ann Arbor: University of Michigan Press, 1993, reprint of Unwin Hyman 1989, pp. 171–94.

LaFaber, Walter. *The New Empire: An Interpretation of American Expansion 1860–1898.* Ithaca: Cornell University Press, 1969, 7th Printing.

Lake, David A. "Powerful Pacifists: Democratic States and War." *American Political Science Review* 86(1) (March 1992): 24–37.

Lake, David A. "Regional Security Complexes: A Systems Approach." In David A. Lake and Patrick Morgan, eds. *Regional Orders: Building Security in a New World.* University Park, PA: Pennsylvania State University Press, 1997, pp. 45–67.

Lamas, Abraham. "Ecuador–Perú: Quién Ganó y Quién Perdió en la Guerra Empatada." *InterPress Service,* March 10, 1995.

Langley, Lester D. *Struggle for the American Mediterranean: United States–European Rivalry in the Gulf-Caribbean 1776–1904.* Athens GA: University of Georgia Press, 1976.

Lanús, Juan Archibaldo. *De Chapultepec al Beagle.* Buenos Aires: Emece, 1984.

Latin American Bureau. *Falklands/Malvinas: Whose Crisis?* London: Latin American Bureau Ltd, 1982.

Layne, Christopher. "Kant or Cant: The Myth of the Democratic Peace." *International Security* 19(2) (Fall 1994): 5–49.

Lebow, Richard Ned. *Between Peace and War: The Nature of International Crisis.* Baltimore: Johns Hopkins University Press, 1981.

Leventhal, Paul L. and Sharon Tanzer, eds. *Averting a Latin American Nuclear Arms Race: New Prospects and Challenges for Argentine-Brazilian Nuclear Cooperation.* New York: St. Martin's, 1992.

Levy, Jack S. "Domestic Politics and War." *Journal of Interdisciplinary History* 18(4) (Spring 1988): 653–73.

Levy, Jack. "The Diversionary Theory of War: A Critique." In Manus I. Midlarsky, ed. *Handbook of War Studies.* Ann Arbor: University of Michigan Press, 1993, reprint of 1989 Unwin Hyman edition, pp. 259–88.

Levy, Jack. "The Offensive/Defensive Balance of Military Technology: A Theoretical and Historical Analysis." *International Studies Quarterly* 28(2) (June 1984): 219–38.

Lipjhart, Arendt. *Democracies.* New Haven: Yale University Press, 1984.

Lipjhart, Arendt. "Presidential Address." Western Political Science Association, Annual Meetings, March 1995, published in: *American Political Science Review* 91(1) (March 1997): 1–14.

Little, Walter. "Public Opinion in Britain." In Wayne S. Smith, ed. *Toward Resolution? The Falklands/Malvinas Dispute.* Boulder: Lynne Rienner, 1991, pp. 63–80.

Loftus, Joseph E. *Latin American Defense Expenditures, 1938–1965.* Santa Monica: RAND, 1968 RM-5310-PR/ISA.

Looney, Robert E. *The Political Economy of Latin American Defense Expenditures.* Lexington, MA: D.C. Heath, 1986.

Loveman, Brian. *The Constitution of Tyranny: Regimes of Exception in Spanish America.* Pittsburgh: University of Pittsburgh Press, 1993.

Lukes, Steven. *Power: A Radical View* New York: Macmillan, 1974.

Machiavelli, Niccolo. *The Prince.* edited and translated by David Wootton Indianapolis: Hackett Pub. Co., ca. 1995.

Mainwaring, Scott and Timothy R. Scully, eds. *Building Democratic Institutions: Party Systems in Latin America.* Stanford: Stanford University Press, 1995.

Makin, Guillermo A. "Argentine approaches to the Falklands/Malvinas: Was the Resort to Violence Foreseeable?" *International Affairs* (1983): 391–404.

Maldifassi, José O. and Pier A. Abetti. *Defense Industries in Latin American Countries: Argentina, Brazil, Chile.* Westport CT: Praeger 1984.

Mansfield, Edward D. and Jack Snyder. "Democratization and the Danger of War." *International Security* 20(1) (Summer 1995): 5–38.

Manwaring, Max G. and William J. Olson, eds., *Managing Contemporary Conflict.* Boulder: Westview, 1996.

Manwaring, Max G. "Monitoring Latin American Arms Control Agreements." In Morris and Millan. *Controlling Latin American Conflicts.*

Maoz, Zeev and Ben D. Mor. "The Strategic Structure of Enduring International Rivalries." Paper presented at the Workshop on Processes of Enduring Rivalries. Indiana University, Bloomington, IN May 1993.

Maoz, Zeev and Bruce Russett. "Normative and Structural Causes of the Democratic Peace, 1946–1986." *American Political Science Review* September 1993 87(3): 624–38.

Maoz, Zeev and Nasrin Abdolali. "Regime Types and International Conflict, 1816–1976." *Journal of Conflict Resolution* 33(1) (March 1989): 3–35.

Marcella, Gabriel. "Epilogue: The Peace of October 1998." In Gabriel Marcella and Richard Downes, eds. *Security Cooperation in the Western Hemisphere: Resolving the Ecuador-Peru Conflict.* Coral Gables, FL: University of Miami, North-South Center Press, 1999, pp. 231–35.

Marcella, Gabriel. "War and Peace in the Amazon: Strategic Implications for the United States and Latin America of the Ecuador-Peru War of 1995." MS US Army War College, Department of National Security and Strategy. September 1, 1995.

Mares, David R. and Steven A. Bernstein. "Explaining the Use of Force in Latin America." In Jorge I. Domínguez, ed. *International Security and Democracy* (1998): 29–47.

Mares, David R. ed. *Civil-Military Relations: Building Democracy and Regional Security in Latin America, Southern Asia and Central Europe.* Boulder: Westview, 1998.

Mares, David R. *Penetrating the International Market: Theoretical Considerations and a Mexican Case Study.* New York: Columbia University Press, 1987.

Mares, David R. "Deterrence Bargaining in the Ecuador-Peru Enduring Rivalry: Designing Strategies Around Military Weakness." *Security Studies* 6(2) (Winter 1996/97): 91–123.

Mares, David R. "La Disuasión y el Conflicto Ecuador-Perú." At the Air Force War College, Quito, August 1995.

Mares, David R. "Latin American Economic Integration and Democratic Control of the Military: Is There a Symbiotic Relationship?" Forthcoming in David Pion-Berlin, ed. *Civil-Military Relations in Latin America: New Analytical Perspectives.* Chapel Hill: University of North Carolina Press.

Mares, David R. "Middle Powers Under Regional Hegemony: To Challenge or Acquiesce in Hegemonic Enforcement." *International Studies Quarterly* 32 (1988): 453–71.

Mares, David R. "The Logic of Inter-American Cooperation on Drugs: Insights from Models of Strategic Interaction." In Peter S. Smith, ed. *Drug Policy in the Americas.* Boulder: Westview, 1992, pp. 329–42.

Martin, Lisa L. *Coercive Cooperation: Exploring Multilateral Economic Sanctions.* Princeton: Princeton University Press, 1992.

Masterson, Daniel M. *Militarism and Politics in Latin America: Peru from Sánchez Cerro to Sendero Luminoso.* Westport, CT: Greenwood, 1991.

Mauceri, Philip. *State Under Siege: Development and Policy-Making in Peru.* Boulder: Westview Press, 1966.

May, Ernest R. *The Making of the Monroe Doctrine.* Cambridge: Belknap Press of Harvard University Press, 1975.

Mayer, Arno J. "Internal Causes and Purposes of War in Europe, 1870–1956: A Research Assignment." *Journal of Modern History* (September 1969): 291–303.

McCann, Frank D. Jr. *The Brazilian-American Alliance, 1937–1945.* Princeton: Princeton University Press, 1973.

McCann Frank D., Jr. "The Brazilian General Staff and Brazil's Military Situation, 1900–1945." *Journal of Inter-American Studies and World Affairs* 25(3) (August 1983): 299–324.

McClintock, Cynthia. "Presidents, Messiahs, and Constitutional Breakdowns in Peru." In Juan J. Linz and Arturo Valenzuela, eds. *The Failure of Presidential Democracy: The Case of Latin America.* Baltimore: Johns Hopkins University Press, 1994, pp. 286–321.

McGann, Thomas F. *Argentina, The United States, and the Inter-American System 1880–1914.* Cambridge: Harvard University Press, 1957.

Mearsheimer, John J. *Conventional Deterrence.* Ithaca: Cornell University Press, 1983.

Mearsheimer, John J. "Back to the Future: Instability in Europe After the Cold War." *International Security* 15 (Summer 1990): 5–56.

Mearsheimer, John J. "The False Promise of International Institutions." *International Security* 19(3) (Winter 1994): 5–49.

Mecham, J. Lloyd. *The United States and Inter-American Security, 1889–1960.* Austin: University of Texas Press, 1962.

Mendez, Juan E. and Luis Alberto Cordero. "Presentación." In Juan Rial and Daniel Zovatto G., eds. *Elecciones y democracia en América Latina, 1992–1996: Urnas y Desencanto Político.* San José, Costa Rica: Instituto Interamericano de Derechos Humanos, 1998, pp. xi-xii.

Meneses, Emilio. *Ayuda Económica. Política. Exterior y Política de Defensa en Chile, 1943–1973.* Santiago: Centro de Estudios Políticos, Documento de Trabajo 117, 1989.

Middlebrook, Martin. *Task Force: The Falklands War, 1982.* London: Penguin, 1987, revised edition.

Milet, Paz V. "La desmilitarización en Haití." *Paz y Seguridad en las Américas.* No. 12, July 1997, pp. 14–15.

Mill, John Stuart. *Considerations On Representative Government.* Indianapolis: Bobbs Merrill, 1958.

Millan, Victor and Michael A. Morris. *Conflicts in Latin America: Democratic Alternatives in the 1990s.* London: Research Institute for the Study of Conflict and Terrorism, 1990.

Millett Richard. "The Limits of Influence: The United States and the Military in Central America and the Caribbean." In Louis W. Goodman, Johanna S. R. Mendelson, and Juan Rial, eds. *The Military and Democracy: The Future of Civil-Military Relations in Latin America.* Lexington, MA: Lexington Books, 1990, pp. 123–40.

Moneta, Carlos J. "The Malvinas Conflict: Some Elements for an Analysis of the Argentine Military Regime's Decision-Making Process." In Heraldo Munoz and Joseph S. Tulchin, eds. *Latin American Nations in World Politics.* Boulder: Westview, 1984, pp. 119–32.

Montgomery, John D. *The Politics of Foreign Aid: American Experience in Southeast Asia.* New York: Published for the Council on Foreign Relations by Praeger, ca. 1962.

Morgan, T. Clifton and Kenneth Bickers. "Domestic Discontent and the External Use of Force." *Journal of Conflict Resolution* (1992): 25–52.

Morgan, T. Clifton and Sally Howard Campbell. "Domestic Structure, Decisional Constraints, and War: So Why Kant Democracies Fight?" *Journal of Conflict Resolution* 35(2) (1991): 187–211.

Morgenthau, Hans J. *Politics Among Nations: The Struggle for Power and Peace.* New York: Knopf, 1973, 5th ed.

Mueller, Dennis C. *Public Choice.* Cambridge: Cambridge University Press, 1979.

Mueller, John E. *Retreat from Doomsday: The Obsolescence of Major War.* New York: Basic Books, 1989.

Munro, Dana G. *Intervention and Dollar Diplomacy in the Caribbean, 1900–1921.* Princeton: Princeton University Press, 1964.

Munro, Dana. *The United States and the Caribbean Area.* Boston: World Peace Foundation, 1934.

Muñoz, Heraldo. "Beyond the Malvinas Crisis." *Latin American Research Review* 19(1) (1984): 158–72.

Mytelka, Lynn Krieger. *Regional Development in a Global Economy: The Multinational Corporation, Technology, and Andean Integration.* New Haven: Yale University Press, 1979.

Navarro, Miguel. "Equilibrios estratégicos en el Cono Sur: una aproximación chilena." In Francisco Rojas Aravena, ed. *Balance Estratégico y Medidas de Confianza Mutua*. Santiago: FLACSO, 1996, pp. 271–302.

Needler, Martin C. "United States Government Figures on Latin American Military Expenditures." *Latin American Research Review* 1973 8(2) pp. 101–3.

North, Douglass C. and Barry R. Weingast. "Constitutions and Commitment: The Evolution of Institutions Governing Public Choice in 17th Century England." In *Working Papers Series, Domestic Studies Program*. Hoover Institute, Stanford University, P-88–11, November 1988.

North, Douglass C. *Institutions, Institutional Change and Economic Performance*. New York: Cambridge University Press, 1992.

Nunn, Frederick M. *The Military in Chilean History: Essays on Civil-Military Relations, 1810–1973*. Albuquerque : University of New Mexico Press, 1976.

Nunn, Frederick M. *The Time of the Generals: Latin American Professional Militarism in World Perspective*. Lincoln: University of Nebraska Press, 1992.

Nunn, Frederick M. *Yesterday's Soldiers: European Military Professionalism in South America, 1890–1940*. Lincoln: University of Nebraska Press, 1983.

Obregón T., Liliana and Carlo Nasi L. *Colombia Venezuela: Conflicto o Integración*. Bogotá: FESCOL, 1990.

Oren, Ida. "The Subjectivity of the 'Democratic' Peace: Changing U.S. Perceptions of Imperial Germany." *International Security* 20(2) (Fall 1995): 147–84.

Organski, A.F.K. and Jacek Kugler. *The War Ledger*, Chicago: University of Chicago Press, 1980.

Owen, John M. "How Liberalism Produces Democratic Peace." *International Security* 19(2) (Fall 1994): 87–125.

Oye, Kenneth A. ed. *Cooperation Under Anarchy*. Princeton: Princeton University Press, 1986.

Paarlberg, Robert. "Domesticating Global Management." *Foreign Affairs* 54(3) (1976): 563–76.

Pala, Antonio L. "Peacekeeping and Its Effects on Civil-Military Relations: The Argentine Experience." In Domínguez, ed. *International Security & Democracy*, pp. 130–50.

Palmer, David Scott. "Peru's 1995 Elections: A Second Look." *LASA Forum* 26(2) (Summer 1995): 17–20.

Pan American Union. *Segunda Conferencia Internacional Americana*. México: Tipografía de la Oficina Impresora de Estampillas, 1901.

Parenti, Christian. "Making Prison Pay: Business Finds the Cheapest Labor of All." *Nation* 262(4) (January 29, 1996): 11–15.

Paul, T.V. *Asymmetric Conflicts*. Cambridge: Cambridge University Press, 1994.

Peralta Ramos, Mónica. "Toward an Analysis of the Structural Basis of Coercion in Argentina: The Behavior of the Major Factions of the Bourgeoisie, 1976–1983."

In Mónica Peralta Ramos and Carlos H. Waisman, eds. *From Military Rule to Liberal Democracy in Argentina*. Boulder: Westview, 1987, pp. 39–68.

Perkins, Dexter. *The Monroe Doctrine, 1823–26*. Cambridge: Harvard University Press, 1927.

Pike, Frederick B. *The United States and the Andean Republics: Peru, Bolivia, and Ecuador*. Cambridge: Harvard University Press, 1977.

Pike, Frederick B. *The Modern History of Peru*. New York: Praeger, 1967.

Pion-Berlin, David. "From Confrontation to Cooperation: Democratic Governance and Argentine Foreign Relations." In Mares, ed. *Civil-Military Relations*, pp. 79–100.

Pons Muzzo, Gustavo. *Estudio Histórico sobre el Protocolo de Rio de Janeiro*. Lima: n.p., 1994.

Portales, Carlos. "Seguridad regional en Sudamérica: escenarios prospectivos." In Augusto Varas, ed. *Paz, Desarme y Desarrollo en América Latina*. Buenos Aires: Grupo Editor Latinoamericano 1987, pp. 333–82.

Posen, Barry R. "Measuring the European Conventional Balance." *International Security* 9(3) (Winter 1984–85): 47–88.

Posen, Barry. *The Sources of Military Doctrine: France, Britain, and Germany between the World Wars*. Ithaca: Cornell University Press, 1984.

Potash, Robert A. *The Army and Politics in Argentina, 1928–1945*. Stanford: Stanford University Press, 1969.

Prieto Celi, Federico. *El golpe*. Lima: B&C Editores, 1992.

Princen, Thomas. *Beagle Channel Negotiations*. Pew Case Studies in International Affairs, Case 401. Institute for the Study of Diplomacy, Georgetown University, 1988.

Princen, Thomas. *Intermediaries in International Conflict*. Princeton: Princeton University Press, 1992.

Rabkin, Rhoda. "The Aylwin Government and Tutelary Democracy: A Concept in Search of a Case? " *Journal of Inter American Economic and World Affairs*, 34(4) (Winter 1992/93): 119–94.

Ramberg, Bennett ed. *Arms Control Without Negotiation: From the Cold War to the New World Order*. Boulder: Lynne Rienner, 1993.

Rapoport, David C. "A Comparative Theory of Military Political Types." In Samuel P. Huntington, ed. *Changing Patterns of Military Politics*. New York: Free Press, 1962, pp. 71–101.

Rattenbach Commission. *Informe Rattenbach: El Drama de Malvinas*. Buenos Aires: Ediciones Espártaco, 1988.

Redick, John R. "The Tlatelolco Regime and Nonproliferation in Latin America." *International Organization* 35(1) (Winter 1981): 103–34.

Reed, W. Robert. "A Retrospective Voting Model with Heterogeneous Politicians." *Economics and Politics* 6(1) (March 1994): 39–57.

Rhea Dulles, Foster. *Prelude to World Power*. New York: Macmillan, 1971, 2nd edition.

Rial, Juan and Daniel Zovatto G. "La Política, Los Partidos y las Elecciones en América Latina." In Juan Rial and Daniel Zovatto G., eds. *Elecciones y democracia en América Latina, 1992–1996: Urnas y Desencanto Político.* San José, Costa Rica: Instituto Interamericano de Derechos Humanos, 1998, pp. xxxvii–xlvi.

Roett, Riordan ed. *Mercosur: Regional Integration, World Markets*. Boulder, CO: Lynne Rienner, 1999.

Rojas Aravena, Francisco. "Centroamérica: Nueva Agenda de Seguridad." In *Paz y Seguridad en las Américas* No. 9, (December 1996): 3–7.

Rojas Aravena, Francisco. "Chile y el gasto militar: un criterio histórico y jurídico de asignación." In Francisco Rojas Aravena, ed. *Gasto Militar en. América Latina Santiago:* CINDE & FLACSO, 1994, pp. 239–78.

Rojas, Francisco and Claudio Fuentes. " Civil-Military Relations in Chile's Geopolitical Transition." In Mares, ed. *Civil-Military Relations* 1998): 165–86.

Rosenberg, Mark, et al. *Honduras: Pieza clave de la política de Estados Unidos en Centro América*. Tegucigalpa: Centro de Documentación de Honduras (CEDOH), 1990.

Rothstein, Robert. *Alliances and Small Powers*. New York: Columbia University Press, 1968.

Rouquie, Alain. *The Military and the State in Latin America*, trans., Paul E. Sigmund Berkeley: University of California Press, 1987.

Rout, Jr., Leslie B. *The Politics of the Chaco Peace Conference, 1935–39*. Austin: University of Texas Press, 1970.

Rummel, R.J. "Libertarian Propositions on Violence Within and Between Nations: A Test Against Published Research Results." *Journal of Conflict Resolution* 29(3) (September 1985): 419–55.

Rummel, R.J. "Libertarianism and International Violence." *Journal of Conflict Resolution* 27(1) (March 1983): 27–72.

Russell, Roberto. "El Proceso de toma de decisiones en la política exterior argentina." In Roberto Russell, ed., *Política Exterior y El Proceso de Toma de Decisiones en América Latina*. Buenos Aires: Grupo Editorial Latinoamericano, 1990, pp. 13–60.

Russett, Bruce with William Antholis. "The Imperfect Democratic Peace of Ancient Greece." In Bruce Russett. *Grasping the Democratic Peace*. Princeton: Princeton University Press, 1993.

Russett, Bruce. *Grasping the Democratic Peace*. Princeton: Princeton University Press, 1993.

Saad Herrería, Pedro. *La Caída de Abdalá*. Quito: El Conejo, 1997.

Saba, Raul P. *Political Development and Democracy in Peru: Continuity in Change and Crisis*. Boulder: Westview 1987.

Salisbury, Richard V. *Anti-Imperialism and International Competition in Central America*. Wilmington, DE: Scholarly Resources, 1989.

Sarmiento, Domingo F. *Facundo, or Civilization and Barbarism*. trans. Mary Mann, introduction by Ilan Stevens. New York: Penguin Books, 1998.

Sater, William F. *Chile and the United States*. Athens: University of Georgia Press, 1990.

Scheggia Flores, Carlos E. *Orígen del Pueblo Ecuatoriano y Sus Infundadas Pretensiones Amazónicas*. Lima: Talleres de Linea, 1992.

Schelling, Thomas C. *The Strategy of Conflict*. Cambridge: Harvard University Press, 1980.

Schlesinger, Jr., Arthur M. *The Imperial Presidency*. Boston, Houghton Mifflin, 1973.

Schmitter, Philippe C. "Foreign Military Assistance, National Military Spending and Military Rule in Latin America." In Schmitter, ed. *Military Rule in Latin America*. Beverly Hills: SAGE, 1973, pp. 117–87.

Schmitter, Phillipe C. "Introduction." In Phillipe C. Schmitter, ed. *Military Rule in Latin America: Function, Consequences, and Perspectives*. Beverly Hills: Sage Publications, 1973.

Schulz, Donald E. and Gabriel Marcella. *Reconciling the Irreconcilable: The Troubled Outlook for U.S. Policy Toward Haiti*. Carlisle Barracks, PA: U.S. Army War College, Strategic Studies Institute, March 10, 1994.

Schumacher, Edward. "Behind Ecuador War, Long-Smoldering Resentment." *New York Times*, February 10, 1981, p. A2.

Sealey, Raphael. *A History of the Greek City States, 700–338 B.C.* Berkeley: University of California Press, 1976.

Selcher, Wayne A. *Brazil's Multilateral Relations: Between First and Third Worlds*. Boulder: Westview, 1978.

Selcher, Wayne A. "Brazilian-Argentine Relations in the 1980s: From Wary Rivalry to Friendly Competition." *Journal of InterAmerican and World Affairs* 27(2) (Summer 1985): 25–54.

Sellers, Charles. "Hard War Averted—Easy War Gained." In Archie P. McDonald, ed. *The Mexican War: Crisis for American Diplomacy*. Lexington, MA: D.C. Heath, 1969, pp. 13–22.

Sereseres, Caesar D. "The Interplay of Internal War and Democratization in Guatemala since 1982." In Mares, ed. *Civil-Military Relations*, pp. 206–222.

Sheinin, David. *Argentina and the United States at the Sixth Pan American Conference (Havana 1928)*. London: Institute of Latin American Studies, University of London, 1991 Research Papers 25.

Shugart, Mathew Soberg and John M. Carey. *Presidents and Assemblies*. Cambridge: Cambridge University Press, 1992.

Sigmund, Paul E. *The United States and Democracy in Chile*. Baltimore: Johns Hopkins University Press, 1993.

Siles, Juan Ignacio ed. *La Política Exterior de Bolivia, 1989–1993*. La Paz: Ministerio de Relaciones Exteriores y Culta, Government of Bolivia, 1993.

Silva, Eduardo. "The Political Economy of Chile's Regime Transition: From Radical to 'Pragmatic' Neo-Liberal Policies." In Drake and Jaksic. *The Struggle for Democracy in Chile*, pp. 98–127.

Singer, J. David ed. *The Correlates of War*. New York: Free Press, 1979.

Sirkin, Gerald and Natalie Robinson Sirkin. "John Stuart Mill and Disutilitarianism in Indian Education." *Journal of General Education* 34(4) (January 1973).

Sklar, Holly. *Washington's War on Nicaragua*. Boston: South End Press, 1988.

Smith, Joseph. *Unequal Giants: Diplomatic Relations Between the United States and Brazil, 1889–1930*. Pittsburgh: University of Pittsburgh Press, 1991.

Snyder, Jack. *The Ideology of the Offensive: Military Decision-Making and the Disasters of 1914*. Ithaca: Cornell University Press, 1984.

Solingen, Etel. "Economic Liberalization, Political Coalitions, and Emerging Regional Orders." In David Lake and Patrick J. Morgan, eds. *Regional Orders*. Pennsylvania State University Press, 1997, pp. 68–100.

Spiro, David E. "The Insignificance of the Liberal Peace." *International Security* 19(2) (Fall 1994): 50–86.

St. John, Ronald Bruce. *The Boundary between Ecuador and Peru*. Vol 1. No. 4 of *Boundary & Territory Briefing*. Durham, UK: International Boundaries Research Unit, University of Durham, 1994.

St. John, Ronald Bruce. *The Foreign Policy of Peru*. Boulder: Lynne Rienner, 1992.

Stein, Arthur. *Why Nations Cooperate: Circumstance and Choice in International Relations*. Ithaca: Cornell University Press, 1990.

Steinmo, Sven, Kathleen Thelen and Frank Longstreth, eds. *Structuring Politics: Historical Institutionalism in Comparative Analysis*. New York: Cambridge University Press, 1992.

Stepan, Alfred. *The Military in Politics*. Princeton: Princeton University Press, 1971.

Stockholm International Peace Research Institute. *1982 World Armaments and Disarmament*.

Stokes, Susan. "Peru: The Rupture of Democratic Rule." In Jorge I. Dominguez and Abraham F. Lowenthal, eds. *Constructing Democratic Governance: South America in the 1990s*. Baltimore: Johns Hopkins University Press, 1996, pp. 58–71.

Stuart, Graham H. *Latin America and the United States*. New York: Appleton-Century-Crofts, 1955, 5th edition.

Tamir, Yael. *Liberal Nationalism*. Princeton: Princeton University Press, 1993.

Thompson, William R. and Richard Tucker. "A tale of two democratic peace critiques." *Journal of Conflict Resolution* 41(3) (June 1997): 428–54.

Thucydides. *The Peloponnesian War*. Translated by Rex Warner. London: Penguin, 1972 revised edition.

Tilly, Charles S. *From Mobilization to Revolution*. Reading MA: Addison-Wesley Publishing Company, 1978.

Tóbar Donoso, Julio and Alfredo Luna Tóbar . *Derecho Territorial Ecuatoriana.* Quito: Ministry of Foreign Affairs, 1994, 4th edition.

Trachtenberg, Marc. "The Meaning of Mobilization in 1914." In Steven E. Miller, Sean M. Lynn-Jones, and Stephen Van Evera, eds. *Military Strategy and the Origins of the First World War.* Princeton: Princeton University Press, 1991 revised and expanded edition pp. 195–225.

Tuesta Soldevilla, Fernando. *Perú Político en Cifras.* Lima: Fundación Friedrich Ebert, 1994, 2nd edition.

Tulchin, Joseph S. *Argentina and the United States: A Conflicted Relationship.* Boston: Twayne, 1990.

Tulchin, Joseph. *The Aftermath of War: World War I and U.S. Policy toward Latin America.* New York: New York University Press, 1971.

United Kingdom, Foreign Office files, Public Records Office, London, 1906–14.

United Nations, Centro Regional Para la Paz, El Desarme y el Desarrollo en América Latina y el Caribe.

United States Government, Arms Control and Disarmament Agency. *World Military Expenditures and Arms Transfers.* Vols. 1985 and 1993–94. Washington: U.S. Government Printing Office.

United States Government, Department of State. *Foreign Relations of the United States* 1910.

United States, Department of Defense. *United States Security Strategy for the Americas.* Washington, D.C.: The Pentagon, Office of International Security Affairs 1995.

Valenzuela, Arturo. "The Military in Power: The Consolidation of One-Man Rule." In Paul Drake and Ivan Jaksic, eds. *The Struggle for Democracy in Chile.* Lincoln: University of Nebraska Press, 1995, revised edition, pp. 21–72.

Varas, Augusto. *Militarization and the International Arms Race in Latin America.* Boulder: Westview, 1985.

Varas, Augusto. "Zonas de Paz en América Latina: Una propuesta factible?" In *Seguridad, paz y desarme: Propuestas de concertación pacífica en América Latina y el Caribe.* Santiago: FLACSO-CLADDE 1992, pp. 81–87.

Vargas Pazzos (ret.), Lt. General Frank. *Tiwintza: Toda La Verdad.* Quito: Color Gráfica, 1995.

Villanueva, Javier. "Economic Development." In Mark Falcoff and Ronald H. Dolkart, eds. *Prologue to Peron: Argentina in Depression and War, 1930–1943.* Berkeley: University of California Press, 1975, pp. 65–78.

Villanueva, Victor. *100 anos del ejército peruano: frustraciones y cambios.* Lima: Editorial Juan Mejía Baca, 1971.

Waltz, Kenneth. *Theory of International Politics.* New York: Random House, 1979.

Waltz, Kenneth. "The Origins of War in NeoRealist Theory." *Journal of Interdisciplinary History*, pp. 615–28.

Waltz, Kenneth. "The Stability of a Bipolar World." *Daedalus* 93 (Summer 1964): 881–909.

Warnock, Mary ed. *John Stuart Mill*. New York: The New American Library, Meridian Books, 1962.

Warren, Harris Gaylord. *Paraguay and the Triple Alliance: The postwar decade, 1869–1978*. Austin: University of Texas Press, 1974.

Weede, Erich. "Democracy and War Involvement." *Journal of Conflict Resolution* 28(4) (December 1984): 649–64.

Wendt, Alexander. "Anarchy Is What States Make of It: The Social Construction of State Politics." *International Organization* 46(2) (Spring 1992): 391–425.

Whitaker, Arthur P. *The United States and the Southern Cone: Argentina, Chile and Uruguay*. Cambridge: Harvard University Press, 1976.

Whitaker, Arthur P. *The Western Hemisphere Idea*. Ithaca: Cornell University Press, 1954.

Wiarda, Howard J. ed. *Politics and Social Change in Latin America: Still a Distinct Tradition?* 3rd ed. Boulder: Westview, 1992.

Wilkie, James L. and Enrique Ochoal. *Statistical Abstract of Latin America*. v. 27 Los Angeles: UCLA Latin American Center Publication, University of California, 1989.

Wood, Bryce. *The United States and Latin American Wars, 1932–1942*. New York: Columbia University Press, 1966.

Woodward, Jr., Ralph Lee. *Central America: A Nation Divided*. New York: Oxford University Press, 1976.

Wynia, Gary W. *Argentina: Illusions & Realities*. New York: Holmes & Meier, 1986.

Zakaria, Fareed. "Realism and Domestic Politics: A Review Essay." *International Security* 17(1) (Summer 1992): 177–98.

Zakaria, Fareed. "The Rise of Illiberal Democracy." *Foreign Affairs* November/December 1997 76(6): 22–43.

Zartmann, I. William. "Prenegotiations: Phases and Functions." In Janet Gross Stein, ed. *Getting to the Table: The Process of International Prenegotiation*. Baltimore: Johns Hopkins University Press, 1989, pp. 1–17/B Government Documents.

Government of Ecuador, Ministry of Foreign Affairs. *Hacia la Solución del Problema Territorial con el Perú: Libro Blanco*. Quito: Ministry of Foreign Affairs, 1992.

Government of Peru, 1979 Constitution.

Government of Peru, 1993 Constitution.

Organization of American States: Working Group on Hemispheric Security, Working Group on Cooperation for Hemispheric Security and the Special Committee on Hemispheric Security.

Interviews

Confidential interviews with Ecuadorian, Peruvian and U.S. military and civilian analysts, Quito and Washington, D.C., August and September 1995.

Confidential interview with a former high ranking Peruvian diplomat. Lima, March 26, 1999.

César Azabache, Defensoría del Pueblo, Lima, April 5, 1999

Ambassador Juan Miguel Bakula, Lima, March 26, 1999

Hugo Barber, Director, PERFILES DE OPINION, July 2, 1996

Dr. Alfonso Barrera Valverde, ex-Foreign Minister, Quito, August 14, 15 & 16, 1995

Adrian Bonilla, FLACSO-Ecuador, April 1997, Guadalajara, Mexico

Fernando Bustamante, FLACSO-Ecuador, Quito, August 14, 1995

Carlos Contreras, Instituto de Estudios Peruanos, Lima, March 25, 1999

Dr. Polibio Córdova, General Director of CEDATOS, Quito, July 18, 1997

Jaime Durn, Director of *Informe Confidencial*, Quito, July 15, 1997

Vitaliano Gallardo Valencia, Third Secretary, Peruvian Embassy, Quito, July 10, 1996

Col. Luís B. Hernández P., Personal Secretary to the Minister of Defense (and commander of the Tiwintza defense during the war), Quito, August 14, 1995

Carlos Herrera Rodríguez, Counselor, Peruvian Embassy, Quito, July 10, 1996

Luís Alberto Huerta Guerrero, Comisión Andina de Juristas, Lima, Peru March 25, 1999.

Ambassador Alfredo Luna Tóbar, Quito, August 17, 1995

Andrés Mejia Acosta, Corporación de Estudios para el Desarrollo, Quito, July 25, 1997

General Paco Moncayo, Army Chief, Quito, August 16, 1995

Santiago Nieto Montoya, Gerente, INFORME CONFIDENCIAL Quito, July 2 & 10, 1996

Enrique Obando Arbulu, President, Instituto de Estudios Políticos y Estratégicos (Peru), Quito, June 18, 1996

Benjamín Ortíz, Director of HOY Quito, July 18, 1997

Julio Prado Espinosa, Ministry of Foreign Affairs, August 16, 1995

Dr. Luís Heladio Proaño, Political Advisor, Ministry of Defense, Quito, August 14, 1995

Fernando Ribadeneira, Director, Academic Diplomatica, Ministry of Foreign Affairs, Quito, August 11, 1995

Julio Cesar Trujillo, Defensor del Pueblo, Quito, July 11, 1997

Gen. Frank Vargas Pazzos (ret.) and Senator, Quito, August 16, 1995

Ernesto Yepes de Castillo, consultant to Foreign Ministry, Lima, March 27, 1999

Newspapers, Weeklies and Flyers*América Vuela* (Santiago)

Análisis Semanal (Ecuador)

Apoyo, S.A. (Lima) via Roper Center for Public Opinion Research, University of
     Connecticut, Storrs, CT.
"Campaña Nacional: 500 anos de resistencia indígena y popular" Folleto 1, Secre-
     taria Operativa, Guatemala November 1, 1990
Chile Information Press, (CHIPnews), subsequently *Santiago Times*
Clarín (Buenos Aires).
Diario
El Comercio (Lima)
El Nacional (Caracas)
El Universo (Quito)
Hoy (Quito)
Informe Confidencial (Ecuador)
Keesings Contemporary Archives
La Nación (San José, Costa Rica)
Latin America Data Base, *EcoCentral: Central American Economy & Sustainable
     Development* Latin American Institute, University of New Mexico
Latin America Data Base, *NotiSur—Latin American Political Affairs,* Latin American
     Institute, University of New Mexico
Latin American Regional Reports
Organización de Pueblos Indígenas de Pastaza, March 10, 1992 #0129-OPIP-92
The Washington Post

Index